AF413809

TAILWIND

PRAISE FOR *TAILWIND*

"In my life with Starbucks, millions of people have worn the Green Apron of the company. So many have honored the company's heritage and offered the lessons of the culture around the world. I count Jim Olson among them. Jim's book pays tribute to a remarkable journey and the wisdom earned over the years from mentors, colleagues, and loved ones. It's a story of courage, of kindness, and of mind over matter that I lovingly recommend to friends, family, colleagues, and anyone who believes in the power of personal transformation."

— Howard Schultz
Chairman Emeritus and Retired CEO, Starbucks
Co-Founder, Schultz Family Foundation
New York Times Bestselling Author

"I once had the good fortune of collaborating with Jim Olson when he was leading communications for United Airlines. From the start, I was struck by his sense of purpose for improving the wellbeing of others. Jim's cancer-defeating journey, which cost him much of his vision, is a triumphant story of restoration, resilience, and renewal. In a world hungry for hope and direction, *Tailwind* is a masterclass in turning life's struggles into a life of significance. With his inspiring story, Jim lights the way forward, showing how to live a life of meaning."

— Arianna Huffington
Founder and CEO, Thrive Global
Founder, *The Huffington Post*
New York Times Bestselling Author

"Jim's book is a treasure trove of resilience, strength, and character, all traits he has mastered. He lays out how to manage and survive life's biggest challenges and come out on the other side, even when you don't think you can. I am inspired by his courage and determination in facing his challenges, and in reading his book, you will be, too."

— Chesley "Sully" Sullenberger
Captain of US Airways Flight 1549 – The Miracle on the Hudson
New York Times Bestselling Author

"*Tailwind* is so much more than a book. It's a compass we all should keep handy for navigating the storms confronting us in life and at work. Jim leaves us inspired to dream big about the joy, love, and whimsy we can offer ourselves and the world. His story of courage, grace, and, above all, faith, gives us the tailwind of hope to chart our own legacy-defining comeback journeys."

— Bob Goff
Founder, Love Does
New York Times Bestselling Author

"Jim Olson's journey is nothing short of extraordinary, and his willingness to share it with others is a genuine act of service. In the face of profound personal adversity, he channeled the courage, clarity, and deep sense of purpose to survive and inspire. His story is a powerful reminder that resilience isn't just about endurance—it's about choosing to keep showing up and holding on to a belief in what's possible."

— Michelle Gass
President and CEO, Levi Strauss & Co.
Board Member, PepsiCo
Former CEO, Kohl's

"I consider Jim's book a gift; not a memoir, but a flight plan for how anyone can meet and master the ocean of storms that we all must navigate in our lives. When you pick this book up you will be unable to put it down, and equally unable to put it out of your mind long after you've finished. Perhaps this book is so powerful not in spite of Jim's lack of sight but because of it. His medical hurdles have only sharpened his vision. These messages strike the reader like thunderbolts to the mind and heart, one after another."

— Oscar Munoz
Former CEO and Chairman, United Airlines
Board Member, Salesforce, Fidelity and Univision
Wall Street Journal Bestselling Author

"With heart and genuine empathy, Jim has produced a book that proves to be critical reading for all leaders and, really, all of us. His journey reminds us that when life throws us the unexpected, we learn the most valuable lessons about how strong we are and the life we can really live!"

— **Poppy Harlow**
Former Anchor, *CNN*
Founder and CEO, Day 2 Media
Chair, *WSJ* Leadership Institute

"This inspiring, un-put-downable book is a testament to Jim's remarkable journey, marked by grit, humility, and an unshakeable sense of hope. He's faced setbacks that would have broken many, yet he's emerged with the same steely resilience and optimism that I've always admired in him. Like Jim himself, every chapter cuts straight to the heart of what it means to Do Hard Things."

— **Fred Swaniker**
TIME 100 Most Influential People
Founder, African Leadership Group and African Leadership University
Founder and CEO, Sand Technologies

"I had the honor and privilege of working alongside Jim at Starbucks and saw firsthand his humility, heart, and deep care for people. In *Tailwind*, that same spirit shines through. His 'Aviate, Navigate, and Communicate' mindset isn't theory, it's hard-won wisdom born from faith, courage, and perseverance. Jim doesn't just write about resilience; he lives it every day. This book will lift you, steady you, and remind you that even in life's ferocious storms, there's always a way forward, and, often, a purpose waiting on the other side. Read it, share it, and then get moving!"

— **Chris Carr**
Chairman of the Board, REI
Board Member, Hilton and Valvoline
Former Chief Procurement Officer, Starbucks

"*Tailwind* is an inspirational story of determination, compassion, and clarity. Drawing on lessons forged in the high-stakes moments of business and personal crisis, Jim offers a playbook not just for surviving cancer, but for living with purpose. His story stays with you long after the last page, reminding you what strength and humanity truly look like. You don't just read his story, you rally behind it."

— Annie Young-Scrivner
Board Member, Yum! Brands
Former CEO, Godiva Chocolatier and Wella Company
Former Global Chief Marketing Officer, Starbucks

"Growing up in the frequent company of my airplane mechanic (and pilot) grandfather, he routinely said, 'Life is 10% what happens to you and 90% how you respond to that.' Somehow, my longtime friend and former colleague Jim Olson has managed to shift that percentage to 1%/99%. This book is filled with lessons born of hardship turned upside down and then transformed into triumph. No matter your line of work or life's pursuit, you'll find something to love, learn, and remember from this extraordinary book."

— Corey duBrowa
CEO, Burson
Former Chief Communications Officer, Google, Starbucks and Salesforce
Former Contributing Editor, *Rolling Stone*

"In his terrific book, Jim chronicles how he concurrently navigated professional and personal health crises. He offers us practical advice on how to maintain stamina and show up for ourselves and our teams every day. Jim's words and stories will bring you to your feet, erupting in applause."

— Linda Rutherford
Executive Adviser, Southwest Airlines
Retired Chief Administration and Communications Officer, Southwest Airlines
Board Member, Frost Bank

"I have had the amazing opportunity to work with Jim Olson and have been humbled by his sense of purpose and deep commitment to working with leaders who are mission focused. Jim has an amazing trait of pulling you into his orbit and helping you think through things in a profound manner. *Tailwind* is a masterpiece of showing up daily, not just to do the hard work, but also to learn to solve problems differently while focusing on the things that matter."

— Isaac Kwaku Fokuo, Jr.
Founder and Curator, The Amahoro Coalition
Founder and Curator, Botho Emerging Markets Group
Co-Head Middle East and Africa, Propagate Content

TAILWIND

A COMPASS FOR TURNING YOUR SETBACK STORY INTO YOUR COMEBACK LEGACY

JAMES T. OLSON

Copyright © 2026, James T. Olson

All rights reserved. No part of this book may be used or reproduced by any means, graphic, electronic, or mechanical (including any information storage retrieval system) without the express written permission from the author, except in the case of brief quotations for use in articles and reviews wherein appropriate attribution of the source is made.

Publishing support provided by
Ignite Press
55 Shaw Ave. Suite 204
Clovis, CA 93612
www.IgnitePress.us

ISBN: 979-8-9948613-0-1
ISBN: 979-8-9948613-1-8 (Hardcover)
ISBN: 979-8-9948613-2-5 (E-book)

For bulk purchases and for booking, contact:

James T. Olson
Jim@ComebackCompass.com
www.ComebackCompass.com

Because of the dynamic nature of the Internet, web addresses or links contained in this book may have been changed since publication and may no longer be valid. The content of this book and all expressed opinions are those of the author and do not reflect the publisher or the publishing team. The author is solely responsible for all content included herein.

Library of Congress Control Number: 2026905046

Cover design by Imran Khaliq
Edited by Elizabeth Arterberry
Interior design by Jetlaunch

FIRST EDITION

Contract of Carriage

*T**ailwind* is intended for motivational purposes only and does not constitute medical advice. *Tailwind's* author is not a healthcare professional. The content of this book is not intended to be a substitute for professional medical advice, diagnosis, or treatment. Always seek the advice of a qualified healthcare professional for any questions you may have regarding a medical condition. Never disregard professional medical advice or delay in seeking it because of something you have read in this book.

Tailwind's author and publisher make no representations or warranties of any kind, express or implied, about the completeness, accuracy, reliability, or suitability of the information, ideas, stories, and claims included in this book. Any reliance you place on the content of this book is therefore strictly at your own risk.

Furthermore, neither the author, publisher, nor any contributors, individuals, companies, or organizations mentioned in this book shall be responsible or liable for any loss, damage, or harm—direct or indirect—that may arise from actions taken based on the material presented in this book. You are solely responsible for how you choose to interpret and utilize the information in this book and are encouraged to use your own discretion and consult with professionals as needed.

By reading *Tailwind,* you acknowledge that you have read, understood, and agreed to the terms of this disclaimer.

To my wife, Stephanie, and our daughter, Kaitlyn — You are my compass, you are my North Star, and you are my "Tailwind."

Table of Contents

Foreword

I will begin the foreword to this elegant and inspiring book in the same spirit in which it concludes, with a message of gratitude to the author himself.

My gratitude to Jim Olson flows from many sources of indebtedness, but these above all.

For his friendship over many years, ones that were filled with plenty of triumphs, as well as turbulence, both private and intensely public.

For his service to me during my tenure as CEO, helping a new captain steady the ship and steer it toward our North Star values, the same ones that continue to guide United Airlines to this day.

For his unfailing sense of service and the duty of care he displayed towards the members of our United family. During an uncertain time, they looked to me for words of leadership. In turn, I looked to Jim, and he often helped me find them.

Finally, I am deeply grateful to him for having written this book. I consider it a gift, not a memoir, but a flight plan showing how anyone can meet and master the ocean of storms that one must navigate in one's life.

I found, as I am confident you will also, that when you pick it up, you will be unable to put it down, and equally unable to put it out of your mind long after you've finished.

A masterclass in storytelling

Like a modern-day Milton, Jim wrote this masterpiece without use of his sight. How he did so, I shall never fathom. Yet, he persevered, and the result is a book unlike any other I've ever read.

Every sentence, every word, feels as though Jim is talking directly to you, coaching you, and guiding you, just as he has done for some of the most influential leaders in business over the course of his extraordinary career in corporate communications.

I know how difficult it is to write a book, even under the easiest of circumstances. In my own memoir about the United turnaround journey, in which Jim plays a pivotal role, I explained that "leadership is an act of extended storytelling."

A person's ability to communicate and ability to lead are inextricable from one another. This connection between the role that storytelling plays in both the art of leadership and life is a central theme of this book.

Jim's story would be inspiring all on its own, but he also has a set of lessons he urgently wants to convey. He understands the keys to how to communicate effectively, and he wants you, the reader, to have them and harness them in your own careers and personal lives.

In that, he succeeds.

The book is an object lesson in itself, a masterclass in the artform of storytelling. Don't just study the lessons inside the book, of which there are many. Study how Jim constructs the book, and how he draws you in as a reader with his authenticity, vulnerability, and honesty.

Perhaps this book is so powerful not in spite of Jim's lack of sight but because of it. His medical hurdles have only sharpened his vision. These messages strike the reader like thunderbolts to the mind and heart, one after another.

Messages born out of pain

Of course, the messages resonate all the louder because they are born out of such pain and personal loss. Thus, the book transcends the subject of corporate communications and becomes a meditation on the pains and joys of life, the redemptive qualities of suffering, and the resilience of the human spirit. Jim offers so many soulful and beautiful quotations in this book, and I'd like to add one more that is drawn from history.

When Dr. Martin Luther King, Jr. was shot and killed in Memphis on the night of April 4th, 1968, Senator Robert F. Kennedy arrived in Indianapolis. He was prepared to speak to a large audience composed largely of African Americans. The terrible news had not yet reached them.

To wails of anger and grief, Kennedy conveyed the tragedy to the crowd. He offered them these words as consolation, ones he surely stumbled upon during his own long nights of grief and suffering in the wake of his brother's assassination only five years earlier.

> *"Even in our sleep, pain which cannot forget*
> *falls drop by drop upon the heart*
> *until, in our own despair, against our will,*
> *comes wisdom through the awful grace of God."*
> *— Aeschylus*

That night, cities across the nation burned down in riots, but after these remarks concluded, the city of Indianapolis slept peacefully, allowing the grief to fall drop by drop until it gave way to some measure of wisdom.

Words have the power to help us find meaning in suffering and provide us with a sense of purpose in the face of immense loss that can easily seem purposeless.

Words can be both sword and shield against the slings and arrows of outrageous fortune, to paraphrase Shakespeare. They can provide us a compass when we are lost "midway upon the journey of our life . . . within a forest dark." Perhaps it is no coincidence that Dante chose the poet Virgil to be his guide through Hell and into Paradise.

Why me?

None of us seek out suffering and loss; it finds us. As Jim explains, a person can either run away from this pain or find something instructive, even salvific, from the experience.

I know this from my own experience. I suffered a life-threatening heart attack 37 days into my tenure as CEO of United Airlines. I spent the next week in a medically induced coma. My family had been told to prepare for the most likely outcome, and the worst. Thankfully, I awoke and spent several weeks in the intensive care unit at Chicago's

Northwestern Memorial Hospital. I would need a heart transplant, and soon, if I was to survive.

Those late nights in the hospital were the worst. The pain was almost as bad as the loneliness. At my lowest moment, I was saved by the words of an angel in scrubs. One night, as my night nurse changed my linens, shifting my atrophied body from one side of the bed to the other in an excruciatingly painful routine, she told me something profound.

"Oscar, there are two kinds of patients in your condition. There are those who look at what just happened to them and ask *Why me?* As in, *Why did this misfortune befall me, rather than somebody else?* And then, there are the patients who look at what they just survived, how lucky they are, and they ask *Why me?* As in, *Why was I spared? What's still in store for me? What is it that I should do with this gift?*"

I was determined to be the latter sort of person. So is Jim Olson.

It is that admirable cast of character—resolve mixed with irrepressible good humor—that drew me to him when we first met. He arrived at my temporary apartment building in downtown Chicago only weeks after I had been discharged from the hospital. I was still recovering, but I was determined to continue building my team so we could get right back to work. The airline doesn't stop just because the CEO has had a heart attack. And, to extend the metaphor, as I assembled my team and my strategy, it felt like I was assembling an airplane midflight.

Finding our North Star

For my first 37 days prior to the heart attack, I had embarked on an exhaustive listening tour of our global operations, holding countless town halls in breakrooms, hangars, and common areas across the system. Hundreds of conversations in galleys and concourses with both customers and employees had convinced me of one thing. We had lost our way as an airline because we had lost the engagement of our employees. Unless we won it back, United would remain forever dis-united.

A messy and incomplete merger with Continental had left us as one company with two cultures. Like nomads in the desert, we were wandering aimlessly. We needed to find our North Star values to guide us.

That's where Jim became invaluable. I hired him as our corporate communications chief and he got to work operationalizing my "employee-first" strategy, built on my core leadership philosophy of "listen, learn . . . and only then can you lead."

What resulted was United Airlines' first statement of shared purpose and shared values in our 90-year history: "We connect people and help Unite the world." It remains our mission statement to this day, and it served to organize and measure our efforts and progress toward uniting our airline.

I am proud to say we succeeded. Had we not embarked upon this turnaround journey, I firmly believe that United would never have survived the storm of COVID that lay years ahead.

We had laid the groundwork, and Jim set the first bricks.

For that, I will be forever grateful to him and feel lucky to call him my friend.

The grace with which he has met this most recent storm in his life is awe-inspiring, though not at all surprising to those of us who know him and have had the privilege to work with him. As you read his words, you will find yourself laughing, crying, and constantly underlining sentences to return to later.

Enjoy the ride.

Oscar Munoz
Former CEO and Chairman
United Airlines

Embarkation: Welcome Aboard!

At some point, we all will face a life-altering crucible in our personal or professional lives. These unexpected and disruptive storms come in many forms: illness, job loss, divorce, bankruptcy, addiction, the loss of a family member, or a home-destroying natural disaster. For our organizations, these crises often strike us in the form of an active shooter, cyberattack, financial downdraft, product recall, labor fight, leadership shakeup, or government indictment.

For me, my beautiful life and high-flying career rolled into a perilous nosedive in 2024 in the wake of back-to-back medical crises. I was terrified I wouldn't survive.

We respond to these life-altering derailments differently. In most cases, our inclination is to race through the tempest as fast as possible. Our hope is that the quicker we can get to the other side, the pain and destruction unleashed by the storm will dissipate as fast as it gathered. As the bumper sticker I saw in a gift shop a few years ago read, "When you're going through Hell, keep running."

Embrace the suck

However, when a crisis strikes, rather than attempt to bolt through the storm as fast as possible, slow down and "embrace the suck," as my longtime friend and marketing AI innovator Mark Stouse regularly reminds me. Getting lost in our adversity or, as I call it, "the in-between space" may very well be the best way to find ourselves and our pathway from setback to comeback. In the end, our lives are not measured by the number of storms we avoid, but rather by the magnitude of the storms we ride.

Choosing to ride out the storms in our lives rather than run from them can be a soul-awakening odyssey to an inner space of self-reflection and self-realization. It is during these extended periods of in-betweenness that we learn to evoke a mindset of certainty in times of uncertainty, fearlessness in moments of fear, motivation in the wake of devastation, and, as my good friend and three-time cancer survivor Lynann Bradbury is fond of saying, "brilliance in the radiance of resilience."

I wrote *Tailwind* to be a compass for helping individuals, leaders, and organizations turn their setback stories into comeback legacies. Whether you, your team, or your organization is facing a significant setback, *Tailwind* will help you transform your calamity into your destiny.

Unlike most "self-help books," this one doesn't chart a fast track or profess a magic quadrant for helping you quickly bounce back from your setback. To the contrary, *Tailwind* is what I call a "self-discovery compass," a reminder for us to throttle back as we navigate the storms swarming us.

Aviate, navigate, and communicate

I have plotted this journey into four stages. The initial three—*Aviate, Navigate,* and *Communicate*—come from the first critical safety lesson every student pilot learns before taking flight. In the event of an in-flight emergency, aviators are trained to follow those three rules, in that order.

Aviate — Fly the plane. First and foremost, a pilot confronted with an in-flight emergency must first do everything in their power to keep flying the plane and keep it in the air while mitigating the problem. The same rule applies to us, whether we're facing a crisis in our personal life or at work. It's critical to stabilize the situation before worrying about what will happen next. I will begin our time together by sharing my story of adversity and how I aviated through the high-stakes medical emergencies that blindsided me.

Navigate — Once a pilot stabilizes their situation, the next rule of thumb in an in-flight emergency is for a pilot to find the closest airport or location (which may be a highway, cornfield, or even a river) to safely land their plane. "Stage Two" of *Tailwind* is the bedrock of this book.

It is here where we take a deep dive into the virtues of slowing down and riding the storm you are in rather than fighting or dodging it. In this stage, I will introduce you to ten "Compass Headings" to help you navigate from setback to comeback.

These ten directional bearings are drawn from the lessons I've learned from my current comeback journey, other struggles I've slayed over the years, and from the setback victories of others. Here are the ten Compass Headings we'll explore together to help guide your purpose-fulfilling comeback trek:

1. Find Your Intego
2. Make Every Day Count
3. Switch Off Your GPS and Turn On Your Curiosity
4. Don't Ask "What If?" Declare "Why Not!"
5. Be a Zelensky
6. Do Hard Things
7. Discover Your Next Mountain
8. Turn Your Resolution into Resolve
9. Hopelessness is Finite. Hope is Infinite.
10. Share Your Blanket

Communicate — Once a pilot has identified a safe spot to land, they need to communicate their situation to all pertinent parties (air traffic controllers, other crewmembers, and passengers). In "Stage Three" of our journey, I'll discuss the importance of sharing your comeback story with others so they can learn from your experience. As a master storyteller, I'll reveal my pro tips for helping you plot and communicate your own inspiring comeback narrative.

Appreciate — While this is obviously not one of the three pilot crisis management steps (although it probably should be), it is a critical stage in our comeback journeys. None of us, no matter how accomplished, smart, strong, or independent any of us think we may be, can make a successful comeback on our own. As the saying goes, "it takes a team to make the dream," and it is imperative that we express our gratitude to those who have helped us make our comeback possible.

In addition to my hard-charging comeback story, *Tailwind* is packed with alluring, instructive, and inspiring tales of other heroic

Stormriders. They turned their setbacks into comebacks by not being discouraged by all the potential *"what-ifs"* and instead boldly and bravely pursued their dreams by proclaiming *"why not!"*

So, for those of us with a F5 twister barreling towards us, *Tailwind* is the ideal field guide for ensuring we emerge not victimized, but victorious; not doubtful, but determined; not discouraged, but encouraged; not shackled by grief, but soaring with joy; and not empty, but abundant in hope.

As Australian musician, writer, and actor Nick Cave surmised in a 2024 interview on *The Late Show with Stephen Colbert:*

"It took a devastation to teach me the precariousness of life and the essential goodness of people. It took a devastation to reveal the preciousness of the world, of its soul and that the world was crying out for help. It took a devastation to understand mortal value. And it took a devastation to find hope."

Sit back, buckle up, and have a great flight!

Stage 1

Aviate

CHAPTER 1

Fly Your Plane

On the evening of December 29, 1972, as the crew of Eastern Airlines Flight 401 fussed with a burnt-out landing gear indicator light during final approach to Miami International Airport, the Lockheed L-1011 jumbo jet they were supposed to be flying gradually descended towards the Florida Everglades. By the time the distracted pilots realized the autopilot had been accidentally turned off amidst the chaos on the flight deck, it was too late. The plane slammed into the shallow swampland seconds later, killing 101 people onboard.

The preoccupied crew failed to follow the most fundamental in-flight crisis protocol: they neglected to fly their plane.

When an unexpected crisis blindsides us in life or business, I cannot help thinking about the lessons we can learn from the emergency training pilots receive when learning to fly and practice during their recurrent training throughout their careers.

The first—and most important—set of priorities that pilots are taught to follow when something goes wrong is: *Aviate, Navigate,* and *Communicate.* Fly the aircraft first, *Aviate.* Safely flying the plane is followed by *Navigating,* determining where you are and where you can safely land. Then, *Communicate.* Pilots know if they don't keep the plane in the air and it crashes, it won't matter how well they were navigating and communicating.

What would Sully do?

The first stage of this book explores the emotions and reactions we have when we first encounter a crisis. These encounters often knock the wind out of us, leaving us startled and uncertain as to what to do next. Let's look at what we can learn from a skilled pilot when he or she is confronted with an in-flight emergency.

There is no one more qualified to study than one of the world's most skilled aviators, US Airways Captain Chesley "Sully" Sullenberger. In case his name doesn't ring a bell, Sully was the captain of US Airways Flight 1549. You might remember it as the airplane which safely ditched into New York's Hudson River on January 15, 2009. I was the Vice President of Corporate Communications at US Airways at the time, where I played a lead role in the airline's crisis communications response, which *Businessweek* called a "case study in crisis management."

Unlike the distracted crew of the doomed Eastern Airlines flight I mentioned above, Captain Sullenberger and First Officer Jeff Skiles provide us with a textbook example of how to aviate when encountering a monumental crisis that we can all learn from: they flew the plane.

Just two minutes into Flight 1549's climb into the clear skies above Manhattan, a flock of Canada Geese collided with the Airbus A320, crippling the jet's two engines. It was such an unlikely scenario that pilot training for low-altitude dual-engine failure wasn't even mandated by the Federal Aviation Administration (FAA) at the time.

Without pause, Captain Sullenberger embraced the "Aviate, Navigate, and Communicate" crisis management protocol he was trained to follow. First, he avoided an imminent stall by easing the thrustless plane's nose down to regain momentum. He aviated. Sully flew his plane first.

Once adequate momentum was achieved, Sully quickly took stock of the plane's position and where he could safely land. After considering several airfields, he determined that the only survivable option was landing on the Hudson River. He navigated. Finally, as the jetliner descended, the Captain calmly informed the three flight attendants and 150 passengers to "brace for impact." Sully communicated. Most importantly, however, he flew the plane first, giving him the precious time he needed to determine where he could safely land the plane and where he couldn't.

Suffocating under doubt, grief, and shame

Just like in aviation, if we get distracted by the collateral damage and emotions of a crisis, we can be blinded to the real priority: keeping our life or business airborne.

When life takes an unexpected swing at us that brings us to our knees, it often unleashes a crusade of emotions. Our personal misfortunes are accompanied by feelings of fear, betrayal, loneliness, grief, denial, shame, and doubt.

Like many of you reading this book, I have had the wind knocked out of me by my fair share of personal hardships: the passing of my father, the loss of a job I loved, and my recent medical traumas. In each of these instances, I was brought to tears upon their initial onset. Sometimes we just need to cry and hug someone. In many cases, it may be whoever is standing next to us when we first hear the news. This period of sadness can be longer or shorter for each of us and will vary depending on the magnitude of the crisis. It is not my place to profess how long this "draining of the swamp of sadness" should last. That is up to each of us, and no one else. But it is a critical part of aviating the arrival of the personal storms in our life.

Beyond sadness, when many of us encounter a consequential crossroads in our lives, at times, it can feel like we are suffocating under the grief, fear, doubt, and uncertainty about what to do next. Sometimes I felt like I was running away from my problems, but I was just running away from myself with no place to go. The reality is we can either confront the storms we are facing now or later. In the end, we can never outrun or outsmart the crises in our lives or those in our organizations.

Turn fear into focus

As we fly into the storm, there comes an inflection point where we must turn the page on these paralyzing emotions. Let me be clear, I am not suggesting we deny or ignore the implications of the crisis at hand, but we must have the courage to close the door to the demoralizing shame, denial, and anger knocking at it and open a window to the inspiring determination, possibility, and hope necessary to move forward. Pivoting from destructive to constructive thoughts starts with believing that our situation is not permanent, no matter how devastating our circumstances may be. In business and life, I've always believed we must each control our own destiny—or someone or something else will.

Deporting these negative emotions and importing the positive ones will ensure we will have the clarity, focus, and cool-headed judgment to make the right calls and summon the right help to stabilize the situation at hand. To aviate. To fly our plane with the same composure, courage, and conviction as Sully.

In many cases, the judgement we demonstrate at the onset of a crisis has life-altering consequences, not unlike those of the world's aviators. So, don't let an obsession with a broken landing gear light distract you from effectively navigating your crisis; fly your aircraft first. It seems like a simple rule to follow, but like the preoccupied crew that crashed Eastern Airlines Flight 401 into the Florida Everglades, it's easy for us to forget to keep focused on flying our plane amidst the distractions, panic, and anxiety in the fog of the moment.

As I navigated my own personal crisis that I share in the following pages, I constantly reminded myself, "Jim, fly your plane!"

CHAPTER 2

Calm Before the Storm

On January 20th, 2024, my wife Stephanie and I were led by a young blonde nurse into a windowless white treatment room in a nondescript medical facility north of Houston. The news we were bracing for would change the rest of my life. Until that day, my life was a remarkable personal and professional journey that had catapulted me to the pinnacle of my profession, taken me to every corner of the world, and blessed me with a beautiful family.

My on-the-move early years

I grew up in a modest middle-class household. My father, mother, younger sister, and I were constantly on the move as my dad pivoted between various government and non-governmental organization (NGO) roles. I was born on New York City's Staten Island. This was the start of a childhood migration that would take me to eight cities across the U.S. and abroad before I was 18.

Along the way, we lived in New Mexico, New Jersey, and Washington, DC. Six of my most formative years were in Charleston, West Virginia, where I emerged as one of the state's fastest young distance runners. Growing up in this blue-collar community, which was perched along the factory-lined and pollution-soiled Kanawha River, I gained an appreciation for the hard-knuckle life so many American families endure. It was also in Charleston where I learned the virtues of self-discipline and teamwork, as well as good old-fashioned grit and determination from my time running track and playing football.

From West Virginia, we were off to Los Angeles, where we resided for my high school years. However, of all the places I lived growing up, none was more fascinating or impactful on my life than Cartagena, Colombia, where we lived for two years. I'll share more about my time in South America later.

Whenever I am asked where I grew up, I reply "everywhere and nowhere." I explain that my upbringing was 3,000 miles wide and 3 feet deep. While many other families enjoyed multi-generational childhood experiences rooted in a single community, I had the opportunity to discover new places and people across the country and beyond.

It was my always on-the-move childhood that set the stage for the adventure ahead of me. Over the past 35 years, my career has taken me to work for some of the biggest names in business and to more than 60 countries across six continents.

My roaring 20s

After graduating from Syracuse University with a bachelor's in public relations, I returned to LA, where I devoted much of the first decade of my career working in the automotive business.

I started my PR career with Thousand Oaks, California-based J.D. Power and Associates, the pioneer of modern-day customer satisfaction research. I regularly wrote for the company's customer satisfaction magazine, *The Power Report*. The publication's Editor was an obnoxiously loud, chain-smoking, whisky-sipping smartass named Jack Feuer. "Chief," as I affectionately called him—who passed away a few years ago—took me under his wing during my two years at the firm. This 40-something fellow Syracuse grad's handwritten edits to my draft articles were a bloodbath. But Jack was one of my early mentors who made me a more efficient and eloquent writer and graciously introduced me to some of LA's most influential advertising executives. He was a far less reliable source of dating advice during my early twenties.

I spent the next seven years working with Nissan North America in various PR and advertising agency roles. This was a meteoric stretch in my early career. It was the mid-90s, and digital media and the world wide web were making their debut. While I was initially focused on conventional PR and advertising for Nissan at the iconic LA ad agency Chiat/Day, it wasn't long before I found myself spearheading the car company's early online media endeavors, including the creation of their first corporate website, employee intranet, and digital newsroom. These pathbreaking endeavors led to a coveted role on Nissan's inaugural Interactive Media Taskforce—working alongside my fellow digital forerunners (including my longtime friend and mentor Neil Patel).

I was quickly promoted to West Coast Director of New Media at Nissan's PR agency, Porter Novelli—where I partnered with interactive media vanguards Jason Teitler and Jim Healy to launch the firm's digital media practice.

When I turned 27, one of the PR profession's luminaries and Nissan's Chief Communications Officer at the time, Don Spetner, approached my boss Craig Caldwell (who led the Nissan account at Porter Novelli) and me about establishing our own boutique agency to support the automaker's product and digital PR efforts. Shortly after, Lost Dog Communications was born, and Craig and I set up shop with some Ikea furniture and a Sony Playstation in a scrappy loft in the wind-swept beachfront LA neighborhood of Playa del Rey. While I departed Lost Dog a few years later, Craig and the firm continued to serve Nissan for the next 25 years.

It was during what I called my "Nissan Years" that Stephanie and I got married. We tied the knot in 1995 a few years after meeting at a PR conference in New York City. It took time for me to come to my senses, but on May 13, 1995, on a postcard-perfect Southern California afternoon, we committed to a life together in a small white chapel perched above the Malibu coastline at Pepperdine University, Stephanie's alma mater and where her father was a Professor of Biology. It was the start of a love-fueled adventure that continues to this day.

My stride-gaining 30s

In 2000, I was called by a recruiter about a position to lead communications at an Internet startup called GoTo.com, which would later change its name to Overture. Overture was a pioneer of search engine marketing, coming of age at the same time as Google. Leaving Lost

Dog was one of the toughest decisions I had to make over the years. It was hard to walk away from a firm I had co-founded at such a young age. I was so proud of what Craig and I had built and the work we were doing for Nissan. Even more difficult than saying goodbye to Lost Dog was parting ways with Craig.

While I had learned a lot from Jack about writing, it paled in comparison to the influence that Craig had on my writing and creativity. Craig started his career writing for some of the world's best-known car magazines and top advertising agencies. I had the privilege of helping Craig develop speeches and presentations for Nissan's top U.S. and global executives, including its former Chairman and CEO Carlos Ghosn. Serving as an understudy to such an extraordinary writer during these formative years of my career elevated my writing to a new level.

Craig was and continues to be so much more than a valued mentor. He is a dear friend. We would take lunchtime rides together along the breezy Playa del Rey bike path, we would shoot hoops at the neighboring beachfront park and vent about our favorite clients, and we would enjoy heart attack-inducing burgers at The Shack across the street. So, it wasn't surprising Craig didn't talk to me for a couple months after I told him I was taking the job at Overture. Thankfully, it didn't take long for us to reconcile. I continue to look forward to our visits to this day and the chance to share a good laugh over war stories from our "Nissan Years."

Being the VP of Global Communications at Overture was one of the most endurance-testing jobs I've held. When I started in the summer of 2000, Overture was in a head-to-head battle with Google. The "Search War" was reminiscent of the Coke vs. Pepsi "Cola Wars" of the '80s and the Windows vs. Mac "PC War" of the '90s. Our small and fierce PR team traveled the country and world to put Overture on the map. In the wake of the 1999 dot-com bubble implosion, Overture— led by CEO Ted Meisel— was one of the few Internet companies to emerge vibrant and profitable. Shortly after changing our name to Overture, we were acquired by Yahoo! for $1.6 billion.

Speaking of the "Cola Wars," it was a former VP of PR at Pepsi that GoTo brought in to oversee investor relations and communications to lead the Overture rebranding and fight against Google. Ken

Ross, who went on to lead communications at Netflix after Overture, would become one of my most trusted mentors. We had quite the ride at Overture, co-creating the company's brand identity, mission, and values. But it was the enduring PR war stories and lessons Ken shared with our team at epic Beverly Hills steak dinners and Vegas team off-sites that rekindle my fondest memories. He is unequivocally one of the PR profession's quiet legends and a giant of a friend.

However, what made my time at Overture one of the most fatiguing experiences of my career was pursuing my Executive MBA at the University of Southern California at the same time. For two years, on every other Friday and Saturday, I would venture to USC's downtown LA campus for a full day of classes—in many instances a day after returning from a trip to New York, Tokyo, or Seoul. But I did it, and emerged as one of only a handful of PR executives in the world with an MBA.

After Yahoo!'s purchase of Overture, Stephanie and I learned to sail and bought a 34-foot Beneteau. It was during those sails along the Southern California sun-kissed coast that we decided it was time to start our family, and LA was not where we wanted to do that.

I recall thinking that LA is for three kinds of people:

1. the rich and famous, as it is one of the most expensive cities in the country to live in;
2. the very poor, because for the homeless, it's warm all year and there is an abundance of food banks; and,
3. the young, as it's a great city if you're in your twenties and launching your career, meeting other young and ambitious people, and having a lot of fun in the process.

After departing Overture at 35, I realized that I wasn't any of those three. It was time for us to find a new city to call home.

In June of 2004 Stephanie and I moved from our Santa Monica townhome to the Emerald City of Seattle, where I accepted a senior position with We. Communications. Founded by tech PR trailblazers Melissa Waggener Zorkin and the late Pam Edstrom, We. is one of the world's largest and innovative independent PR agencies, and Microsoft's first and longstanding agency of record.

My boss there was Corey duBrowa, who would be my boss twice over the course of my career and, if I'm lucky, I'll have a shot to work for him a third time. I quickly recognized Corey was the tempo setter everyone at the agency wanted to keep up with. So, it's not surprising he would later lead communications at Starbucks, Salesforce, and Google. Today, he is the CEO of Burson, one of the world's largest and most iconic PR agencies. He is also widely recognized as one of the PR profession's most admired leaders. To this day, when I'm confronted with a consequential decision, I ask myself, "What would Corey do?"

A year after moving to Seattle, our daughter, Kaitlyn, was born. Over time, we became known to friends and family as "The Olson Three." For the next 20 years, we explored the world together.

My high-flying 40s

In the years that followed my time at We. Communications, I was invited to take on a series of back-to-back senior corporate communications leadership roles.

In 2008, I joined US Airways as VP of Corporate Communications. The hallmark of this experience was playing a lead role in the crisis response to the emergency water landing of US Airways Flight 1549 on New York's Hudson River, known as the "Miracle on the Hudson." This accident would become one of the aviation industry's highest-profile crises.

During my time at US Airways, I had the privilege of working with three admired leaders who later became the CEOs of two of the largest airlines in the world. Doug Parker, the Chairman and CEO of US Airways, became Chairman and CEO of American Airlines following its acquisition by US Airways. Scott Kirby, US Airways' President, later became Chairman and CEO of United Airlines, the world's largest airline. And Robert Isom, US Airways' Chief Operating Officer, succeeded Doug as American's Chairman and CEO.

However, it was my boss Elise Eberwein—US Airways' EVP of HR, Communications, and Community Relations—who had the biggest impact on me. In an industry notorious for professional "hard landings," Elise went above and beyond to ensure I succeeded in a role that is impossible to prepare for. Elise exemplified servant leadership more than anyone I've ever worked for; she was a badass executive by every measure, but beneath her Harley-riding and black-diamond snowboarding fearlessness, Elise demonstrated empathy for her team—and more importantly our families—unmatched by any other executive at the airline. Which explains why I continue to consider Elise and her pilot husband, Russ Webber, cherished friends.

Four years later, I departed Phoenix (where US Airways was based) for Seattle again. I rejoined Corey duBrowa, who had left We. Communications to be Chief Communications Officer at Starbucks. Corey recruited me to the world's largest coffee retailer to serve as VP of Global Corporate Communications and Public Affairs. The opportunity to work with Starbucks' CEO Howard Schultz during the largest growth streak in the company's 40-year history was just too enticing to resist. And the chance to work alongside Corey again—who had become a dear friend and mentor—was an equally enticing invitation I couldn't decline.

Following half a decade at Starbucks, I was recruited back to the airline world for the opportunity of a lifetime to serve as Chief Communications Officer at the world's largest airline, United Airlines. I worked with the carrier's new CEO and Chairman, Oscar Munoz, to develop and introduce United's 21st century mission and values, unite a disgruntled global workforce, restore the airline's iconic brand, and mitigate a drumbeat of reputation-threatening issues, including the forced removal of a customer from a United Express flight that sparked global attention.

My admiration for Oscar began during my interview with him on December 26, 2015. I was still at Starbucks then, flying into Chicago under the cloak of darkness after a ten-day trip to Chengdu, China. Oscar was recovering in his downtown apartment, still regaining strength after a near-fatal heart attack just two months earlier. What struck me immediately was his disarming authenticity—his genuine curiosity about other people, businesses and the world around him.

After a few minutes of warm small talk, he cut straight to the heart of it. "Jim, I've already spoken with enough people to know you can do this job. What I need to understand this morning is whether we share the same purpose and values." The next ninety minutes unfolded as a powerful exchange—questions, stories, lessons, and insights that revealed not just what we believed, but who we were.

I was offered the job a couple weeks later.

It was a remarkable ride—marked by turbulence and triumph—that concluded two years later in the wake of a leadership restructuring. In the weeks and months following my departure from United, I reminded myself that when we get knocked off one mountain, there is always another one ready for us to climb.

My purpose-discovering 50s

Indeed, it was my exit from United that set the stage for a three-year global sabbatical that took me on an international teaching, speaking, writing, and consulting journey. Along the way I visited, worked, and lived in more than a dozen countries spanning five continents. This included an executive residency at African Leadership University (ALU) on the Indian Ocean island of Mauritius, serving as a Public Relations Professor at Syracuse University, keynote speaking engagements around the world, and writing leadership articles for *Fortune* and *Fast Company*.

Our family's year in Mauritius was life-changing for all three of us. It was especially enlightening for Kaitlyn, who had just turned 14 when we sold our North Shore Chicago home, packed our nine suitcases, and headed to Africa. Mauritius was an extraordinary experience, but the chance to visit other countries across Africa, including our ten-day Kenya camping safari, made this an experience like no other.

More than anything were the incredible people we met along the way, many of whom will remain lifelong friends. Two of the most impactful people we met were ALU Founder Fred Swaniker and ALU President Christopher O.H. Williams. I'll come back to ALU, Fred, and Christopher later in this book, but there are few people in this world that I hold in a higher esteem than these two courageous, world-improving leaders. Thanks to Fred, Christopher, and the countless others our family encountered along the way, we discovered like so many before us, you can leave Africa, but Africa never leaves you.

We returned from the sun-soaked turquoise waters of Mauritius to the snow-blanketed streets of upstate New York, where I joined the faculty of Syracuse University's S.I. Newhouse School of Public Communications. It was during this experience that I received a call from Andrew Levy, the former Chief Financial Officer at United Airlines. We worked together at the airline, where we bonded over our shared appreciation for the unrivaled value of PR. We departed United around the same time. However, instead of embarking on a global sabbatical, Andrew began raising money to start a new airline. As the former Co-Founder and President of Allegiant Air, building new airlines was in his blood.

Andrew was ready to launch his new venture—Avelo Airlines—and was inquiring about my interest in leading communications. As much as I enjoyed teaching, I ultimately decided to join Andrew's startup airline. I still had jet fuel in my veins. I carefully contemplated the offer and determined that there will always be teaching roles for me to pursue, but new airlines only come along every ten to 20 years.

When Avelo took flight on April 28, 2021, it became America's first new airline in 15 years. The chance to build an airline and its brand story from scratch was just too seductive of an opportunity to pass up. My five years with Avelo were a breathtaking ride as we vaulted the airline from obscurity to broadscale admiration. At the time of my departure (May 2025), Avelo operated 20 737s, flew to 50 destinations across the U.S. and abroad, and employed more than 1,000 people. Avelo has also flown nearly 10 million travelers, earned top marks in customer satisfaction, and achieved industry-leading on-time reliability. I'll share more later about Avelo and the team-building leadership that has earned Andrew the distinction of being one of the aviation industry's most admired entrepreneurs.

I feel blessed to have enjoyed such a remarkable career, one that has enabled me to visit so many places across the globe, meet and work with some of the world's most respected leaders, collaborate with some of America's most influential journalists, and make a positive difference in so many people's lives. At the same time, I am humbled by the recognition my endeavors have received. I've been named one of the world's top 100 communicators and honored by Syracuse University's S.I. Newhouse School of Public Communications as one of their 50 most influential graduates. The organizations, leaders, and teams I've worked with have also received many of the world's top honors.

It is hard for me to find words to capture how grateful I am for the family, jobs, and experiences my life has gifted me over the past 57 years. However, no one, including me, could have predicted what was in store for the next chapter of my storied life.

CHAPTER 3

Houston, We Have a Problem

November 10, 2023 was a quiet and uneventful Friday evening in The Woodlands, Texas, the leafy suburb north of Houston I called home when I wasn't traveling, which was about 60% of the time. I was flying solo that weekend—Stephanie was in San Antonio visiting friends, and Kaitlyn was at college. So, I ventured out to dinner at one of my favorite local seafood restaurants on my own. I saddled up to the bar next to a couple enjoying a bottle of champagne and a pair of crabcakes. I ordered a dozen freshly caught Gulf oysters, a Caesar salad, and a full-bodied glass of cab. It was delicious, as usual.

Around 9 p.m., I pulled into the driveway of our white brick two-story home situated at the end of our tree-lined street at the top of the cul-de-sac. After wrapping up a quick chat with Kaitlyn, who had called to update me on her day, I crawled into bed and quickly fell asleep.

Two hours into my slumber, I woke up to a sharp, jabbing pain in my lower back just above my hip. I tried stretching it out and massaging the area to no avail. The pain increased at a rapid rate. I took some Advil, but it only got worse. It became unendurable. I felt like an organ was going to burst. I have a high threshold for pain, but this was alarming.

At that moment, the sage advice of United Airlines' former CEO and Chairman Oscar Munoz, who I worked for a few years ago, echoed in my mind. A few weeks after Oscar joined United, he experienced a catastrophic heart attack in his Chicago apartment. He ultimately survived following multiple surgeries and a heart transplant. In the weeks, months, and years following his remarkable recovery, Oscar made it his mission to share with others the advice he received from a cardiologist neighbor shortly before his heart attack. The friend told Oscar, "If you ever feel anything strange or different with your body—and you'll know it when you feel it—go to the ER or call 9-1-1." He explained to Oscar that most people, guys in particular, are reluctant to call for help because they fear the embarrassment of paramedics arriving and determine nothing is wrong. Oscar would remind us it is better to be embarrassed than dead. Calling 9-1-1 after Oscar felt a strange sensation in his leg saved his life.

Like Oscar, I knew something was off that evening. I scraped myself out of bed, put on some sweatpants and a T-shirt, got in my car, and raced off to the hospital. It was a short drive—about three miles—but it felt like an eternity. The pain continued to intensify. I've never been stabbed, but it felt like someone pierced my lower abdomen with an electric screwdriver.

The pain was so bad, I was worried about passing out on my drive to the ER, so I concentrated on my breathing to keep my mind on the road. Around 2:30 a.m., I screeched into the empty parking lot at The Woodlands Memorial Hermann Medical Center. I stumbled into the brightly lit ER and flopped onto the reception desk.

I sheepishly cried out that I thought I was having appendicitis. She ushered me through a gurney-lined hallway to a treatment room. An awaiting nurse directed me to change into a blue hospital gown and lay on the treatment table. He placed a warm blanket over me and, within a few minutes, he was pumping me with morphine to mitigate the pain. He told me to relax and that a doctor would be in soon. The pain quickly subsided. I can now appreciate why this high-octane painkiller is so effective on the battlefield—and so addictive. The pain vanished in a matter of minutes.

The doctor quickly dismissed my speculation of appendicitis. "Your appendix is on the other side. But we still need to figure out what is going on." I thought to myself, *of course it's on the other side.*

The doctor drew my blood and ordered a CT scan. I returned to the ER treatment room, nudged in my AirPods, alerted Stephanie and Kaitlyn to my hospitalization, and drifted away to a chorus of nerve-soothing tracks on my phone as the morphine did its thing.

My moment of reckoning

Two hours passed and the doctor returned.

"I have some good news and bad news," he began. "The good news is I don't see anything wrong with your abdominal organs or lower back. It was a perfect scan, and your bloodwork looks good."

I contemplated what the bad news could possibly be.

"Here is the bad news. While it wasn't our intention, the CT scan captured part of your lung, which revealed a large and concerning mass."

I had a thousand questions. "I don't smoke—is it lung cancer?"

He sensed my panic and tried to temper my concern by explaining that it isn't necessarily cancer: it could be scarring or an infection. But he underscored the urgency of getting it checked. "It's a very large spot. You need to take this very seriously."

My next question was, "What caused the pain in my lower back?"

The doctor said that was a mystery to him. "There is no direct connection between the spot on your lung and the lower back pain you experienced. But it got you in here and alerted us to the spot on your lung. That is the important thing."

I left the ER that morning never experiencing even the slightest pain or tenderness in my lower back ever again, not in the days, weeks, months, or years that followed.

The verdict

Over the course of the next eight weeks, I underwent additional CT and PET scans, and, ultimately, a biopsy of my lung. The moment of truth had arrived. The office of the Oncologist I had been referred to called to set up an urgent appointment to discuss the biopsy results.

For the two days leading up to the appointment, I felt like a defendant awaiting the jury to return with their verdict. In my case, I feared a death sentence. In the meantime, I prayed and did everything I could to keep positive.

We fear a lot of things in our lives and jobs, but the fear that haunted me at this moment made everything else insignificant.

On a mid-January afternoon, Stephanie and I sat in the sterile, windowless office of my Oncologist at The Woodlands Cancer Institute.

Even saying the word "Oncologist" was hard to muster—I was 55 and in great shape. I had lost 30 pounds the year before and was working out on a regular basis. I was at the peak of my career. *This isn't happening to me*, I told myself.

Dr. Krishna Pachipala entered the room in his white doctor's coat and stethoscope around his neck. He pulled up a chair next to us and cut to the chase. "Your lung biopsy turned out not to be lung cancer. It appears to be Stage 4 metastatic melanoma."

At that moment, the conversation switched into slow motion. All I heard was "Stage 4 cancer." I knew very little about cancer, but I knew Stage 4 was not good. I was glad Stephanie was there to take notes, as I was in a parallel universe at that moment.

The verdict had been rendered.

As he began explaining the treatment plan, I snapped out of the fog I was in. Dr. Pachipala explained he was going to administer a cutting-edge cancer treatment called immunotherapy. He told us unlike chemotherapy, which is similar to a 20th century nuclear bomb that destroys your good and bad cells, causing massive collateral damage, immunotherapy is like a 21st century military drone that only targets the cancer. I asked him how effective it was.

"Very effective," Dr. Pachipala replied. "My patients have experienced a 90%–100% success rate with immunotherapy. Prior to immunotherapy, the survival rate for Stage 4 metastatic melanoma patients was 10%–20%. You are in good shape, so I'm very optimistic you will respond positively to this approach."

I had a thousand questions racing through my head, including whether there would be the same debilitating and demoralizing side effects so common with chemotherapy.

He explained that there are many potential side effects. "Some people get fatigued. Rashes and itchiness are also not unusual. But again, you are overall in great shape, so I do not anticipate you will have a negative reaction."

I was also curious how long and frequently I would have to undergo the treatment. He explained it really depends on the patient: it can take a couple years for some, while others achieve remission in less than a year.

A life ring from God

While I've admittedly spent a lifetime enjoying time in the sun—Hell, I lived on an exotic island in the Southern Indian Ocean for a year—I was baffled how I ended up with melanoma with no prior diagnoses of questionable spots on my body during annual physicals. He explained it is rare, but in about 5%–10% of cases melanoma metastasizes in one or more organs with no surface area spots, or spots so small or residing on the skin so briefly they go undiagnosed. Even after my diagnosis, a Dermatologist's reexamination found no surface-area spots.

I asked, "Do you think the pain in my lower back was a symptom of the tumor on my lung?"

Dr. Pachipala replied the same as the other doctors I had asked. "I've never seen that before. I don't believe there is a direct correlation, especially since you haven't experienced the pain again since the first instance."

I followed up with the obvious question: If there were no visible signs of melanoma, how would I have known to get this checked if that CT scan in November hadn't accidentally caught it?

"There is no way you would have known. That's why they call melanoma *the masquerading cancer*; there are often no symptoms of the tumors until it's too late to effectively treat in most patients. You are very lucky to have caught it when you did."

I thought, "lucky?" That lower back pain and the accidental scan of my lung were nothing short of a miracle. A message from God to get your ass into the hospital: "I just threw you a life ring."

As I processed this unexpected news, I recalled a similar but far less alarming conversation with a different doctor in Chicago six years earlier. As part of a nose-to-tail executive physical, a spattering of microscopic spots was found on my lung. However, my doctor at the time believed they were too small to be cancerous. He concluded they were likely residual scarring from a prior lung infection or exposure to toxins earlier in my life (after all, pollution-belching FMC and Union Carbide chemical factories flanked West Virginia's Kanawha River where I grew up and ran several miles almost every day).

I was in great health as far as that doctor was concerned, and he told me to carry on with my life. Since the doctor didn't believe a biopsy was necessary, I'll never know if this was a precursor to my melanoma diagnosis or simply the residual infection scarring my doctor at that time had indicated it was.

As I stared at the wall, trying to make sense of everything, I told myself that second-guessing whether I should have been more concerned about those previous spots was only going to compound the grief and fear hijacking me.

I had many more questions, but I knew this was just the first of many visits to come with the doctor. As we gathered our stuff and stood up to leave, Dr. Pachipala turned to us and said, "One last thing. Out of an abundance of caution, I want you to get a brain MRI to make sure the cancer has not jumped to your head. It's doubtful, but let's just be certain we have a full picture of what we are up against."

The relief I felt after learning about the high success rate of immunotherapy was quickly replaced by a new wave of unfathomable fear and uncertainty. A brain tumor, I thought to myself, would be too much to handle. However, as the doctor emphasized, it's better to know the full picture—and pray a brain mass is not part of it.

As my mind spiraled toward the worst outcomes, I steadied myself with the words of Apollo 13 Commander Jim Lovell: "There are people who make things happen; there are people who watch things happen; and there are people who wonder what happened." If a tumor was waiting in my brain, I was determined to meet it as that first kind of person.

CHAPTER 4

It Will Get Worse Before It Gets Worse

Over the course of my three-decade public relations career, I've been in the foxhole for some of the most high-profile, high-stakes crises of our time. These include plane crashes, a terrorist suicide bombing, union battles, and a hostile corporate takeover by activist investors, to name just a few. There are many lessons I've learned from these experiences, but the most compelling of them is that when you are dangling in the jaws of a crisis, I can assure you, *it will get worse before it gets worse.* In other words, when you think the crucible you are facing can't get worse, I assure you, it can and will.

This mantra doesn't just apply to the business world. The same holds true in the adversities that confront us in our personal lives. Whether it's being fired, a life-threatening medical diagnosis, financial misfortune, or a deteriorating relationship, in most instances, the setbacks we face on the home front get worse before they get better.

This unfortunate but time-tested truth was about to cast its dark shadow on my life.

Let's roll!

On a Friday afternoon in early February, it was time for my first immunotherapy infusion. With Stephanie by my side, the nurse directed me to an oversized blue leather reclining chair in the front row of two dozen similar chairs, about half of which were occupied by other patients receiving either chemo or immuno infusions. It was a surreal scene—one that I had never envisioned myself in.

Here we go, I thought to myself. I consider myself a "cancer warrior," so to commemorate my first strike against the enemy that invaded my body, I wore an olive-colored T-shirt like the trademark green tee worn by Ukraine President Volodymyr Zelensky. If anyone knows something about fighting a heartless and ruthless opponent, it's that badass.

The nurse took my blood pressure, verified my name and date of birth, and then proceeded to inject an IV in my left arm. For the next hour I laid back, inserted my Air Pods, and drifted into deep thought as the double cocktail of cancer-vaporizing drugs dripped into my vein.

I fired up the soothing music of Spanish DJ Jose Padilla, kicking off with a selection appropriately titled *Day One*. I closed my eyes and imagined the drugs racing through my body to the frontline of the battle of my life, the 2.5" mass on my left lung.

However, I was about to learn about a second, even more consequential, battlefront.

Brace for impact

As my first infusion session drew to a close, Dr. Pachipala emerged to check in on me. He asked how it was going; I told him I didn't feel a thing. I joked that it felt like a placebo. He smiled.

The smile was short-lived. His voice lowered as he told me he got the brain MRI results back that morning. "You have a 1.5" tumor."

I was speechless, so he filled the silence with the battle plan he had mapped out. He directed me to his practice partner, Radiation Oncologist Dr. Jason Berilgen, or "Dr. B," as his staff and patients affectionately call him. His office reached out to me that afternoon to schedule an emergency appointment for the following Monday. I took the first opening they had at 8:00 a.m. Like Dr. Pachipala, Dr. B had a very compassionate but direct bedside manner. I could tell he had engaged in similar conversations to the one he had with me hundreds of times before. He reassured me everything was going to be okay and that he was going to eradicate this "guber," as he called it, with a single 15-minute radiation blast.

He made it sound so easy. But I knew this was much more serious—and dangerous—than the mole I had removed from my nose when I was 14. My mind was flooded with terrifying thoughts of having my head shaved and a burning laser penetrating my skull. Or what if they miss and I'm paralyzed for the rest of my life.

Dr. B quickly calmed my fears. He explained the procedure from start to finish, answering every question I had with remarkable patience.

First, "You're going to get a really cool mask made. You'll wear this during the procedure to hold your head still. You'll need to get that done tomorrow, and we'll do the procedure on Thursday."

Dr. B proceeded to explain what would take place during the procedure. "You'll lay on a table and the laser will circle your head for 15 minutes."

Will they have to shave my head? "No."

Will it hurt or burn? "No—you won't feel a thing."

Will I need my wife to drive me home? "No—you'll be in the same condition as when you arrived."

This seemed way too simple, but I trusted he knew what he was doing. I had no other options. Winning was the only option, and a "shock and awe" radiation blast sounded like an effective battle plan to me.

As Dr. B stood up to leave, I asked him about the effectiveness of radiation.

Without hesitation, he said, "We should have the tumor eliminated with this single session. However, it will take about 90 days for the radiation to dissolve the tumor."

I thanked the doctor and left his office feeling cautiously optimistic.

The next day, I drove to the hospital to have my mask fitted. A couple of young and chatty nurses escorted me back to a large room with a gigantic futuristic-looking machine in the middle. I asked if that was the machine that would be delivering the radiation blast.

"Yep, that's her," one of the nurses quipped.

After filling out some paperwork, which included a five-page waiver outlining a hundred potential side effects and risks to undergoing this treatment, from nausea to paralysis to death, they asked me to lay down on the table.

They placed a warm, soft plastic mold on my face that would serve as the foundation for the much larger mask. It took about ten minutes for the mold to solidify, and I was done. They said my mask would be ready for Thursday. I grabbed my car keys and wallet off the table and headed home.

Star Wars

I returned to the hospital on Thursday afternoon wearing jeans and a black T-shirt. I was once again in battle mode. The same two nurses presented me with my mask. It was impressive. They placed it on me, and I felt like a *Star Wars* Stormtrooper. I hopped on the table and laid back. They bolted the mask to the table to keep my head from moving. One of the nurses placed a warm blanket over me and inquired what kind of music I wanted to hear. I asked what my options were; they said they had everything. I suggested classic rock.

"You got it, Jim!"

The nurse asked me if I was ready. I said, "Let's roll!"

She gave me a smile that I could barely see through the mask, patted me on the shoulder, and said she would see me in 15 minutes.

They cranked up the tunes, turned down the lights, and I was off to battle, again. This time, I was armed with *Star Wars*-like green and red lasers I could see rotating around my head as Guns N' Roses' "Welcome to the Jungle" and Bruce Springsteen's "Thunder Road" played in the background.

It was over before I knew it, and pain-free, as Dr. B had promised. No smoke and fire. No shaved head, no hole in my skull. The nurse returned, unbolted my mask, and helped me off the table.

"How did it go?" she asked.

I replied, "One of the best laser shows I've seen."

As I left the room, she called out, "Don't forget your mask!"

"What a great consolation gift," I said.

I placed it in my trunk and drove it home. It sits in my home office today as a symbolic medal from that early—but consequential—battle.

For the next three months, I continued to receive my immuno infusions every three weeks. I prayed that the radiation was dissolving the tumor in my head like the body of a gangster in a Sopranos episode melting in a barrel of acid.

All I could do was wait, pray, and keep my positive attitude flying at a high altitude. I was scared; what if it didn't work? For the next 90 days, my mind toggled between envisioning the tumor's complete eradication to nightmares of defeat and the terrifying consequences of an untamed tumor growing in my head.

Fast forward 12 weeks. Dr. B's office called and asked me to schedule a follow-up brain MRI. This was it: the images revealed from this x-ray of my brain would be the definitive evidence of whether we had eliminated the uninvited enemy that was trespassing on my brain.

This MRI, like the first one that revealed the tumor, is one of the more unpleasant experiences of this journey. They laid me down on a table, gave me some ear plugs, and slid the table back into the MRI "donut." For nearly an hour, I stared at the top of the spinning magnetic x-ray machine as it belched out a symphony of the most obnoxious noises you can imagine. It was as if my head had been placed in a metal trash can as someone banged the can with a hammer. This was accompanied by a chorus of other teeth-clinching noises, including an Amber alert, fire alarm, dentist drill, a construction site jack hammer, among many others. The sounds rang in my head for the rest of the day.

My early win

Two days later, I was back in Dr. B.'s office. As I waited, I said a final prayer. I heard a light knock on the door and Dr. B entered with a beaming smile.

"It's a ten," he exclaimed.

I asked what that meant.

He explained, "It's the best possible outcome we could have hoped for. The tumor is essentially gone."

He showed me side-by-side images of the first MRI with the new one. There were still a few very small spots at the bottom of the image that I asked about. He said it was the residual scar tissue from the radiation. "That's not unusual to see."

I asked what's next. He said, "You're done. We just need to keep an eye on it to make sure it doesn't return."

I was on top of the world. I spent the rest of the day calling and texting family and friends the great news, thanking them for their support and prayers. I had won my first consequential cancer battle. My confidence in my ability to win this war was now stronger than ever. I was confident the immunotherapy was going to yield the same victorious outcome. It was just going to be a longer fight.

Friends and family asked how I was able to achieve such an early win. I tell people it is the powerful trifecta of modern medicine, an unshakeable positive attitude, and a deep faith in God that what can't be healed through our human superpowers will be healed through His supernatural restoration.

I felt victorious, but it was far too early to hang a "mission accomplished" banner. I was up against a formidable enemy called cancer. While I won the first round, friends who had either survived their own cancer fight or knew others who had reminded me that cancer is a wicked and sneaky disease that strikes back when you least expect.

"Keep your guard up," they warned.

I went home that night, thanked God for expelling the tumor from my head, and prayed for the miraculous interventions to continue.

In the days and weeks that followed, I drew the courage to forge ahead from the words of British Prime Minister Winston Churchill, who reminded the world in his 1942 speech after the Allied victory at El Alamein: "This is not the end. It is not even the beginning of the end. But it is, perhaps, the end of the beginning."

CHAPTER 5

Blindsided

I entered the summer of 2024—six months into my diagnosis—with an abundance of hope and enthusiasm. My brain tumor was gone, my lung tumor had shrunk 70%, and, with the exception of a few minor episodes of fatigue, I was feeling great. I was working out on a regular basis—if you placed me in a lineup of ten guys pulled off the streets of Houston, I would likely be the last one you would say is fighting Stage 4 cancer.

As I battled forward, I continued to thrive at my job as the Head of Brand and Communications at Avelo Airlines. Except for doctors' visits and treatments, I only took one day off work. I was traveling and working harder than ever. In the first half of the year, we launched more new destinations and routes than at any other period in our airline's young three-year history. I was crisscrossing the country multiple times a month to introduce new destinations and inaugurate new routes. Our growing company was soaring: we were delivering industry-leading on-time reliability and customer satisfaction, best-in-class employee engagement, and healthy financial performance.

I felt unstoppable!

As the peak summer travel season ramped up, I was flying high and saw nothing but blue skies on the horizon. However, my turbulence-free summer was about to hit a violent high-altitude clear-air wake that would send my life into a horrifying and uncontrollable nosedive.

In the days leading up to July 4, 2024, I was in LA on business to conduct a TV interview at the city's largest TV station and celebrate flying our one millionth customer from our base at Burbank Airport.

Then, on Wednesday, I was off to Santa Rosa to join our team at Avelo's Northern California base to celebrate Independence Day on Thursday, ready to overindulge in an abundance of festive food and snacks with our pilots, flight attendants, and airport crew.

It was a fun day, and I was now looking forward to squeezing in some Napa wine-tasting before heading back to Houston on Saturday.

Ambushed

As I prepared to return to my hotel that afternoon, I struggled to summon my Uber. My sight dimmed as a soft haze drifted across my vision—making it difficult to see. I brushed it off as fatigue. I had been up since 4:30 a.m. to ensure I was at the airport to support our crew for Avelo's first bank of flights. I also thought it might be a bad pair of contacts; I had just received a new package of lenses following my uneventful annual eye exam a week earlier.

I went to bed optimistic I would awake to my normal vision. I woke up the next morning to more distorted sight. I looked in the mirror—I could barely recognize myself.

I was scared. I called my Optometrist. She asked me a series of questions and scheduled an emergency appointment for me on Monday when I was back in Houston. I continued with my wine tasting. I may have lost my sight, but my sense of taste and appreciation for California's finest vintages was stronger than ever.

I returned to Houston a couple days later. I explained to my eye doctor what happened and what I was seeing. She conducted a battery of tests and determined nothing was wrong with my physical eye or retina (beyond an existing retina condition I've had since childhood that required contacts, but didn't disrupt or limit my livelihood in any significant way). She referred me to Houston's top eye center for further evaluation. She said my situation was beyond her abilities and required a deeper level of expertise.

The next day, I was off to the Retina Consultants of Texas, the state's leading vision and blindness prevention clinic. It is an impressive operation staffed by the state's leading Ophthalmologists and equipped with state-of-the art vision testing and imaging technology.

For the next several weeks, I underwent a tsunami of tests and two additional brain MRIs. I also visited a Neurologist and met with my Oncologist to determine if the immunotherapy might be the culprit.

Six weeks passed without a conclusive diagnosis. My vision remained in the same fog. My team of doctors ultimately determined the dramatic bilateral vision deterioration I was experiencing was the result of severe optic nerve damage. The diagnosis was nonarteritic anterior ischemic optic neuropathy (NAION), a rare condition resulting from swelling of the optic nerve. It is most common in men in their 50s—me! It is typically caused by a sudden disruption of blood flow to the optic nerve. I was told there are many things that could have triggered this that were outside my control. Very small seizures or strokes that you would never notice or a brief spike in blood pressure are the most common causes.

My Ophthalmologist who specializes in vitreoretinal surgery and medical retina, Dr. Effie Rahman, believed it was possible my immunotherapy treatment could have triggered a dramatic spike in my blood pressure, resulting in the disruption of blood flow to my brain. After consulting with my Oncologist, they concluded it would be best to suspend immunotherapy treatment out of an abundance of caution. However, Dr. Rahman acknowledged, "we'll never know what the underlying cause was."

During my last visit with her, she said "The good news is I believe that we have solved the mystery behind what likely caused your vision loss. The bad news is there is no cure. While I don't want you to lose hope, it is rare that the optic nerve regenerates."

She leaned over, gently placed her hand on my shoulder, and said, "This will very likely be your vision for the foreseeable future. You've been through a lot this year; you are handling all of this incredibly well. Hang in there."

Nosedive

I left her office in a state of trauma. Since the loss of my sight prevented me from driving, Kaitlyn picked me up. I was lucky to have her home from college during the summer to drive me to my frequent doctor appointments. It was a quiet ride home. I felt like I had just been condemned to a life sentence of blindness. With no cure or corrective lenses to improve this condition, I feared I would never drive or work again, enjoy a California sunset, or watch Kaitlyn perform in her musicals or in a Broadway show someday.

For several weeks, I wanted to shrink into the sheets of my bed. I woke up each morning praying that I would open my eyes to a clear world. It never happened. Cancer was now the least of my concerns. I was confronting a Category 5 hurricane of biblical proportions, and I had no idea what to do.

A firestorm of emotions ambushed me, a paralyzing Molotov cocktail of fear, denial, shame, and grief. I wanted to blame something or someone, most notably myself. While my doctors had assured me there was nothing I could have done to prevent this catastrophe and that the small size of my optic nerve cells made me predisposed to this nightmare, I was haunted with the sense of self-betrayal that there was something I could have done, as well as the self-doubt that I could never return to the PR career that I love so much and that has been my self-identity for the majority of my life.

The self-worth that had steadied me since childhood had slipped away—replaced by a lingering ache of unworthiness. I not only had difficulty recognizing my face in the mirror each morning, I no longer recognized who I was.

I felt like this additional 20,000 feet added to my climb might finally break me. As a lifelong gritty and hungry grinder who has always bravely chased doing hard things and choosing the road less traveled—I feared this might just be too much—even for me.

Turning trauma into triumph

Standing on the edge of this dark and terrifying abyss, I summoned strength and inspiration from the enduring words of President Theodore Roosevelt, who said:

> *"It is not the critic who counts; not the man who points out how the strong man stumbles, or where the doer of deeds could have done them better. The credit belongs to the man who is actually in the arena, whose face is marred by dust and sweat and blood; who strives valiantly; who errs, who comes short again and again,*

because there is no effort without error and shortcoming; but who does actually strive to do the deeds; who knows great enthusiasms, the great devotions; who spends himself in a worthy cause; who at the best knows in the end the triumph of high achievement, and who at the worst, if he fails, at least fails while daring greatly, so that his place shall never be with those cold and timid souls who neither know victory nor defeat."

As time passed and I transitioned from denial to acceptance, I realized I needed to flip the script.

I had to swap the demoralizing story of hopelessness that was traumatizing me into a motivating story of hope. It was time to replace doubt with determination, turn this obstacle into an opportunity, and turn my biggest disability into my biggest differentiator. I've always believed the greater our challenges, the greater our destiny.

Rather than retreat from the storm that was turning my world upside down, I was ready to saddle up and ride this storm to the other side and, in the process, turn this unimaginable struggle into unrivaled strength, confidence, and purpose.

On a late August afternoon walk, as I reflected on my perilous freefall, I was listening to Post Malone's new album *F1 Trillion*. One of the tracks caught my attention. It was titled "Nosedive." I wept for a moment as I listened intently to lyrics that bluntly capture the unexpected beauty we can all discover in our respective tailspins.

CHAPTER 6

Blue Sky

It was the last day of 2024 as the platform I was laying on slowly eased into the donut-shaped CT scanner. A wave of warmth washed through my body as the contrast the technician had injected in my left arm raced through my veins. An automated male voice directed me to take a deep breath and hold it for 30 seconds as the spinning scanner hummed away. The automated voice returned, directing me to breathe normally. This sequence of events continued several times before the technician informed me the session was complete, removed the IV from my arm, and escorted me to the door.

This was my 6th CT in 13 months. This time, I was especially anxious. This scan was going to reveal whether I was cancer-free.

Three months earlier, I underwent five consecutive days of targeted radiation blasts to my left lung. The radiation was what my doctors and I hoped would be the capstone treatment to my year-long cancer fight. The immunotherapy treatment had successfully shrunk the tumor on my lung 70%, from 2.5" to 0.75". This was exceptional progress, according to my doctors.

Unfortunately, as I explained in the prior chapter, they believe the immunotherapy may have triggered or contributed to the optic nerve damage last summer that blinded me. So, instead of continuing with the immunotherapy, as effective as it was, they determined the risk to the vision I had left was too great to continue. Radiation was their treatment of choice for this final battle.

I was sad that I could not continue the immunotherapy. It was working so well, and I'm certain a couple more infusions would have slain the lung tumor all together. But losing more of my vision was not worth the risk. I was adapting to my new low-vision world, and the fear of losing more of my sight or going completely blind scared me almost more than death.

Nevertheless, I was excited about the radiation alternative. After all, it quickly and painlessly eliminated my brain tumor earlier in the year. Radiation was certainly a far safer and less intrusive treatment than surgery, which my doctors also considered.

Back into the foxhole

In early October 2024, I prepared for five consecutive days of radiation that entailed a single 15-minute, high-dose blast of radiation to my left lung each day. Targeting the lung with radiation is complex business. Our lungs are in perpetual motion as we breathe, so aligning the radiation laser with my ⅓" tumor was truly a game of four-dimensional chess for my doctor and his technicians. Two weeks prior to the start of my radiation treatment, I underwent a four-dimensional simulation scan where technicians tracked my breathing and mapped the precise location of the tumor. This included marking multiple spots on my chest and ribcage with small permanent ink tattoos to plot the targets for the laser.

The day finally arrived for my first of five radiation sessions. Physically, emotionally, and spiritually, I was ready for battle. It was a warm and sunny morning as the Uber pulled up to the Woodlands Cancer Institute where I would undergo this treatment (I could no longer drive because of my optic nerve damage). After checking in, a nurse escorted me back into a cold, dimly-lit room with the colossal gray radiation machine staring me down as I entered. She directed me to take my shoes and baseball cap off and lay face up on the sheeted platform beneath the laser apparatus. One of the technicians lifted my shirt as the other one aligned the laser with the small "x" tattoos that had been etched on my torso during the simulation session a couple weeks earlier.

Unlike the new, Space Age-looking radiation machine used on my brain nine months earlier at a different location, this machine reminded me of a vintage Russian tank. When I received my brain radiation, I felt like a *Star Wars* Stormtrooper. However, on this day, I felt more like a

D-Day Marine storming the beaches of Normandy. I asked the technician if this dinosaur was just as effective as the shiny sleek machine I had previously used.

"It will get the job done."

They told me to lay back and relax. The two young female technicians exited the room to the "command center" behind a large window and fired up Old Sparky. As I stared at the ceiling, I could hear them cranking up the big guy as its steady hum turned into a snarling growl. For the next 15 minutes, the laser arm circumnavigated my torso, briefly pausing for a minute or so several times along the way.

It was hard to lay there and not contemplate whether it was working or not. But my doctors hadn't let me down yet. I closed my eyes and thanked God for the miracle he was performing. Instead of praying for him to remove the cancer from my body, which I had already done countless times since the onset of this crucible, I expressed my gratitude for the successful extraction that I believed was already underway.

Too often, we beg God for things He is already making happen.

The next four days' sessions were carbon copies of the first day. The only exception was the third day, when Dr. B, the same Radiation Oncologist who treated my brain tumor with a single dose of radiation, emerged from the command center behind the glass window to say hello. He said everything was tracking perfectly. I also asked him about the vintage machine they were using this time, and, like the technician a few days earlier, he reassured me it was the same technology, just in an older package. I slept better that night after both of those reassuring responses.

As I exited the room after my fifth and final session, the staff applauded and shouted out congratulations. I smiled sheepishly as I opened the door to step outside for my awaiting Uber. I wasn't sure how to respond to the unexpected recognition. Did they know something I didn't know? Or were they congratulating me for completing five sequential radiation sessions? I wasn't going to know whether the treatment was successful or not for 12 weeks. It takes at least that long for the radiation to dissolve the tumor, and the radiation blasts themselves are painless. In fact, it was rather relaxing, having 15 minutes of solitude each day. I was perplexed by the pre-verdict applause, but it made me feel good.

The euphoria of completing the radiation was short-lived. As proud of myself as I and those around me were for my having gone through this, I was numb with anxiety. Despite my best efforts to eat well, exercise, and project an upbeat attitude, on the inside, my stomach felt hollow and my mind was occupied by contemplative thoughts of best- and worst-case scenarios. I felt like I was back in that courtroom of life, pensively awaiting the verdict on my life by a deliberating jury. The daily uncertainty of not knowing whether the radiation was melting the tumor away or whether my body had surrendered was emotionally paralyzing at times. There was an invisible war underway inside my body, and I had no idea whether I was winning or losing.

Yet, I carried on, continuing to surround myself with life-illuminating family, friends, and colleagues and casting aside people and things in my life that detracted from my singular cancer-destroying mission. Most of all, as scared as I would sometimes get, I never lost my faith. I never lost my courage to fight on. I never lost hope. I never stopped believing.

I believed the impossible was possible.

The ruling

In January 2025, one year into this unthinkable journey, here is where I stood:

- First and most importantly, I was alive and in remission. The historical five-year survival expectancy of people with similar Stage 4 metastatic melanoma to mine is between 10%–20%. I was well on my way to beating the odds.
- In late December 2024, almost one year after being diagnosed with a 1.5" tumor on my brain, only residual scarring from the initial radiation treatment 11 months earlier remained. My Oncologists believed these small spots were not cancerous, but since a biopsy on my brain (while I'm alive) is not possible, my doctors could not say for certain whether the small residual spots were benign.
- In January 2025, almost one year to the day of my cancer-revealing lung biopsy, my doctors were confident the remaining visual arti-

facts on my lung (that the New Year's Eve CT scan revealed) were benign residual scarring or "shadowing" from the recent radiation. A subsequent PET scan performed in April 2025 reported no indications of cancer on my lung or any other organs.

- The sudden and dramatic vision loss I experienced in July 2024 persists. While I can still see, the field of vision in both eyes (worse than 20/200) is poor enough that my doctors have designated me legally blind. Unfortunately, barring a divine intervention or medical breakthrough, there is no imminent cure for optic nerve damage and the distorted vision I experience, which is similar to having a double dose of dilation drops applied that never wears off. My vision also cannot be improved with corrective lenses or surgery, since it is the cords that go from my eyes to my brain, not my eyes themselves, that are the cause of this condition.

Emotional turmoil aside, I only took one day off work in the first seven months of 2024 while I was undergoing my immunotherapy treatment. While I did take time off for my 60-minute infusions every three weeks, and for other various medical appointments, I only encountered a major episode of fatigue once that left me in bed most of the day while on a business trip to Connecticut.

Step back to move forward

The personal and professional impact from the optic nerve damage was far more debilitating. I have already shared the emotional nosedive I experienced in the last chapter. However, an incredibly important part of my ability to pull out of that perilous plunge was benching myself in early August 2024 and taking a three-month medical leave of absence. Calling my boss Andrew Levy, the Founder and CEO of Avelo Airlines, and telling him I was sidelining myself to cope with the loss of my sight was one of the hardest calls I've made in my professional life.

I've never quit anything before. I'm a grinder. I'm a fighter. But sometimes surrendering, walking away from the fight, is the stronger, more courageous move.

While on this medical hiatus, it was hard returning from my morning walks with nothing to do beyond the steady drumbeat of doctors' appointments. Each morning, I would settle into my home office with my Starbucks coffee close at hand and start journaling. With Stephanie and Kaitlyn's encouragement, my journaling was the genesis for the book I had been dreaming of penning for 25 years. However, the book I'm authoring today is one I never fathomed I would be writing when I was 30.

Not only did writing give me something to live for every morning, it also served as the occupational therapy I needed to adapt to my new low-vision world. In the days and weeks that followed, I self-taught myself the keyboard commands for quickly zooming in and out on my computer and phone and how to have Siri read back long passages of text. Everything that most people probably take for granted, like video-conferencing, writing and reading emails, managing calendars, drafting Word documents, designing PowerPoint slides, and intuitively texting and seamlessly using phone apps were all fundamental modern-day skills I had to relearn. With limited sight, it was like learning to walk, talk, and, dare I say, breathe all over again.

Writing this book allowed me to explore, practice, and perfect these skills in a safe, non-pressure context. Word by word, sentence by sentence, and chapter by chapter, I regained the basic skills I would eventually need to return to work. Writing this book also enabled me to keep my writing, critical thinking, and creativity challenged. As the saying goes, if you don't use it, you lose it, and what better way to keep all three of those skills in peak condition?

Writing this book helped me reconcile the emotional turmoil accompanying the monstrous storm I was riding. Meeting and speaking with the other Stormriders I spotlight in this book and discovering their respective comeback stories reminded me I'm not alone. As hard as this journey has been—and it is far from over—it has revealed to me there is nothing we will be confronted with that God knows we can't handle. There have been so many times that I thought to myself, just as I was about to summit this mountain, why is the universe adding another 20,000 feet?

I kept climbing. I kept moving forward. I kept showing up. And I kept believing in myself and what I knew in my heart was possible.

This journey has revealed to me what I'm truly made of. A friend recently asked me what my biggest takeaway has been from this experience. Without much hesitation, I explained that, more than anything, this adversity revealed to me the unbending and universal power of *hope*.

Hope kept me going.

Hope motivated me to get up every day.

Hope inspired me to never give up.

Hope restored my self-worth.

This *setback* was the *setup* for my comeback odyssey—and *hope* kept driving me forward in my fight to survive and thrive. After all, the only force stronger than fear is the courage hope breathes into every one of us.

The bigger our challenge the greater our destiny

To characterize 2024 as a setback in my life would be an understatement. But in many cases, the biggest storms that confront us in life are the biggest blessings. In November 2024, at the conclusion of my 90-day medical break, I returned to work as the Head of Brand and Communications at Avelo Airlines. I was ready.

I had nothing, and everything, to prove.

The easy option would have been to exercise my eligibility for long-term disability, but that would have been too easy. I just had to do things differently. But during the six months after I returned to work, there was nothing that I was doing before I lost my sight that I couldn't do now. In fact, I hosted a dozen press conferences after my return, and it is doubtful any of the dignitaries or reporters in attendance had any idea I am blind.

As proud of my professional turnaround as I am, I believe this book is the true measure of my comeback. Over the past year, I've prayed to God every day to give me a chance to illuminate His unrivaled grace and supernatural healing power to the world and devote my life to giving hope to the hopeless. This book is my initial attempt to honor my second shot at life.

Cancer did not make me weaker; it made me stronger.

Blindness did not make my world darker; it made my world brighter.

When we think life has finally dealt us more than we can handle, these struggles are intended to reveal to us what we are capable of handling. Because, at the end of the day, the bigger the challenge confronting us—the bigger our destiny.

I was reminded of the significance of my renewed personal calling in April 2025. I had the chance to attend the season opener of the Hartford Connecticut Yard Goats minor league baseball team. Our Avelo communications consultant in Connecticut (and now a dear friend), Mary Coursey, offered me and a friend tickets to the game. It was the biggest event of the season in the state, not to mention Mary's family has some of the best seats at the field four rows behind home plate.

These coveted seats not only made the evening that much more exciting, as we could clearly hear the crack of the bats and the muffling of the breaking curveballs landing in the pocket of the catcher's mitt with every pitch, but given my substantially reduced vision, having seats so close to the action also made the game much easier for me to enjoy.

A few innings into the game, we noticed a father and son sitting in the row in front of us. Of course, there were likely thousands of father-son pairings at the ballpark that night. However, this boy, likely around ten years old, had what appeared to be a slim, silver blind person's cane leaning against his seat. We also observed him placing his phone very close to his face to read the small screen, just as I do now. It was apparent, he had a significant visual impairment or blinding condition like mine.

As the game played on, I found myself contemplating what this young man must be experiencing. On the one hand, I felt grateful he was enjoying the game with whatever sight he had and, more importantly, this treasured time with his father. I was also glad he had access to seats so close to the field, which I'm certain dramatically improved his ability to enjoy the game.

I was also sad. As pop flies and foul balls soared in the background, my heart sank for a few moments as I imagined all the decades of experiences ahead of him that he won't see with the same majestic clarity so many of us have enjoyed for most of our lives. At that moment, I thanked God for the abundance of beauty I enjoyed before I was blinded, which offers me a vivid catalog of memories I can draw from every day. I prayed for this young man to benefit from a medical breakthrough or miraculous healing that will restore his sight early enough in his life that he can experience firsthand and build his own vividly clear collection of visual memories to summon at will in the future.

I wanted to lean over the seats and give him a flaring fist bump. I had so many encouraging words I wanted to impress upon him and remind him to keep going. To keep doing what he was doing tonight: live life to the fullest of his ability and never let anything or anybody stand in his way. And, most importantly, never lose *hope*.

Because on the days when it feels like life has *turned against us*— God, our families, friends, and millions of others around the world we've never met are *fighting for us*.

They stood up and left before I had the chance to talk to him, but this experience reminded me why I'm writing this book: to blaze a glorious trail of hope that helps us turn our life-detouring struggles into lives of abundant significance.

Get up or give up

As all cancer survivors and warriors know, the battle never ends. I have been warned by many of my fellow cancer slayers to be prepared for this demon to strike back in violent and demoralizing ways, even long after we think this chapter of our life is done and dusted. I was about to learn this lesson myself, just as I thought I had won my battle.

After returning home to Houston from my trip to Connecticut, I woke up that Monday morning and lost my balance stepping out of bed. I found myself bumping into walls, doors, and dressers as I stumbled to the bathroom sink. Something was wrong. Very wrong. I was disoriented and off balance.

I splashed water on my face and gazed into the mirror. My pixelated view of myself from the optic nerve damage was even more distorted. The peripheral vision on the right side of both my eyes was gone—it wasn't black—it was simply invisible. It was a distressing split-vision effect.

I carefully navigated my way to the kitchen to grab a glass of water. I struggled to match my hand with the refrigerator door handle. After opening the door, I slowly weaved my hand, more by feel than sight, to the top shelf and grabbed the filtered water pitcher. I began pouring it into a tall, thin drinking glass.

Icy water soaked my hand as I realized I had missed the glass with my normally perfect pour. I grabbed a hand towel, wiped up the pool of water, and sank into a nearby chair, where I quietly cried as I raced my hands through my hair in a panicked state of fear, confusion, and uncertainty. I had flashbacks to last July, when I lost my sight for the first time. I knew something was going very wrong.

I called my Oncologist as soon as their office opened. I underwent my quarterly brain MRI a week earlier as part of my 90-day progress check. I was scheduled to meet with my doctor later that week to review the results, but I already knew the answer that morning.

My doctor's assistant told me to come in right away.

I struggled to summon an Uber with my progressively worsening vision, but ultimately found my way to the doctor's office. I literally bumped into the nurse who was waiting for me and, with a cracking voice and tears in my eyes, I whispered to her, "Melissa, this isn't good—I'm scared."

She told me, "we've got you," and led me to the treatment room.

A few minutes later, Dr. B knocked and stepped into the room. "I don't like what I see."

I had never heard him utter these words before. He explained that he had reviewed my latest MRI for the past hour and concluded there was "concerning activity and contrast." He was careful to say that this "activity" didn't necessarily mean the spots on the MRI were cancerous—they very likely could be the residual "shadowing" artifacts from the radiation blast a year earlier. He said it's not unusual for that collateral scarring to take new forms or move around. However, Dr. B said this could also be an early indication the cancer was back.

"I think we're going to need to cut this stuff out to be safe," he said.

Within 24 hours, I was meeting with Houston's top Neurosurgeon, Dr. Sabih Effendi. He confirmed what Dr. B had shared with me. "You have two options: surgery or no surgery. It's your life, but in my view, there is only one option. If we don't take care of this now, you'll continue to experience peripheral vision issues from the pressure and swelling in your brain at best, and at worst, the tumor will continue to grow. Treating this will only get more complicated with time."

My worst nightmare—brain surgery—was now a reality.

Brain surgery is risky. There is a long list of side effects, from infection to stroke to paralysis to death, that I had to acknowledge on a five-page waiver. But the risks that haunted my conscience the most were the additional threat to my vision and the loss of the ability to read. While the surgeon assured me there was a slim chance of these complications, it was impossible to shake them from my thoughts.

Bring it on!

Two weeks later, Stephanie drove me to Memorial Hermann Medical Center for a three-hour brain surgery to remove the small, potentially cancerous spots the latest MRI revealed. I walked in, chin up, with the same fearless "Do Hard Things" mindset that had accompanied me on so many times before.

It was a miraculous experience. They rolled me into the operating room at 10:30 a.m. on Tuesday, April 22. As I lay face up on the operating table, soaking in the equipment and people around me, I lost consciousness within moments of my arrival.

I awoke at 2:30 that afternoon in an ICU suite to Stephanie at my bedside and a doctor asking how I was feeling. I didn't feel or remember a thing, despite a 4" incision being carved into my head to remove the back portion of my skull and the subsequent surgery.

I returned to the world of the living with little more than a slight headache—admittedly, I have had far worse hangovers—though the cocktail of high-end drugs was blunting any acute pain. The visiting doctor said the surgery was a "success."

I was relieved. The best part was that my vision was not impacted despite the high-stakes location in my visual lobe, just a hair from a critical artery. The goal of the surgery was not to improve my vision; success, for me, was for it not to get worse. After the doctors and nurses exited, Stephanie made her way back over to my side with a big hug as I cradled my face in my hands, closed my eyes, and cried to God with gratitude.

Forty-eight hours later, they set me free. As the nurse rolled me in a wheelchair through the lobby towards the hospital exit, where Stephanie was waiting in our car, we bumped into my surgeon, Dr. Effendi. He was excited to see me doing so well and on my way home.

"Well, I just looked at your post-surgery MRI and the residual scarring is gone. I'll see you in two weeks to remove the staples from your head."

The lung and brain tumors were gone and the post-surgery pathology test identified no residual cancer in my brain. The remission prior scans had indicated was validated. As this book goes to press, I'm celebrating the second anniversary of the start of my cancer fight with a full year of remission under my belt, knowing well that, as cancer warriors, our fight is never over, whether it's our own or fighting for others entering this brutal arena.

I couldn't have dreamed of more inspiring and hope-filled words as I rolled out of the hospital that day and stepped out of the wheelchair on my own two feet into my car for the short ride home. I departed the same way I arrived, with the fearless and steely "Do Hard Things" mindset that gets me through everything in life. With a slightly smaller brain—but a soul and spirit filled with an abundance of gratitude, love, and joy that tip the scale on the portion of my brain they removed.

Limitless

Since returning to work in November 2024, I proved to myself, my Avelo Airlines colleagues, and the world I could do everything I was doing before—and as effectively as before. My return to my executive post at Avelo as a blind person was a potent reminder that the only limits holding us back are the limits we place on ourselves.

I had lost my sight—not my mind. My childhood friend Doug Camp (who also lost most of his vision several years ago) reminded me of this during a call a year earlier.

This latest medical setback was a blessing in disguise that gave me a big shove to wrap up this book and fulfill the comeback legacy I endeavored to achieve when I first put pen to paper on this hope-sharing authoring odyssey.

With that confidence and inspiration, a few days before my surgery, I offered my resignation as Head of Brand and Communications at Avelo so that I could have the runway to fully recover and finish this book.

Here we go again! Back into the eye of the storm of professional ambiguity. As I have shared with you already, and will many more times in the pages ahead, our lives are not measured by the number of storms we avoid, but by the magnitude of the storms we confront.

The past two years have been the fiercest tempest yet in my 57-year journey, but I faced it with the hope, optimism and courage that has been courageously summoned by so many before me, very often under far more treacherous and hopeless circumstances.

Few people exemplify the resilience of the human spirit more than South Africa President Nelson Mandela, who assures us in a letter he wrote to his wife during his 27-year incarceration that "hope is a powerful weapon even when all else is lost."

Indeed it is—there is blue sky on the other side of every storm.

Stage 2

Navigate

CHAPTER 7

Ride Your Storm

When I was in college I drove across the U.S. six times. Twice a year, I would fuel up my Sahara Beige Mitsubishi Montero for the 3,000-mile haul between my Los Angeles home and upstate New York, where I attended Syracuse University.

It was my personal *Cannonball Run*. Each September, I would stretch my Southern California summers as long as possible, squeezing in a few final days on Santa Monica's sun-soaked coastline before heading to Syracuse's gray and blustery winters. When it was time to depart, I plotted the fastest route, blowing through cities and towns along the way, oblivious to their histories, stories, and people. When I did stop, it was simply to refuel, whip through a drive-through, or lay my head on a crunchy motel pillow for a few hours.

The same cross-country rally occurred each spring as I blazed a path back to Southern California like a stallion returning to his stable.

I was proud of how many hours and miles I would pack into each day's drive. Often, I completed my destination-obsessed journey in as little as four days, remarkably without ever receiving a ticket. Although, I did get a stern warning from an Oklahoma State Trooper on one occasion.

Mission accomplished, I boasted to myself and friends. I had successfully traversed our magnificent country saying little more than "supersize, please" to the McDonald's drive-through employee and "checking out" to the motel front desk clerk.

In hindsight, I won the race. But I lost out on the more important journey.

I've been reminded of those road trips over the past three years on the much shorter six-hour drives from Houston to visit our daughter in the small West Texas community of Abilene, where she is attending Abilene Christian University. For the tens of thousands of drivers who barrel through this small whistlestop city along I-20 each day, Abilene is a pitstop for gas or food at best, and a rapidly appearing and vanishing blip on their GPS screen at worst.

Abilene is the quintessential "in-between place." Like the tens of thousands of other communities like it that form the tapestry of America, it is easy for us to overlook the remarkable people, culture, heritage, natural beauty, and contributions these seemingly unremarkable places offer. And, above all, the unifying connection to people we might once have ignored, dismissed, or avoided.

Turn in-between places into think-spaces

The importance of in-between places in our personal journeys extends well beyond the "flyover states" and "truck stop towns" so many of us have unjustly and regrettably bypassed over the years. The power of "in-between" can also be harvested in the in-between moments and spaces in our lives: the career downturns, destructive addictions, relationship dustups, and healthcare scares. The same can be said about the in-between periods of perpetual transition, transformation, ambiguity, and disruption that leaders and organizations encounter every day

Whether at home or at work, these in-between periods may very well be the Think Spaces we need to restore, renew and reclaim our lives and organizations.

Consider the remarkable storm-riding turnaround journey of Scott Harrison, the founder of charity: water, a nonprofit on a mission to bring clean water to everyone on the planet. However, for Scott fulfilling his destiny to start charity: water was a harrowing ride. His 20s were spent partying until dawn as a New York nightclub promoter.

Scott recalls, "I moved from club, to club, to club, filling up the VIP sections and flashing my Rolex to photographers. For almost ten years, I smoked two packs of cigarettes a day and was out drunk almost every night. I was into strip clubs, gambling, and about every drug except for heroin. I was spiritually bankrupt, emotionally bankrupt, and I was certainly morally bankrupt. I wanted things to be different."

Scott decided to leave night life. He sold almost everything he owned and took one year off to try serving others instead of himself.

Scott found his in-between think space volunteering as a photo-journalist telling stories on a hospital ship that was headed to Africa to treat people in medically deprived Liberia. As Scott visited villages across the continent, he discovered the absence of clean water. People were drinking from scummy ponds and rivers. He saw kids getting sick and dying.

Dirty water is responsible for more deaths in the world than all forms of violence, including war. Nearly 1 billion people are drinking dirty water—that's twice the population of the U.S. and one out of ten people worldwide. Scott told himself, "This is not okay."

He returned to New York, threw a big party for his 31st birthday, and raised $15,000 to go build three clean water wells in Uganda. The 700 people who donated $20 each to attend his party proved he could make a difference. This was the beginning of charity: water.

In 19 years, with the help of more than 1 million donors world-wide, charity: water has raised $1 billion and funded over 186,000 water projects in 29 countries. When completed, those projects will provide 20.3 million people with clean, safe drinking water. You can learn more about Scott and charity: water at CharityWater.org.

Then there is the redemptive comeback odyssey of my childhood friend Cheryl Laws.

Cheryl grew up in South Charleston, West Virginia, where we attended junior high school together in the early '80s. Cheryl was smart and popular, a cheerleader who sang in her church choir, was always smiling and laughing, and, above all, was friendly and welcoming to everyone, even those of us who weren't hip enough to hang with "the cool kids" that Cheryl ran with. Everyone, including me, adored her.

Looking back on our younger years, I always sensed something special about Cheryl. Yet it was only recently that the depth of her grace, the magnitude of her courage, and the radiance of her caring spirit would be fully revealed to the world.

"On the outside, I succeeded at projecting a happy, positive, and healthy identity. But on the inside, I felt like an imposter. No one knew the soul-draining pain I was suppressing and the destructive choices I was secretly making," Cheryl recently shared with me. "The version of me my mom and the world saw was a carefully constructed mask."

At age 11, Cheryl's world took a life-derailing turn. Her father left and Cheryl's mom was thrust into single motherhood. That's the moment she became a latchkey kid and her life rolled into a dark tailspin.

In 6th grade she was already smoking cigarettes. At 13, Cheryl was experimenting with marijuana. On most weekends throughout junior high, she was drinking and, at 16, she tried cocaine for the first time. When she got to college, she added recreational pills to the mix and got pregnant. Not long after that, Cheryl dropped out of school, suffered a miscarriage, and began freebasing cocaine.

Cheryl's life spiraled out of control.

Years later, Cheryl's day of reckoning arrived.

"After a severe panic attack, I found myself at a crossroads. I was at a turning point."

That was the last day Cheryl smoked crack.

"The universe landed me on the doorstep of destruction. It spared me so I could heal, and eventually guide others to heal."

At 42, Cheryl discovered her own transformative in-between space when she returned to college, earning her bachelor's and master's degrees. Her graduate thesis became the business plan for what would become Pollen8, which is on a mission to end the spiraling trajectory of opioid addiction and relapse across West Virginia. With the highest rate of opioid addiction of any state, Pollen8 is building a better future and helps women with substance use disorder understand their value, their purpose, and get them into safe environments.

"This is my calling. I know what it's like to feel lost, ashamed, and unseen. I also know what it's like to rise from that place and discover purpose on the other side. Pollen8 is proof that healing is possible and that recovery is contagious. When one woman is given the tools to thrive, she becomes a beacon of hope for others."

Through Pollen8, Cheryl is helping women struggling with substance addiction by providing wraparound support, including safe housing, workforce training, peer recovery coaching, case management, and a community that doesn't just talk about second chances. Pollen8 actually makes second chances possible.

"Just as a bee pollinates flowers so that life can grow, we seek to pollinate hope, opportunity, and healing across West Virginia. In doing so, we're changing the narrative about addiction one life at a time."

Scott and Cheryl's stories are powerful reminders that none of us are broken beyond repair.

They aviated through their personal crises and pulled out of their destructive nosedives. They then embarked on course-correcting journeys that led them to their purpose-defining destinies. Scott and Cheryl rode their storms and navigated their way to world-improving comebacks. It was this critical in-between space—Scott's purpose-enlightening voyage on that hospital ship and Cheryl's mission-revealing midlife return to college—that transformed their soul-draining setback stories into their soul-reviving comeback legacies.

CPU time

Similarly, it was in-between space that inspired Bill Gates in the 1990s to disappear to a small, nondescript cabin of his own perched along Oregon's Hood Canal for what he called "Think Week." The Microsoft co-founder would whisk himself from Seattle to his secret hideaway by seaplane for what he called "CPU Time." An appropriate metaphor for a software titan.

In the 2019 *Netflix* documentary *Inside Bill's Brain*, Gates reflected on his need for his Think Week:

"You think okay, do I need to read some books about this? Or who do I need to talk to about that? Some things, I say to myself—hey, I just need to think."

An unaccompanied Gates would bring boxes of emails, books, and proposals that he didn't have time for the rest of the year. No one was allowed to visit except for a staffer who would deliver meals to him twice a day and restock his fridge with Diet Orange Crush and Diet Coke. He would bunker down for 18 hours a day and read, think, and dream.

So successful was the concept that Gates institutionalized Think Week as a grassroots ideation process among the company's top 50 engineers. In fact, it was Gates' Think Weeks, according to a 2005 *Wall Street Journal* story, that ultimately inspired the development of Microsoft Internet Explorer 95.

Turn down the volume to turn up your creativity

When I worked at Starbucks as the head of global corporate communications, we described the warm and welcoming ambiance of our stores as the "Third Place," that familiar place *in-between* work and home where you can connect with a friend, colleague, or client over a Grande Iced Caramel Cloud Macchiato.

But the vibrant coffee shop atmosphere that makes Starbucks the perfect Third Place for convening with others is a far cry from the quiet space we need to distill our biggest problems and brew our most audacious dreams. According to a University of California San Diego study, the average American is exposed to 34 gigabytes of information every day across print, online, digital, audio, video, and in-person channels. That translates into about 100,000 words every 12 hours.

The magnitude of news, information, and noise we are exposed to provides us with little, if any, capacity for our brains to do what they are intended to do—think.

Consequently, I've come to believe what we need more than anything today is a "Fourth Place" in our lives. Or, put another way, an "in-between place mindset"—the attitude that we must disconnect to connect with the best of ourselves, our ideas, and our aspirations.

This "Think Space," as I call it, provides a sanctuary from the noisy places that restrain our best thinking and detain our wildest ideas. And we don't need a seaplane or hospital ship to get there. There are an abundance of quiet Think Spaces all around us. You may even be reading this book in one.

When I lived in Chicago, I would ride the Metro North train to and from work between our Northshore home and downtown Chicago. During the morning and evening rush hours, the railway designated every other car a "quiet space." That meant no calls and no talking. Unless I bumped into a colleague at the train station whom I wanted to continue a conversation with or was expecting an important call, I would find my way to an upper deck seat on one of the designated quiet cars, put on my noise-cancelling headphones, lean back, and just think for the 50-minute ride. If I was headed into work, I would use the time to frame my thoughts or ideate for a meeting that day. On the ride home, I would often try to decompress by staring out the soot-stained window, watching the landscape transition from Chicago's bustling downtown into the sleepy tree-lined lakeshore villages.

One of the loudest places in Chicago—the train—was ironically one of my favorite Think Spaces.

Speaking of transportation, airplanes are another one of my favorite Think Spaces. There are few experiences I look forward to more than the solitude that accompanies a long flight. The longer the better. I often bring a small notebook on every flight (two for the longer ones) and, after sliding on my headphones and opening my tray table, I pull out my pen and notebook and let my ideas flow. In fact, many of the chapters, ideas, and inspirations in this book were born in my uninterrupted Think Space above the clouds.

Take your imagination on a walk

But we don't have to book a trans-Pacific flight to enjoy the imagination-sparking benefits of a Fourth Place. One of the most convenient and catalyzing sources of Think Space is right outside our front doors. Whether we reside in a fourth-floor flat in Brooklyn, a countryside estate in Ireland, or a condominium in Nairobi, we are just steps away from the ultimate Fourth Place: a quiet walk. Not only is a 30-minute stroll every day great for our health, it's also one of the best creative stimulants around.

Let's look at research spearheaded by Marily Oppezzo and Daniel Schwartz, behavioral scientists at Stanford University. Their 2014 study concluded that if we want to be more creative, we should take a walk. In fact, the study concluded that people who ideate while walking alone generate twice as many creative ideas as those who participate in traditional small group brainstorms.

Most importantly, our quest for Think Spaces can be a soul-awakening odyssey to an inner space of self-reflection and self-realization. I have found that it is the solitary experiences enabled by a Think Space-mindset that evoke certainty in times of uncertainty, fearlessness in moments of fear, and motivation in the wake of devastation.

Often, we believe that at the critical, game-changing crossroads that confront us in work and life we must seek the wisdom of others. In many of these instances, others feel equally obligated to seek us out.

Yet, all too often, the volume of those well-intended voices around us mute the most important voice of all—our own.

Turn inflection points into reflection points

Indeed, it is often the most consequential inflection points that catalyze the most illuminating reflection points in our journey. As Harvard leadership historian Nancy Koehn and her research assistant Eugene Kogan observed in a 2020 *Fast Company* article, "thoughtful crisis leaders recognize that even in the urgency of an intensifying crisis, they can adjust the pace of decision-making, thus creating space for reflection and—more often than not—for the most effective options to emerge."

Koehn and Kogan point to the Think Space that U.S. President John F. Kennedy created at the apex of the 1962 Cuban Missile Crisis, ordering a naval quarantine of Cuba to prevent Soviet ships from transporting any more offensive weapons to the island. They suggest that the quarantine's most important contribution was the extra time it created for leaders from both the U.S. and the Soviet Union to contemplate the catastrophic consequences of nuclear war. It was the Think Space that JFK created through the quarantine that resulted in the deescalation of one of the most high-stakes military showdowns in modern history.

Onward!

As we race to the important events, places, and people in our destination-obsessed lives, getting lost in the in-between places, spaces, and moments along the way may very well be the best way to find ourselves, our stories, and the map to our comeback legacy in the wake of the life-altering adversities confronting us.

It was this critical multi-month in-between stage as I navigated my medical setbacks that empowered my comeback journey. It was during this period of self-reflection and restoration I evicted the dream-shattering barriers in my mind and invited in the dream-achieving determination and tenacity to pursue my purpose-fulfilling legacy, which was completing this book, answering my calling to help you answer yours.

In the pages ahead, I'll introduce ten "compass headings" to help you navigate your own storm.

1. Find your Intego
2. Make every day count
3. Switch off your GPS and turn on your curiosity
4. Don't ask "What if?" Declare "Why not!"
5. Do hard things
6. Turn your resolution into resolve
7. Be a Zelensky
8. Discover your next mountain
9. Hopelessness is finite. Hope is infinite.
10. Share your blanket

These directional bearings are drawn from the purpose-fulfilling lessons I've learned from my current comeback quest, other crucibles I've slayed over the years, as well as from the setback victories of other Stormriders I'll introduce you to.

It is my aspiration that these destiny-enlightening and enabling beacons of hope will equip you with the courage and conviction to be the setback-slaying, comeback-chasing Stormrider you are, and that the world needs you to be.

As 19th century German philosopher Friedrich Nietzsche wrote, "He who has a *why* to live for can bear almost any *how*."

So, let's marinate in the silence and solitude of the Think Spaces in our lives.

Discover the unexpected in-between places—and people—in our journeys.

Remember that what got us here—won't get us where we want to go.

Lean into the fears that frighten us.

Divorce the doubt, shame, and betrayal that hold us back.

Fly head-on into our headwinds with grit, gratitude, and grace.

And ride the storms that move us onward, forward—and set us free.

Last summer, as I listened to country music legend Cody Johnson's 2025 single "The Fall"—it reminded me that life is worth the ride, and the fall.

Stormrider

Cheryl Laws

None of us are broken beyond repair.

I grew up in South Charleston, West Virginia in the late 1970s and early 1980s, a time and place where opportunity felt abundant. Our town was a close-knit community, and my childhood should have been marked by security and stability. But life took a different turn when I was 11. My father left, and my mother—a stay-at-home mom until that point—suddenly became a single parent of four, working full time to keep us afloat. She was doing her very best just to survive. That was the moment I became a latchkey kid. My teenage sisters looked after me when they could, but much of the time I was left to my own devices.

On the outside, I succeeded at projecting a happy, positive, and healthy identity. But on the inside, I felt like an imposter. No one knew the soul-draining pain I was suppressing and the destructive choices I was secretly making. The version of me my mom and the world saw was a carefully constructed mask.

I was smoking cigarettes in the 6th grade. At 13, I was experimenting with marijuana. Most weekends in junior high, I was drinking alcohol. And at 16, I tried cocaine for the first time. I was hiding the pain and chaos I didn't know how to process.

At 18, I left for college and added recreational pills to the mix. I didn't last long. I failed out, came home pregnant, then suffered a miscarriage at 14 weeks. Everyone told me I had "dodged a bullet," but to me, it felt like losing a child. The grief pushed me into even darker places. I began using cocaine regularly and, within weeks, I was freebasing.

My turning point came several years later after a severe panic attack. That was the last time I ever smoked crack. It was a moment of reckoning. I was at a crossroads. I believe now that the universe brought me close enough to destruction that I could heal, and eventually guide others to healing.

The next part of my life was about cleaning up my own messes. I wasn't a savior, and I didn't become a "do-gooder." I became a survivor who slowly, painstakingly learned how to thrive.

A sociologist is born

In 2010, I began working at Kanawha County Drug Court. For the first time, I was exposed to participants' biopsychosocial assessments: raw, unfiltered accounts of trauma that told a story deeper than crime or drug use. These were my first encounters with the concept of adverse childhood experiences (ACEs).

Suddenly, addiction no longer looked like moral weakness. I could see it for what it was: a coping mechanism, an attempt to survive the pain inflicted by the very people who were supposed to love and protect them. In those moments, I understood not just them, but myself, in a completely new way. It felt like an original thought, an epiphany. At that moment, a sociologist was born.

I went back to college at 42, earned my Regents Bachelor's degree with a minor in Sociology, and, immediately upon graduation, enrolled at Appalachian State University in Boone, North Carolina. In 2016, I graduated with a Master of Arts in Appalachian Studies because I wanted to understand how the opioid epidemic spread like wildfire in my community, in Appalachia.

My graduate thesis became the business plan for what would become Pollen8. Returning home to South Charleston, I invited the people and places that thought they knew me to meet the healed, authentic version of me. I called on those very relationships and community resources to bring Pollen8 to life.

Through my research across the United States, Canada, and Brazil, I identified three environmental cues that cause 86% of those in their first year of recovery to relapse:

1. Living life without a sense of purpose.
2. Remaining in poverty.
3. Returning to people, places, and things associated with active addiction.

Pollen8 was built to address these three triggers head-on, offering a path that restores purpose, creates economic mobility, and builds a new community of belonging.

The birth of Pollen8

Pollen8 is more than a program, it is a movement. Just as a bee pollinates flowers so that life can grow, we seek to "pollinate" hope, opportunity, and healing across West Virginia. Through our Reintegr8 program, we provide wraparound support: safe housing, workforce training, peer recovery coaching, case management, and a community that doesn't just talk about second chances, it actively makes them possible. Our approach is rooted in the same principle that saved me: sharing experience, strength, and hope.

Why this work matters

Every day, I meet women who remind me of myself at 16: funny, smart, full of potential, but quietly hurting. Some have already lost children, homes, or freedom. Many have been written off by society. At Pollen8, we tell them there is always hope. We walk with them as they navigate the hardest work they will ever do: rebuilding themselves.

This is my calling. I know what it's like to feel lost, ashamed, and unseen. I also know what it's like to rise from that place and discover purpose on the other side. The women Pollen8 has helped are proof that healing is possible and that recovery is contagious. When one woman is given the tools to thrive, she becomes a beacon for others.

Living the philosophy

Over the years, working with the women we have served and applying the principles of both our programming and the 12 Steps to my own life, I have learned three powerful truths:

1. We are all in recovery from some sort of trauma (what didn't go right in our childhood).
2. We replaced those wounds with an addiction (alcohol, drugs, food, sex, shopping, work).
3. And, more than anything, remember that healing is daily work.

My philosophy is this:

- Do the work.
- Expose the negative behaviors that no longer serve you.
- And ask your Higher Power to not just remove them but replace them with the innate gifts you were born with, the ones that these negative behaviors have been covering up for a very long time.

Be willing. Be humble. Be of service. Recognize that your behaviors affect others, for good or for harm, and stay in constant connection with your highest self. Above all, heal. Then take these principles and show them through your behavior, the way you live, and the way you treat others. If you do this, you become an example that recovery (healing) is possible—not just possible, but worth it.

None of us are broken beyond repair.

Learn More: You can discover more about Cheryl and Pollen8 at Pollen8WV.org.

CHAPTER 8

Compass Heading 1 – Find Your Intego

Living in Mauritius for a year as an Executive In Residence with the African Leadership University (ALU) presented me with many extraordinary experiences. One of those was attending the 2019 Kwita Izina Baby Mountain Gorilla Naming Ceremony in the foothills of Rwanda's Volcanoes National Park.

Every year, tens of thousands of men, women, and children travel by foot, bike, bus, and car from across the country to participate in this time-honored tradition. This year's celebration, as in years past, was officiated by Rwanda's President Paul Kagame and attended by many of the country's highest-ranking government officials. Over the years, the ritual has also attracted diplomatic, business, and social justice leaders; championship athletes and coaches; and artists, philanthropists, and entertainers from across the globe.

This year's Kwita Izina was no different. Among the 25 honorary "gorilla namers" were the Undersecretary General of the United Nations, a Princess from Jordan, the former Prime Minister of Ethiopia, supermodel Naomi Campbell, English football legend Tony Adams, and Israeli Ambassador and pop star Ne-Yo. Each bore the heavy responsibility of naming one of the young primates handpicked by Rwandan park rangers for this year's ceremony.

As I observed the naming procession from a few rows behind President Kagame, one name struck me more than the others, "Intego." In the Rwandan national language of Kinyarwanda, Intego means "purpose." It was the name given to one of the infant gorillas by renowned *National Geographic* photographer Ronan Donovan.

Amidst the fanfare, I thought to myself, *What a fitting name for an animal, symbolizing the perseverance, pride, and hope of a nation that has authored one of the great humanitarian comeback stories of our time.*

As you navigate your storm and immerse yourself in your in-between space, it is the perfect time to reflect on your own personal *Intego.* If you've previously declared a purpose, *is it still relevant?* And if your life is missing a galvanizing North Star, now is the time to find it. Or maybe, if you create the right conditions and keep your eyes (and heart) open, your purpose will find you.

What is our purpose?

Discovering your purpose can take time. In my case, it took three decades. What I thought was my purpose for many years was well-disguised ambition. Let there be no mistake, there is nothing wrong with ambition: it's ambition that fueled my extraordinary career. But ambition without purpose is like a sailboat without a compass.

The fruits of our ambition may bring us happiness, but it's purpose that gives our life meaning.

So, what is the pathway to discovering our purpose? There are countless books and articles on the topic, but one of the best blueprints for living a life of meaning is the Venn diagram painted on the wall that greeted me in early 2020 at the entrance of the Ikigai coworking space in Nairobi, Kenya. *Ikigai* is a Japanese concept meaning "a reason for being." Many Japanese believe that everyone has an *Ikigai*, but finding it can be a lengthy journey of self-discovery.

The search for purpose begins with three important questions:

1. **What do you love doing?** In other words, *how would you spend your days if money were not a necessity? What would you do if you had*

no fear? Michael Jordan would tell you his passion for hoops is not dependent on multi-million-dollar sponsorships; the joy Bono gets from writing and performing is not derived from owning a sprawling villa on the French Riviera; and Captain Chesley Sullenberger's love for flying was not inspired by fame or fortune. For Michael, Bono, and Sully, and so many others like them, they don't see their work as work. Their vocation is a labor of love.

2. **What are you great at doing?** You must be brutally honest with yourself on this one. The question is not *what do you think you are great at?* Nor is it, *what do you want to be known for?* Rather, *what are you known for being great at by others?* For example, I love planes and when I was growing up, I wanted to be a pilot. Like an artist who loves the aroma of dripping paint, I relish the travel-inspiring fumes of jet fuel. But there was one problem. My eyesight, while adequate for driving, was not good enough to fly. The harsh reality for me was that no matter how obsessed I was with aviation and no matter how good of a pilot I thought I could be, I would never qualify to fly. I would never be known as a great aviator. This is by far the hardest of the three purpose-defining questions to answer as it requires ruthless self-awareness that is often dream-shattering to accept.

3. **What does the world need you to do?** Put simply, *what problem does the nexus of your passion and talent solve? How will your passion and talent make the world a better place? What grand challenge in the world would be irresponsible for you to turn your back on?* While I was the VP of Global Corporate Communications at Starbucks, CEO Howard Schultz would regularly remind us that the pursuit of profits without purpose was a shallow aspiration. In doing so, he would challenge our company as well as the broader business world to contemplate our role and responsibility as a for-profit 21st century corporation.

In one of my early meetings with the Starbucks chief, he asked me how I was enjoying my job.

I replied without hesitation, "Howard, it's the most exciting job I've ever had."

He turned away for a minute, then glanced back at me with a paternal look on his face and said, "And don't forget—*why* we are here is really important."

I realized at that moment I had just failed my first essay exam with one of the world's most admired leaders. What Howard was telling me was that, as excited as I was about the high-profile job I had just landed, I was not there to fulfil my ambition. As leaders at Starbucks, we are there to improve the lives of our 300,000 employees and make a positive difference in the communities we serve around the world.

Living our purpose

As we survey our personal and organizational impact in the world, we must ask ourselves the same question: *what is our role and responsibility as 21st century citizens and leaders?*

Consider the mission-driven founders of Boston architectural firm MASS Design Group. In 2008, a small group of Harvard design students set out to build a different kind of architectural firm, one that uses the power of architecture to build justice and human dignity. Over the past decade, MASS has designed hospitals, schools, and museums around the world, including the Pulse Night Club Shooting Memorial, the Ellen DeGeneres Gorilla Conservation & Research Center, and ALU's six-story campus in Kigali, Rwanda.

MASS and their architects love what they do, are known around the world for their talent, and fulfill a deep need in the world for humanity-inspiring architecture. In short, they exemplify the world-changing power of fusing ambition and meaning together with the unbending alloy of purpose.

Similarly, while I was at ALU, I worked with a number of fellow "Second-Curve Leaders" (as I call us) who have pivoted from accomplished First-Curve business careers to purpose-driven Second-Curve missions. Leaders like Fred Swaniker—a serial entrepreneur who pivoted from a rising-star career at the global management consulting firm McKinsey to spearhead a new era of higher education and lifelong learning as the founder and CEO of the African Leadership Group (which established ALU, the African Leadership Academy for high school-age students, and ALX, a continent-wide higher education distance-learning platform).

Then there was Christopher O.H. Williams, a globe-spanning leader who left the corporate suite as one of adidas' top strategy and marketing executives to serve as ALU's first President. And Mawulom Essel-Koomson, who led Vodafone Ghana's customer experience function and served as chief of staff to the company's CEO before joining African Leadership Group where she served as Chief Operating Officer. The list of First-Curve leaders at ALU—like Fred, Christopher, and Mawulom, who have discovered and bravely followed their purpose to Second-Curve missions—is long and impressive.

As I revealed in the last chapter, my calling is to help other people and organizations answer theirs. I love helping people (and organizations) discover, live, and share their leadership stories. People tell me I'm pretty good at it. And there is a ferocious appetite in the world for people to be part of something bigger than themselves or the organizations they work for. It's the calling that summoned me to Africa in 2019 and the North Star that illuminates my path forward.

It's the same calling that invited Coldplay Co-Founder Chris Martin to devote his life to music. In a 2024 *CBS Sunday Morning* interview, when asked why he keeps going a quarter of a century after launching the band, Chris answered, "That's like asking an apple tree why you make apples. Because that's what I'm made to do. And I'm really happy doing it."

As you contemplate your *Intego*—your purpose—at whatever station in life you are in, ask yourself: *What would I love to be doing if money, fear, or professional ascent were not standing in my way?*

With the right North Star lighting your way, this is your chance to turn your soul-depleting downturn into a soul-filling *Intego*-inspired mission.

As Etty Hillesum, the Dutch author of confessional diaries describing the German occupation of Amsterdam, wrote: "I no longer believe we can change anything in our world until we change ourselves."

Stormrider

Fred Swaniker

*How I am turning my moment of obligation
into a century of positive impact.*

I experienced my first coup d'état at the age of four.

Because of the coup d'état, my family left my native home of Ghana and moved to Gambia. As luck would have it, six months after we arrived, they too had a military coup.

I vividly remember being woken up in the middle of the night, gathering my few belongings, and walking for about two hours to a safe house. For a week, we slept under our beds because we were worried bullets might fly through the window.

Then at the age of eight, we moved to Botswana. This time, it was different. There were no coups. Everything worked. And they had a great education system. They had such good infrastructure. Even at that time, they had a fiber-optic telephone system, long before it reached Western countries.

The only thing they didn't have was their own national television station. So, I remember watching TV from neighboring South Africa, watching Nelson Mandela in jail being offered a chance to come out if he would give up the apartheid struggle. But he didn't. He refused to do that until he achieved his objective of freeing South Africa from apartheid. And I remember feeling how just one good leader could make such a big difference in Africa.

Then, at the age of 12, my family sent me to high school in Zimbabwe. Initially, this too was amazing. It had a growing economy, excellent infrastructure, and it seemed like it was a model for economic development in Africa. I graduated from high school in Zimbabwe and went off to college in the U.S.

Six years later, I returned to Zimbabwe. Everything was different. It had shattered into pieces. Millions of people had immigrated, the economy was in shambles, and 30 years of development was wiped out. How could a country go so bad so fast? Most people would agree it's all because of leadership. One man, President Robert Mugabe, is almost single-handedly responsible for destroying this country.

These experiences of living in different parts of Africa growing up did two things to me:

First, it made me fall in love with Africa. Everywhere I went, I experienced the wonderful beauty of our continent. I saw the resilience and spirit of our people. At the time, I wanted to dedicate the rest of my life to making this continent great.

But I also realized making this continent great meant addressing this issue of leadership. You see, all these countries I had lived in, with the coups and corruption I had seen in Ghana, Gambia, and Zimbabwe, were contrasted with the remarkable examples of good leadership in Botswana and South Africa.

Africa's leadership crisis

I realized that Africa would rise or fall based on the quality of its leaders.

Now, one might think, of course, leadership matters everywhere. But the difference that one good leader can make in Africa is greater than anywhere else in the world. Here's why. In Africa, we have weak institutions like the judiciary, constitution, and civil society. In societies where there are strong institutions, the difference a single leader can make is limited. But when there are weak institutions, a single leader can make or break a country.

So, where to from here?

I believe that the next generation of leaders has a unique opportunity to transform the continent. Specifically, they can do two things that prior generations haven't done. The first thing they need to do is create prosperity for the continent. Why is prosperity important? Because none of the prior generations have been able to tackle this issue of poverty. Africa today has the fastest-growing population in the world, but also the poorest. By 2030, Africa will have a larger workforce than China, and by 2050, it will have the largest workforce in the world. One billion people will need jobs in Africa. So, if we don't grow our economies fast enough, we're sitting on a ticking time bomb. Not just for Africa, but the entire world.

Now, all of this sounds great, but where are we going to get this new generation of leaders from? Do we just sit and hope that they emerge by chance or that God gives them to us?

No, I don't think so. It's too important an issue to leave to chance. I believe we need to create African institutions. Homegrown ones that will identify and develop these leaders in a systematic, practical way.

Preparing the next generation of African leaders

I saw the tremendous hunger that existed for this leadership training, but it was not being satisfied anywhere on the continent. So, we're doing just that, one school, one partnership, one country, one student, and one new leader at a time.

We've now been doing this for the past 15 years. Today, we have hundreds of thousands of young women and men being groomed for the African continent through the African Leadership Academy in South Africa, the African Leadership University with campuses in Rwanda and Mauritius, and ALX, a continent-wide hybrid learning and leadership development platform with education hubs in major cities across Africa.

In doing so, we created a new blueprint for 21st century education. Our leadership-focused curriculum is centered around preparing a new generation of African leaders to solve Africa's biggest challenges, such as wildlife conservation, unemployment, agribusiness, and education. We're doing it by having students declare missions, not majors, and in doing so, unlock their full leadership potential.

Our ecosystem of leadership development across these campuses and through our state-of-the-art distance learning platform is developing 100,000 emerging leaders at any given time. We are well on our way to achieving our goals of equipping the continent with 3 million ethical and entrepreneurial leaders by 2050.

My hope is that half of them will become the entrepreneurs that we need who will create the jobs that we need. And the other half will go into government and the nonprofit sector, and they will build the institutions that we need.

Building Africa's Ivy League

They aren't just learning academics. They are learning how to become leaders. And they are developing skills as entrepreneurs. Think of this as Africa's Ivy league. But instead of getting admitted because of your SAT scores or which family you come from, the main criteria for getting into these programs is the potential you have to transform Africa.

What we're doing is just one group of institutions. We cannot transform Africa by ourselves. My hope is that many other homegrown African institutions will blossom. These institutions will all come together with a common vision for developing the next generation of African leaders, and they will teach them this shared message—create jobs and build institutions.

What we are doing is working. In 2019, *Fast Company* honored ALU as one of the 50 most innovative organizations in the world (no other university on the planet made the cut). *CNN* has described ALU as "The Harvard of Africa." *The New York Times* spotlighted ALU as one of the eight places in the world "where history is being made." I was humbly named one of *TIME*'s 100 Most Influential People in the world. And our endeavors have caught the attention of the world's most admired and influential leaders, including Bill Gates, Melinda French Gates, Richard Branson, and U.S. President Barack Obama, to name a few.

So, it's not surprising world-changing nonprofit organizations like Mastercard Foundation, Conservation International, Michael and Susan Dell Foundation, BESTSELLER Foundation, and Omidyar Network (among many others) have loaned their voice and invested hundreds of millions of dollars into our endeavors and shared sense of purpose.

Nelson Mandela said, "Every once and then, a generation is called upon to be great. You can be that great generation."

I believe if we carefully identify and cultivate a new era of African leaders, this will be the greatest generation that Africa and, indeed, the entire world has ever seen.

Our moment of obligation

Let me leave you with this: We are all put on Earth for a purpose. We go through life confronted with "Moments of Obligation," as I like to call them. Sometimes you see a problem that needs solving—a grave social injustice that enrages, saddens, or angers you. Other times you may see inspiring and exciting opportunities—like Bill Gates' moon-shot, when he saw the chance to put a computer on every desk around the world. However, every minute you spend chasing these things takes you away from your true purpose here.

How do you know what you should be doing? You need to ask yourself three questions before taking the leap:

1. **Is it big enough?** Those of us with the education, talent, network, health, and wealth shouldn't be doing small—or easy—things. We need to be doing big, hard things. If it isn't hard enough, don't do it. If it isn't big enough, don't do it!
2. **Am I passionate enough?** Does the opportunity keep you up at night? Are you sleeplessly obsessed about it? If not, don't do it!

3. **And do I have the right expertise?** Am I uniquely qualified and more talented than anyone in the world to do this? If not, don't do it!

If you answer "yes" to all three questions, then do it! But that's only about 1% of the time.

Don't be seduced by the easy and small things. We are here to do the big, hard things the world needs us to do. So, don't quit your job. Keep preparing yourself and searching for that true Moment of Obligation. Trust me, if you don't find it, your world-changing purpose will find you!

Learn More: You can discover the extraordinary work Fred is spearheading through the African Leadership Group at ALGroup.org.

Compass Heading 2 – Make Every Day Count

In May 2024, while visiting my mom in Pittsburgh, I returned to my hotel for a nightcap in the lobby bar. It was a bustling evening at the airport Marriott as I found my way to the last vacant stool.

I wedged myself between a group of three strangers who had just sparked up a conversation as the final innings of the Pirates game played in the background. Seated to my left was a young guy who described himself as a "green-tech entrepreneur." To my right was a woman who said she was a management consultant, and next to her was an older gentleman who told us he was a retired Exxon fracking employee.

Thirty minutes and two beers into our lively conversation, the green-tech investor inquired about our ages.

I told him I was 55. The woman next to me shared that she was in her mid 40s. Then, it was the retired oil fracker's turn.

"I'm 26,395 days old," he said.

I quipped, "How many years is that?"

"I'm 72, but I measure my age in days, not years," he said.

My new friend explained to us he didn't believe our accomplishments in life are achieved on an annual basis. "Our progress and milestones in life are an accumulation of the choices and actions we take every day. We need to make every day count. That's why I measure my life in days instead of years."

Tomorrow is not promised

No one cherishes this philosophy more than my friend Caroline Bowen.

For three decades, Caroline was a successful pharmaceutical sales executive. In 2019, the 50-year-old Atlanta resident was enjoying a long summer weekend in the north Georgia mountains boating and swimming with her family—until she suffered a near-fatal heart attack.

Caroline recalled, "The next thing I knew, the medics were racing as fast as they could to get me to the hospital. Before I knew it, I was in recovery. I was alive! I pinched myself hard. I needed to know if I was alive or if I was dead. I was alive! Praise God! He was not done with me just yet. I knew in that instant that God had big plans for me. I had no idea what that plan was, but I was not questioning it."

It didn't take long for that plan to reveal itself to Caroline. A few weeks after completing rehabilitation, she turned to her passion for cooking—in particular, baking her grandmother's sacred apple pie recipe. She began selling the pies from her front porch and never looked back.

Caroline moved her pie-baking business from the family kitchen to a shared community kitchen near her suburban Atlanta home. Today, Sweet Kaki's Apple Pies are baked in a standalone commercial kitchen and available at 60 retailers across the country.

Caroline didn't waste a day following her second shot at life. She turned her passion into her purpose. Day by day, pie by pie, Caroline turned her perilous life-altering setback into her legacy-defining comeback.

She reminds us, "Life is short, do not live with regret. Use your fine china, wear your pretty pajamas, spray the heck out of your expensive perfume and start your pie business! We are not promised tomorrow."

As we contemplate how to ensure every day counts in our own lives, there are three imperatives we can embrace.

Be a grinder

One of my fondest memories growing up is from when I attended the Virginia Tech All Sports Camp in Blacksburg, Virginia. It was an awesome camp that encompassed virtually every individual and team sport you could imagine. I spent five summers there as a camper, followed by two summers as a junior counselor while I was in high school.

The camp was run by Virginia Tech's Head Track & Field Coach, Russ Whitenack. Coach Whitenack was an accomplished distance runner himself who raced competitively during his college days. Every camp has its rallying cry, and at this camp, it was "What a day!"

At the end of each meal, Coach Whitenack would take five minutes for announcements. He would conclude his updates with a full-throated "What a day!" This was echoed in thunderous unity by the 250 campers, "What a day!" This ritual would occur three times a day for the totality of the six weeks of camp.

At the start of each summer, Coach Whitenack would share the story behind the "What a day!" battle cry for new campers.

The tale went something like this:

"Many years ago, on a dark, cold, and wet fall morning, as I slept in the cross-country dorm, I heard a guy yell from the street below 'What a day!' I put a pillow over my head and went back to sleep. The next morning, I heard the same obnoxious lone voice shout out 'What a day!' into the darkness of the morning. This continued for several days, until one morning, I grabbed some of my teammates and scrambled down the dorm steps to confront the morning yeller.

"As we approached the hooded man, we realized he was a fellow cross-country teammate. We asked him why he was up screaming 'What a day!' at 5 a.m. He told us it was his personal rallying cry. He shared with us that, no matter how dark or bleak the day looked—rain, snow, or hail—it was a great day to run. You ought to pay to run on a day like today. He pulled the strings tight on his hood and disappeared into the morning mist for the start of his five-mile run.

"The next morning, several of us woke early to join our teammate. As we set off on our run, we shouted in unison: What a day!"

Legend has it that the mystery "What a day!" runner was, in fact, Coach Whitenack. Regardless of who the runner was, the moral of the story is the same. Which is that grit, the unrelenting blend of passion and determination, will fuel our motivation to go above and beyond in life. Whether it's the inspiration to rise before dawn on a rainy day for a morning run, the persistence to keep knocking on the closing doors of investors to raise money for that entrepreneurial venture, or the resilience to return to school to complete that degree abandoned years earlier, when we embrace a "What a day!" mindset, anything is possible.

After all, it is grit that motivates us to get up in the morning even as thoughts of giving up paralyze us. It is grit that drives us to dig in, in order to dig out of our deepest holes. And it is grit that feeds our hunger to win the most important race of all: the human race.

Pursue potential over perfection

In October 2022, I accompanied Avelo Airlines CEO Andrew Levy (where I led communications at the time) to Lansing, Michigan for a "courtside chat" about team leadership with Michigan State Head Basketball Coach Tom Izzo. Seated on stools in the film room adjacent to the Spartan locker room, the two discussed a wide range of leadership priorities for winning on and off the court.

In our perfection-obsessed world, it was refreshing to hear these two accomplished leaders profess the virtue of seeking "excellence" over "perfection."

Coach Izzo—one of college hoops most enduring leaders— explained, "Being good is one thing. Being great is another. But being elite is what I'm looking to do, and I'm a long way from that. You always need to find people who have accomplished more. Our players want to do things with people who are at the elite level. I'm making progress, but still have a long way to go."

Similarly, the culture at Avelo was about continuous improvement. Andrew built on the championship coach's advice with his own perspective on pursuing world class excellence:

"We are always trying to get better. You want to have an organization that buys into that. That's core; if our people buy into a shared standard of excellence, our customers see that. I hold myself to a very high standard. That's what motivates me and the continuous pursuit of getting better and seeking excellence. You shouldn't ever 'get there.' If you do, that's when mediocrity sets in."

You don't have to be an airline executive, college hoops coach, or elite athlete to benefit from Tom and Andrew's wisdom. While perfection is a finite destination, excellence is a never-ending journey. Excellence rallies us to press forward faster, harder, higher, and farther every day.

Wherever we are headed, now more than ever is the time to swap our perfection obsession for a growth mindset. One of my all-time favorite movie scenes is the half-time pep talk Al Pacino delivers in the 1999 film *Any Given Sunday*. During this epic scene, the players—and all of us—are inspired to claw our way forward inch by inch, yard by yard, and day by day:

"You know, when you get old in life, things get taken from you. I mean, that's part of life. But, you only learn that when you start losing stuff. You find out life's this game of inches. So is football. Because in either game, life or football, the margin for error is so small—I mean one-half a step too late, or too early, and you don't quite make it. One-half second too slow, or too fast, and you don't quite catch it. The inches we need are everywhere around us. They're in every break of the game, every minute, every second. On this team, we fight for that inch. On this team, we tear ourselves and everyone else around us to pieces for that inch. We claw with our fingernails for that inch, because we know when we add up all those inches that's gonna make the. . . difference between winning and losing! Between livin' and dyin'!"

Evict the dream slayers

We know who they are. They are all around us. They are our friends, relatives, colleagues, and teachers. Whether they are well-intentioned or intent on holding us back for their own self-interest, they share the same name in my view: dream slayer.

I encountered the first of many dream slayers in my life when I was 15. Growing up, I dreamed of being a journalist. I loved reading the newspaper and watching the evening news with my parents. However, I will never forget the day my 9th grade English teacher told me "You'll never be a great writer." She gave me a "C" in the class and her words haunted me for years.

When I saw that grade on my report card, I was devastated. From that day forward, I was on a mission to prove that dream-assassinating teacher wrong.

Day by day, class by class, assignment by assignment, article by article, I turned her demoralizing doubt in me into relentless determination. In the years that followed, I went on to serve as editor of my high school newspaper, never earned a grade below an "A" in a writing or English class in high school or college, soared to the top of a writing-focused communications career, and wrote a book that is inspiring people around the world.

That 9th grade teacher was not the only dream slayer in my life. Many followed her. Over time, however, I learned to distance myself and eventually evict the dream killers from my life and invite in fellow dream-chasers.

These are the people who encourage us to push forward, aim higher, run faster, travel farther, and dream bigger. They are the ones who lift us up after others knock us down, stick with us when others are against us, carry us forward when others are holding us back, and illuminate us as others cast shade.

Our dreams are too big, and our destinies are too consequential, to let others shrink, discourage, or distract us. So, as we strive to make every day count, it is critical that we make every relationship, every interaction, and every person count.

Chinese philosopher Laozi wrote, "A journey of a thousand miles begins with a single step." Coach Izzo knows this. Coach Whitenack knows this. Andrew Levy knows this. My new friends from the Pittsburgh Marriott know this. As do so many others we've met in this book. They all evoke the drive to take our respective hills, step by step, mile by mile, and day by day. We do this by seeking excellence in everything we do, evicting the dream slayers in our lives, and getting up every time we feel like giving up.

Because this is what storm-riding grinders like us do. And we never forget second-chancer Caroline Bowen's sobering warning—we are not promised tomorrow.

Stormrider

Caroline Bowen

We are not promised tomorrow.

My name is Caroline Bowen. I'm also known as Kaki.

I grew up in Darlington, South Carolina. A sweet, small town. My parents still live in the same house I grew up in with my two brothers. We were and still are a very close-knit family.

Growing up, my mama was a great cook. She always had home-cooked meals for us. There was never anything out of a box. Everything was made from scratch. Now that I'm a mama, I look back at those days and I realize that was my mama's way of showing us that she loved us. Food brings people together and it means love. Some of my best memories growing up are from sitting around that old oak table, eating and sharing stories with my family.

However, I didn't share my mama's love for cooking. I could appreciate a good meal, boy, oh boy, did I appreciate my mama's cooking, but I hated cooking. I was going to grow up and leave that small town and be a huge executive.

When I got my first job out of college, it moved me to Atlanta. I was thrilled! It was my big break to begin my journey to becoming a big-time corporate executive. My mama was so worried about me leaving home, and she was even more worried that I would starve to death because I didn't know how to cook.

When this small-town girl hit Atlanta, things were not as exciting as I had dreamed they would be. Work was a lot, and Atlanta was big and scary. I decided that I would stay in my small and safe apartment and learn how to cook. Who was I kidding? I couldn't cook. I would call my mama every night and ask her how to cook this or that. She would listen with a patient ear and tell me exactly what to do. I began to enjoy cooking. I was an amateur, but I learned to at least bake a potato and boil a pot of white rice.

When I got married, my mama gave me the most precious gift. It was a handwritten cookbook of all our family recipes that we shared growing up around that old oak table. I have loved and enjoyed that cookbook more than any gift that I have ever received. Mama even drew a picture of how to "cut out" the bunny ears on the family-favorite bunny cake we had every year on Easter.

One evening, as I was searching for a dessert to make for my husband and young son, I came across my grandmama's beloved apple pie recipe in my mama's cookbook. It seemed simple to make, but it had me sweating trying to make it. I failed several times in my attempts to make it. One day I made it where it was okay to eat, but no one asked for seconds. If you do not ask for seconds, it must not be good, right?

Baking therapy

In October of 2007, I slipped into a deep depression. I lost all interest in life. The only thing that kept me going was my three-year-old son. The depression was so severe that I could not sleep. One night, I started cooking and I cooked the entire night until the next morning. I found myself cooking and baking day after day, night after night, all day and all night. I was concentrating on measurements and flour. I was finding ways to change a recipe to make it taste different.

Cooking became my therapy. Cooking and baking saved me. My husband would wake up each morning to a kitchen full of casseroles, stock pots of soup and spaghetti sauce, pound cakes, and a dozen apple pies. The food multiplied. We would pack his car and, on the way to work, he would drop food off to friends, neighbors, and teachers. There was enough food to feed a community.

That was the year I mastered the apple pie! From that day on, I always had 10–15 apple pies in my freezer.

I grew up feeling and knowing that food was love. Now, as an adult, it took on a whole new meaning to me. Food does mean love. It also became my salvation. Cooking saved me from drowning in my sadness and depression. It brought joy to my heart to feed people. I loved to make someone's day with sausage and cheese muffins or a pie. I praised and thanked the dear Lord for saving me through the therapy of cooking.

I was able to return to work. I had a wonderful sales career in the pharmaceutical industry. I loved my work family and my customers.

Is this the end?

In May of 2019, my life changed again.

It was a beautiful day on the lake in the North Georgia Mountains. My family was on vacation. We were all so excited to be out of school and together on the lake. I had packed a delicious picnic lunch for my husband, two children, and mother-in-law. We ate at the dock and spent the entire day swimming, boating, waterskiing, and tubing.

After lunch, I had a funny feeling in the center of my chest. Not anything serious, just an uncomfortable feeling. It felt like my sandwich was stuck in my chest. I remember thinking this odd feeling would go away soon. I kept drinking water in hopes that whatever was stuck in my chest would move on. It became a small pain, and then a not-so-small pain. I could not get rid of it.

That evening, I had the most horrific pain that I've ever experienced. It was paralyzing. My body became numb and hot to the touch. My body was drenched. I could not move or speak. I felt like I was having an out of body experience. I was about to die in front of my precious two children. How could this happen so fast? How could this be the end?

My family called 9-1-1 and the rest seemed to move in slow motion. I was taken to a small local hospital where the physician on call saved my life. I know that God placed that wonderful doctor in my path that night. He assessed me quickly and confirmed I was having a heart attack. He knew I needed a life flight to a larger hospital, and he arranged it quickly.

As a perfectly healthy 50-year-old, I was having a heart attack. It did not make sense.

It was questionable if I was going to make the 17-minute flight. My mind was racing, thinking mainly of my children.

There is nothing like a mama's love and all I could think about was *Dear Lord, my husband cannot raise my children alone.* I could hear the medics telling me to stay with them. Meanwhile, on one side of my mind, I could see my two earthly children smiling at me and they were bright in color. On the other side, I saw the color gray and I was searching so hard for my sweet baby boy in heaven. I knew I was about to join him, and I wanted to find him quickly. I never saw him, only dark gray clouds.

We landed and the medics were racing as fast as they could to get me inside that hospital. Again, I was speechless and having an out-of-body experience. I was calling out for my sweet baby boy in heaven because I needed him to be with me as I gained my wings.

His masterplan

The next thing I knew, I was in recovery. I pinched myself, hard. I was alive! Praise God! God saved me! He was not done with me just yet. I knew that instant, God had big plans for me. I had no idea what, but I was not questioning it. God gave me more time with my family. That is all that mattered.

The horrific pain I felt that day was a blood clot. I had a myocardial infarction to my left circumflex. I am lucky I survived.

My recovery was tough. I was an emotional wreck. You hear stories from one extreme to the other about heart attack recovery. Some bounce back quickly, and others, not so much. Well, lucky me, I was the "not so much." I had zero energy. Walking from the bed to the bathroom was tiring. I had to take a break in the shower between shampooing and conditioning.

Folding the laundry was a daunting task. I tried to go back to work, only to have to extend my leave. Playing games with my children was out of the question. Walking outside was a definite no.

Standing to cook drained me. The one thing I loved the most, cooking, was off limits. Cooking brought me joy, cooking was my therapy, cooking saved me from such darkness several years earlier. I was sad, incredibly sad.

When my husband would take the kids to school and head to work, that was my time to mourn my loss. I would cry and cry. I would try "one more time," to stand up and bake. But, no, no, no! I would have to quickly find a seat and rest.

One day, while washing my hair, I rinsed and started to put the conditioner through my hair, and I had to stop. I needed a break. I stopped and became so incredibly frustrated. Why did God save me, only for me to be 100% miserable with zero energy? I was so angry. I wasn't sure who or what I was angry with. I was just angry!

I sat on that stupid stool, resting with shampoo and water running down my eyes, and I had a complete meltdown. I cried out to God to hear my prayers, to help me, to please help me. I was not asking for $1 million. All I wanted was to be myself again! I wanted my energy back. I wanted to laugh and play with my children. I wanted to do the darn laundry. I wanted to cook, sweep the kitchen floor, go shopping, buy groceries, and walk down the driveway to check the mail. I wanted to go back to work and I wanted to cook supper. I wanted to bake an apple pie!

No regrets

At that moment, something hit me like a ton of bricks: regret. My mind shifted to all the things I wished I had done in my life. We all have things in our life we wish we had done, but we put off or would "save" for another day. That is where my mind was going. I was haunted by regret.

I cried out to God if it was His will, to please give me my life back, 100%. I promised Him I would do all of these things I wished I had done, but had been too scared or busy to do.

I pleaded to God from that moment on I was not going to live with any regrets. This was a "Scarlett O'Hara" moment. You know, the "God as my witness" part in the book? No regrets! I was going to use my fine china, not just look at it in the china cabinet. I was going to wear my pretty pajamas, not keep them nicely folded in my chest of drawers. I would spray the heck out of my expensive perfume.

And start my pie business!

At that moment, I knew God was preparing me for bigger things and greater joy. He allowed me to go through a lot to get to where I was meant to be.

A few weeks later, I completed my cardiac rehab; I felt great. My energy was returning, and I was able to cook and bake again. I kept my word to God, and I started doing all those things I had regrets over. I took my fine china out of the cabinet and started using it daily. I wore a different pair of pretty pajamas every night. And I gave myself a healthy spray of my expensive perfume each morning and evening.

Turning pain into pies

Most importantly, I started my pie business. I began by selling my apple pies off my front porch and I never looked back!

My life has not been perfect, but I feel so blessed. After selling my pies for a year from my front porch, local businesses wanted to carry my pies, so we had to move into a commercial shared kitchen. I quickly outgrew the shared kitchen, and my husband and I built a commercial kitchen near our home.

My business name is Sweet Kaki's. My pies are now available in dozens of stores across eight states. I have expanded from just apple pie to nine other sweet pies and a new savory line of pies and muffins.

God has been with me through each pie and each customer. I give God all the glory for this joy He has given me. I am at my happiest when I am cooking. God knew what it was going to take to get me to where He wanted me to be. I am thankful I followed His lead.

Life can take a lot of turns. Grief never gets lighter; we just learn how to carry the weight. Our scars show that we went through something hard, and we made it. Faith can get you through anything. A strong faith not only believes He can, but that we believe God will. I am convinced that I am doing exactly what God intended for me to be doing.

It is my belief that food brings people together. What an honor and a privilege it is, knowing that my pies are served on so many tables. Cooking is my joy, my refuge, my therapy. How blessed I am that God gave me my life and allowed my joy to be a service to others. Food means love, something I learned from a pretty incredible mama.

Life is short, do not live with regret. Use your fine china, wear your pretty pajamas, spray the heck out of your expensive perfume, and start your pie business.

We are not promised tomorrow.

Learn More: You can discover more about Caroline and her famous apple pies at SweetKakis.com.

CHAPTER 10

Compass Heading 3 — Switch Off Your GPS and Turn On Your Curiosity

The bus drivers didn't know my name, where I was from, or why I was there, but they knew who I was. Every Saturday for two years, I would head down our red-tiled driveway to the sidewalk in front of our home and wait.

Within a few minutes, a short and squatty blue and white bus would pull up to the curb. The driver would smile and wave me aboard. After handing him the fare, I would find my way to an empty window seat on what the locals called "La Busetta." I would lean back, my toes barely brushing the floor, and just ride, often for hours, with no destination in mind.

Destination unknown

On a dark winter evening a few days before my seventh birthday, my parents sat my younger sister and me down for a family talk in the living room of our three-story townhome in Alexandria, Virginia. They pulled out a globe and pointed to the top of South America. "We're moving to Colombia."

A few weeks later, we were at Washington's National Airport, boarding an Eastern Airlines Boeing 727 for Orlando. My parents brilliantly persuaded us into the move with the promise of a layover at Disney World, which had opened just a few years earlier. After a few spins on Space Mountain, we were on our way to Miami to catch a one-way flight to Cartagena—and a lifetime of exploration and adventure.

As we descended into Cartagena aboard the Avianca Airlines Boeing 707, whitecapped waves danced across the Caribbean's turquoise canvas. We soared over a golden strand of beach as the iconic four-engine jetliner touched down and rolled to a stop at the end of the single-runway airfield.

My dad had accepted an assignment with Project Hope, a global humanitarian NGO. After a couple weeks at the Hotel Caribe, in the heart of Cartagena's glamorous Bocagrande district, we moved into a waterfront home across the lagoon in the swanky El Laguito neighborhood. Tucked between a sleek high-rise apartment building and the lively Kiki & Walters Steakhouse, our new equator-straddling home was a world away from the suburban DC life we left behind.

Cartagena's buses were as diverse and colorful as the city itself. There were the brightly painted Chiva buses that were primarily used on rural routes (and also served as my school bus), long, flat-faced city buses that were always overflowing, with passengers hanging out the windows and front door, long-distance luxury coaches with their colorful lights and plush interiors, and the blue and white mini-buses that served our neighborhood and other Cartagena suburbs.

Don't let your destination get in the way of your journey

While my friends back home in DC were riding their bikes up and down Old Town Alexandria's tree-lined streets, I spent my Saturday mornings cruising Cartagena's bustling boulevards on its aging buses—alone.

For a first grader, there was a lot to see on my journeys. But more importantly, I was learning how to see the world differently. Some days, I would head downtown and soak in the sights of street vendors hustling their goods. Other days, I would cruise the majestic coastline or swing by the seafood shop and pick up a lobster for dinner. When I was missing the States, I would venture out to the airport to watch the planes.

There was no shortage of buses or routes to pick from. When I was really feeling adventurous, I would hop on one of the bigger, standing-room-only city buses. I would watch with admiration as the men hanging out the door jumped off as the bus rolled to a stop. I saw this as a rite of passage to manhood and challenged myself to take the leap. It took several tries, and some scraped knees and elbows along the way. For the others on the bus, my ambition was their entertainment.

Their laughs and jeers didn't discourage me. To the contrary, they strengthened my resolve.

A few weeks before my family's return to the U.S., I took my final leap from the front step of the bus as it rolled to a stop down the street from my house. This time, I landed squarely on my feet and jogged to a standstill alongside the bus. The pointing, joking, and laughter turned to cheers, whistles, and applause that day.

At age eight, I learned an enduring lesson about the power of resilience and perseverance. In today's world, my parents would probably be accused of child neglect for giving me so much free rein in a foreign land. But they instilled precisely the kind of curiosity, courage, and cultural dexterity our world needs today.

A passport to curiosity, discovery, and connection

Since my time in Colombia, I've worked in and visited 60 countries across six continents. Whether it was traveling to Tokyo in my 20s as a communications consultant for Nissan, leading the global expansion of a technology startup in my 30s, orchestrating Starbucks' rapid expansion across South America and Asia in my 40s, or living in and traveling across Africa in my 50s as an Executive In Residence at the continent's most prominent university, I have no doubt that my boyhood adventures in Colombia equipped me with the passport to the lifetime of curiosity and global relationship-building that I've developed in the years that followed.

Riding that bus every weekend for nearly two years was an early lesson in leadership unrivaled by any so-called global MBA (which I also possess). My weekly expeditions taught me more about how to navigate the unfamiliar streets of an unfamiliar land than could ever be drawn from a college lecture hall. I left Colombia equipped with something far greater than the cultural experience of a lifetime.

I departed Colombia with an insatiable curiosity about diverse cultures, distant places, and different people, the curiosity to always look around corners, and the personal confidence to be comfortable with the uncomfortable.

Flip your script

No one understands better how to ditch a destination-obsessed GPS-plotted career path for an uncharted entrepreneurial journey than my friend and master storyteller Pat Lore.

Pat spent the first decade of her professional life pursuing her childhood dream of becoming a TV network journalist. By the time Pat was 30, she was on the precipice of breaking into the highly coveted New York City media market. Along the way, Pat interviewed President Clinton, Rod Stewart, and Jerry Seinfeld, among many other high-profile figures.

In the summer of 1996, she was the "go-to" correspondent for the NBC affiliate in Hartford, Connecticut when TWA Flight 800 exploded over the Long Island Sound. Pat recalled, "When I got to the scene, I saw reporters from all the New York stations and the network news correspondents. As I looked around, I started to immediately feel unworthy of standing shoulder to shoulder with the likes of some of the industry greats that I had watched for years."

This is my big moment, she thought, as her producer counted down the seconds in her earpiece to go on air.

But when the time came for Pat to shine, she froze.

"I was completely embarrassed, fumbling through the live shot with just basic information, trying to speak and not really being able to catch my breath."

Despite multiple successful reports that day, Pat returned to Connecticut feeling unworthy of her network news aspirations. "I gave myself permission that day to kill my dream."

Not long after that, Pat signed off from her final assignment and said farewell to her promising broadcast news career. For the next several months, she felt lost and uncertain about what she would do next. Demoralizing doubt and anxiety extinguished the passion and determination that had fueled the first decade of Pat's high-flying TV news career. "My passion has always been meeting people, telling stories, and diving into all kinds of topics. But I wasn't sure how to translate that into a new career outside of the newsroom."

Pat didn't let her prior destination-obsessed ambitions detour the destiny-inspired journey she was about to embark on. Less than six months after the crash of Flight 800, Pat pulled out of her professional and emotional nosedive and started her own video storytelling venture, Headline Productions.

Over the next 25 years, Pat established herself as Connecticut's master storyteller. Along the way, she has crafted stories for some of the country's most admired businesses, nonprofits, and professional associations, giving the people, places, and movements that matter the voice our world needs to hear. Beyond her video storytelling work, Pat is a coveted speaker, meeting facilitator, and media coach. And in 2020, she published her first book, *Be Authentic on Video: The Playbook*.

Pat's journey is a humbling reminder that we can all "flip the script" on our doubt and, in doing so, transform our stories of shame into lives of significance. "We can't rewrite our past, but we can reframe it. It's never too late to change our story."

Pat manifested the change she needed in her life by turning off her GPS-mapped career path and taking a hard left turn into the uncharted, curiosity-fueled world of purpose-illuminating storytelling.

As the wise New York Yankees catcher Yogi Berra once observed, "If you don't know where you are going, you'll end up someplace else." Who knows, you might even find yourself starting your storytelling business as Pat did, or working at the university of the future on a remote African island as I did.

Indeed, what we learn from where we've been will help us understand how we get to where we want to go. That's why, 50 years later, I'm still riding those buses, soaking in everything and everybody around me, with no destination in mind.

Sometimes, not knowing where you are headed makes for the best destination of all. So, switch off your GPS, turn on your curiosity, and see where you go!

Stormrider

Pat Lore

*How I turned my story of shame
into my life of significance.*

When you're a TV journalist on the climb, you get accustomed to waiting for that "big story" to arrive. The one that will put you on the map. What that typically meant was waiting for a sizable breaking news story to unfold.

Disasters seemed to come to me effortlessly, starting with my very first assignment as a television news reporter in Wilmington, North Carolina. I had barely been in the Tar Heel State for 24 hours when I reported to work at WJKA covering the top story of a lifetime: a capital murder crime.

I remember that day vividly. I was sent to the courthouse to capture the suspect being walked down the back hallway to his arraignment.

I got there early to jockey myself into position, dressed in my black pumps, video camera slung over my right shoulder, and a WJKA mic flag in my left hand.

I asked the suspect a question. He didn't answer. But the clip was played repeatedly by the news director who decided that "sound bite" would be the perfect clip to lure new viewers in.

Over the years, as I hopscotched around the East Coast moving from station to station, I went from crime to general assignment to consumer alerts. No matter what my beat was, I was regularly awarded the "Top Story," and I loved it.

During my sixth year as a television news reporter, I was still climbing and making a name for myself. I was 29 years old. I had always set this deadline in my head of being in the New York market by the time I was 30. I was getting close.

My big break

Having grown up in the suburbs of New York City, I was enamored with watching Peter Jennings on *World News Tonight*. My dream was to be a correspondent in the trenches, just like Peter. In my mind, I would know that I had finally "made it" once I landed a job in New York, the number one market in the country.

On a steamy summer day in July of 1996, the story of my career had finally arrived. I was working as a general assignment reporter in Hartford, Connecticut (the 23rd largest media market at the time), when the breaking news came in: TWA Flight 800 had just crashed into the Long Island Sound. My news director sent me to cover "the *big* story."

When I got to the scene, I saw reporters from all the New York stations and the network news correspondents. As I looked around, I started to immediately feel unworthy of standing shoulder-to-shoulder with the likes of some of the industry greats that I had watched for years. Information was barely coming in. Tray tables were floating to the surface. The jet was submerged. I thought, if I could nail this live shot, it would be the quintessential piece for landing in the destination of my dreams.

Unworthy

When the producer in the studio back in Hartford started counting down in my ear, "One minute till we go live," I began to tremble. My mouth was dry, I took a big gulp. My heart was racing. This wasn't how I expected my "big moment" to go. I was completely embarrassed, fumbling through the live shot with just basic information, trying to speak and not really being able to catch my breath. On the painful three-hour car ride back to the station, I decided that I would leave the business.

Despite countless successful live shots, I convinced myself I was no longer worthy of my dream. That was the end of my climb, and the start of a new reality: the coverup. Faking my way through live shots for six months until my contract expired. No one knew that I was suffering with extreme anxiety. I kept second guessing myself. I allowed doubt to win. I kept that story hidden for 24 years.

In retrospect, all it took that day in Long Island was a moment of self doubt to whirl my mind into the abyss of inability. What if I could have ignored my nerves and chosen to trust myself? I remember at the time looking to my left, then looking to my right, surmising that everyone else was more accomplished, more credible, more worthy than me. At least, that's the story I told myself at that moment. I needed to be more grounded in my sense of self. That kind of life ring would have saved me. Instead, I gave myself permission to kill my dream.

As I reflect on those pivotal and painful moments on the shores of the Long Island Sound, I remember my growing disenchantment with the local news industry. I had started my career during the birth and proliferation of the tabloid TV era, and in my news shop, every story had to be "sensational." At first, it was exhilarating. But as the years wore on, and the headlines and sound effects got more "gotcha" and negative, I started to feel sleazy. There had to be a better way beyond the 90 seconds of nonsense that I was spewing daily.

I felt alienated from reality. At the time, I couldn't clearly see any other future. What else would I do? All I knew was how to tell stories. In the end, my higher self swooped in and acted as my life ring, forcing me to no longer be able to do the job.

Unemployed and feeling lost, I had no idea where my future was headed. What I did know was that my passion has always been meeting people, telling stories, and diving into all kinds of topics. But I wasn't sure how to translate that into a new career outside of the newsroom.

I flipped my script

In 1996, I took a bold and unconventional step. I started my own video production company, Headline Productions.

I had no clients, no equipment, and no clue how to run a business.

The journey was both daunting and exhilarating. With each new opportunity, I hesitated, but pushed myself to say yes, even when I had no idea how I would make it work. That leap of faith opened doors I never could have imagined: clients from different industries, projects across the globe, and stories that reached deeper than anything I'd ever reported on.

Most importantly, this path led me to the kinds of stories that could truly transform lives, the stories I had always been seeking as a reporter but could never fully tell.

Instead of rushing to thrust microphones in front of unsuspecting people or going undercover to expose wrongdoing, I embraced a more thoughtful approach—a dance of discovery. I focused on crafting stories with intention, stories that resonated deeply, touched hearts, and sparked real change. These weren't just fleeting moments in the news cycle; they were narratives that lingered, inspiring connection and transformation.

We hold the pen to our story

In 2020, more than two decades after I left the news business, I finally stepped up to the live mic and shared my story of shame. Releasing it into the world and writing a book to help others conquer their fear of the camera has been a deeply healing experience. But more than that, it opened doors to conversations with people across the globe who, like me, are ready to flip the script on fear and shame.

I remember being a 29-year-old woman, constantly asking, *Why me?* What I've learned over the years is that the most powerful stories aren't the ones we tell others, but the ones we tell ourselves. Those stories can either define our limits or shape our potential. I realized I didn't need to rewrite my past. I needed to reframe it. Our stories have the power to ignite our dreams or extinguish them.

The most important narrative we'll ever create is the one we live, and it's never too late to change our story.

Learn More: Pat is a global video storyteller, former TV journalist, and author of *Be Authentic on Video: The Playbook*. She specializes in crafting human-centered stories that connect audiences to brands, destinations, and purpose-driven people and organizations. See her work at HeadlineProductions.com.

CHAPTER 11

Compass Heading 4 — Don't Ask "What If?" Declare "Why Not!"

One of my fondest memories of my grandmother is the comforting and reassuring words she would share with me whenever I would confide in her about one of the many worries that consumed me growing up. She always disarmed my concerns with the same four words: "Everything will be okay."

She was right. As I replay in my mind the dozens of situations I shared with her over the years, I struggle to recall a single instance that didn't turn out okay.

Grams passed away three decades ago; however, her reassuring words continue to echo in my mind at almost every turn in my life. We all carry a backpack of worries around. Let there be no mistake, some of these concerns are very real and life-altering. I'm shouldering a pretty heavy backpack of life-jolting and life-threatening concerns as I write.

Grams hasn't let me down yet. I'm quite certain that won't change.

It's easy for us to get paralyzed by a "what if" mindset, whether it's in our relationships, our work, our health, our hobbies, or our travels. In my mind, there is no greater barrier to living our best lives, achieving our dreams, and fulfilling our purpose than surrendering to the fear and doubt of "what if."

Over the years, I've come to learn the best way to shed our "what if" mindset is to embrace a "why not" state of mind and heart. Reframing our approach to life from a lens of fear to one of courage is harder for some of us than others. Some people become "why not-ers," as I like to call them. Others are born "why not-ers."

Why not now!

No one exemplifies living a "why not" life more than my friend Angee Linsey, an accomplished author, executive recruiter, and career coach. Angee's first bold move was joining the U.S. Army as a journalist right out of high school—the same Cedar Falls, Iowa high school her mother and grandfather attended.

"From an early age, I always knew I wanted to bust out into the world. So, I made sure it was written in my enlistment contract that I would be assigned overseas in Germany."

Angee's military service was just the first of many "why not" moves to come. After completing her military duty, she was accepted to the University of Missouri's journalism program. Like so many other opportunities this chance-taker pursued, Angee didn't hesitate to apply to the world's top journalism school. She shared with me it didn't occur to her that this was one of the most competitive journalism programs in the world and acceptance was a long shot.

"I just figured, why not pick the best J-school? Thankfully, they also picked me."

Unfulfilled by the corporate and agency PR roles she held after college, Angee found herself at a crossroads.

"When living a 'why not' life, sometimes the choice isn't quite the right one, so you change course. You can be great *and* the company can be great, but not a great match for one another. It's okay to say no (or to leave) when something is not a fit."

Angee turned to her childhood dream of working on a cruise ship. *Why not,* she told herself. She sold her car, packed her bags, and, for the next three years, fueled her globetrotting wanderlust soul as the newsletter editor aboard the *Royal Viking Sun.*

Fast forward several years. After serving as an in-house recruiter at a *Fortune* 100 global consumer brand, Angee departed her comfortable and secure corporate job and ventured out on her own, establishing her own headhunting shop in Seattle. Today, you will find Angee running her firm from Ericeira, Portugal, where she had long dreamed of living. In 2021, she sold her Seattle home, packed her bags, and relocated to Portugal's central coast.

"When I was confronted with some health issues that pointed to the possibility that I may not be as mobile in my retirement years, I knew I should consider making that move to Portugal while I still felt good enough to enjoy it. My new mantra was, 'Why not now!'"

For most of us, there is a setback that inspires us to take the kinds of "why not" quantum leaps Angee has. But when I asked her to share some of the burning platforms with me that motivated her decisions to take these leaps of faith, she said, "There aren't any, this is just how I'm wired—I was born saying *'why not now*!'"

What if you don't chase that dream?

Ina Garten, the best-selling cookbook author, is another quintessential "why not-er." In the 1970s, she was in her 20s and working long hours as an economic policy adviser at The White House. To escape the intensity of their work, Ina and her husband Jeffrey would regularly host dinner parties with friends; "I loved cooking." In a 2024 *CBS Sunday Morning* interview, Ina shared, "I thought to myself, I love what I do after hours, and what I do during the day is not that exciting."

Shortly after her 30th birthday, Ina stumbled across an ad for a small specialty food store for sale in The Hamptons. "I went home and told Jeffrey I had to do something creative—that was the beginning of it."

She told herself, why not!

The young couple dismissed the many "what-ifs," took out a second mortgage on their D.C. home, and bought the Barefoot Contessa for $20,000. For the next several years, Ina ran the store while Jeffrey commuted from D.C. to The Hamptons to be with her on the weekends.

In 1996, Ina sold the Barefoot Contessa and embarked on her cookbook authoring career. The rest is history, as they say, but it started with taking that "why not" leap of faith that transformed her after work passion into her legacy-defining purpose.

If we worry about everything—we'll do nothing

I embraced this same "why not" mindset when I was invited to move to Africa to serve as an Executive In Residence at the continent's most prominent university. Like so many others we are reading about in this book and whom we have encountered in our lives, my family faced a tsunami of "what if" concerns.

What if... we couldn't sell our Chicago home in the softening real estate market at the time?

What if... we couldn't find a temporary home for our dog Grizzly before we moved? Bringing him with us was not an option.

What if... we couldn't find a welcoming school for Kaitlyn, who was turning 14 and entering her first year of high school? The devastation of leaving her BFFs behind and the trepidation of making new ones during this critical time in a teen's life was understandably terrifying. Nothing broke my heart more than trying to reassure our precious little girl that everything would be okay as tears rolled down her cheeks before bed each night.

What if... one of us got seriously sick or injured while living on the remote Indian Ocean island of Mauritius, where we were going to reside for the next two years?

What if... one of our aging parents took a sudden turn for the worse while we were on the other side of the world?

What if... I couldn't find a job when we returned to the U.S.?

There were many sleepless nights that summer. The list of "what-ifs" grew by the day as our departure date approached. Then we would rest our heads on our pillows and remind each other that if this move was easy, it wouldn't be worth doing. I would remind myself and my family that we were now part of the African Leadership University family, which embodies the rallying cry "Do Hard Things."

Indeed, doing the most important and impactful things in life demands "hard things" of us. We had been blessed with the privilege of a healthy and prosperous life. The University's Founder Fred Swaniker is fond of professing "find your moment of obligation," the culmination that your life and career have been building towards. The moment the world is calling on you and needs you.

This was my family's moment of obligation, and I wasn't going to let anything stand in the way. I kept telling myself and my family we were going to go. We would make this work. I kept telling myself that this is what people like us do. We fly into the storm, not around it.

In late July 2019, we summoned the moving vans, said goodbye to our friends, finished packing the nine suitcases accompanying us to Mauritius, called a pair of Uber XLs, tearfully locked the door to our beloved home one last time, and raced off to the airport. A few hours later, we were on a jumbo jet climbing into the hazy summer sky above Lake Michigan, carrying us to the other side of the planet.

In the three months that led up to our departure, there were a hundred reasons not to get on that plane. Each one of them would have been a valid reason on their own merit to abort our plans and stay comfortably put in Chicago.

But we never abandoned the one reason we were doing this to begin with—to do our small part to help change the trajectory of a continent with so much potential for itself and the world. And, in doing so, we changed the trajectory of our own lives.

There is a lot to worry about as we navigate the challenges and opportunities of life. However, these circumstances provide us with the possibility—and responsibility—to care for each other, ourselves, our world, and our future.

Everything will be okay

As we navigate these headwinds and crosswinds, we must resist worrying about everything, or we may very well end up doing nothing. Doing nothing simply cannot be an option.

Indeed, it is these moments in our lives when we need to stop contemplating "what if?" and start declaring "why not!" Because, as Grams Olson reminds us from the heavens, "Everything will be okay."

Stormrider

Angee Linsey

How I turned my "what if" dreams into a "why not now" life.

Growing up in Cedar Falls, Iowa is about as wholesome as it gets. I attended the same high school as my grandfather and my mother. I got decent grades in school. Worked at the local movie theater. Babysat neighborhood kids. The usual things kids do growing up in the Midwest.

But, from an early age, I always knew I wanted to bust out into the world. Travel and exploration of places and cultures played a big part in my "bust out" goals, but in hindsight, I see there were also a lot of bold moves that did not conform to the choices made by others in my family or friend groups.

I'd say my bold moves began when I joined the U.S. Army to be a journalist right out of high school. I made sure it was written in my contract that I would be assigned overseas—Germany, to be precise. Given that I was the editor of my high school paper, it seemed like a cool job that I didn't even know was possible in the military.

Busting out

At the risk of aging myself, it was the Cold War era, long before the United States faced two simultaneous wars in the Middle East. The stories and photos I produced were all about training. I flew on helicopters, rode in tanks, and spent time crawling in mud with a camera to get the stories of the soldiers in my unit. Often the only woman in the room, I learned a lot about standing up for and proving myself. I saw the whole experience as fun, exciting, and a great way to spend my formative years.

After four years in the Army, I went on to the University of Missouri Journalism School in Columbia, Missouri. I dutifully researched the best universities for journalism and Missouri just made sense. It didn't occur to me that most people don't get in. I just figured, "why not" pick the best J-school? Thankfully, they also picked me.

I thought journalism would be the road I traveled, imagining a life in New York working for a major magazine. Somehow, I landed a summer internship with *Travel & Leisure* magazine. While spectacular, being a magazine editor and living in the Big Apple probably was not the right match for me. Now what?

One day in my senior year of college, I saw a bulletin about a major company coming to the J-school to recruit for their Communicator Development Program (CDP). This was where I learned about corporate communications. This was the direction I knew I wanted for my future.

The answer is always no—unless you ask for what you want

The only problem: all the interview spots were filled. But my motto has always been, "the answer is always *no* if you don't ask the question," so I talked my way into having the representative from the company add an extra half hour to her day, and she included me in the lineup. My first job out of college was as a CDP at The Dow Chemical Company.

What an exceptional start to a communicator's career this turned out to be! It was at Dow that I witnessed amazing communications leadership. I may have been wide-eyed and innocent to the ways of corporate life, but the people I worked with genuinely seemed to love being there.

Nearly every person I worked for was thoughtful in their leadership style. They mentored, coached, and encouraged. They didn't make life easy, but they made it interesting. I was a sponge, and my hard work paid off on the opportunity to work on award-winning programs.

While all this was going on, I maintained my military affiliation by staying in the National Guard in both Missouri and Michigan as a journalist, earning my way up to staff sergeant before applying for a direct commission in the U.S. Navy Reserve, where I transitioned to becoming a Navy Public Affairs Officer.

Eventually, my career wandering eye got the best of me, and I decided that moving on to a bigger city with more single twenty-somethings like me was a good idea. My motivation was lifestyle in my personal life. I accepted a position at a well-respected, large PR agency—a career move that turned out to be a total mismatch.

I convinced myself the inner voice that said "think twice before taking this job" was just noise. Unfortunately, I didn't pay attention to the signs and within days in the new role, I knew I had made a serious career misstep.

It's okay to pivot

That has happened twice in my career. When living a "why not now" life, sometimes the choice isn't quite the right one, so you change course. In both cases, I stuck it out for a year, then made the leap to something new. Both times, the move was a great one. You can be great *and* the company can be great, but not a great match for each other. It's okay to say no (or to leave) when something is not a fit.

After the first misstep, this was the crossroads where I made a giant leap which would lead me down a very different path for the rest of my life, though I didn't know it at the time. I chose to follow a dream I had of working on a cruise ship. Crazy, right?

When I was 14, my parents took me to the Virgin Islands for vacation. This Iowa girl had never seen the ocean, and I certainly had never seen a cruise ship, of which there were a few in port in St. Thomas. When I got home from that vacation, I went straight to the public library and researched every cruise line I could find.

Back then, there weren't that many. I wrote to them all, explaining that I was 14 years old and wanted to know what kinds of jobs and what kind of education you needed to get a job on a cruise line. No one responded.

If you ask my mother about this story, she will tell you that she should have known then that my career would wind up being in recruiting or career coaching. She says, "Angee always liked figuring out how to get a job more than actually having one."

Landing my childhood dream job

I packed my bags, sold my car, and boarded the *Royal Viking Sun*, number one cruise ship in the world, according to Berlitz in 1992. My title was "Skald Editor," writing a daily publication with features and interviews, not typically the kind of newsletter on cruise lines.

The ship went around the world, rarely hitting the same place twice in a year. While my work was not a journalistic piece of art, my wanderlust was honored. I had incredible experiences and developed lifelong friendships that still exist today.

It was on the ship that I took inventory of my life and career, knowing this was not a "forever job." What did I really want to do? After several self-assessments and reading books like *What Color is Your Parachute?* I figured out that, indeed, I really did like helping others with their careers. After three years of sailing around the world, I moved to California to go to graduate school to earn my Master of Arts degree in Career Development.

Stumbling into my professional destiny

I needed to work while in school and found myself at a staffing agency in hopes of landing a job. As I sat across from the recruiter at this boutique agency, I quipped, "I bet I'd be good at what you do."

She smiled, raised an eyebrow, and introduced me to her boss. My recruiting career was born.

As with all military reserve positions, I simultaneously served part-time as a Navy public affairs officer, where the work included everything from serving as the commanding officer of a small public affairs team during weekend drills, to doing media training for senior officers, to going on incredible assignments, such as joining a Navy medical team in Nicaragua for an exercise that provided medical and dental care in rural areas of the country.

My "part-time" job also included being recalled to active duty after September 11, 2001, and creating an internal communications program for the Sixth Fleet family members so that they would be informed when the ships were deployed during a crisis.

My "civilian life" allowed me to advance from agency recruiting to corporate in-house recruiting leadership roles. I was loving my life and work living first in the San Francisco Bay Area and then Seattle. I suddenly found myself in an admired global company, but in a job where I was misaligned. My strengths were on the backburner, and I spent my days struggling through spreadsheets, program management, and office politics.

My big leap

Of all the bold moves I have ever made in my career and life, the next one was my bravest. I quit my secure corporate job and started my own recruiting and career coaching firm.

I gave myself one year to make it work, or I would go back to the corporate world. Despite a national financial crisis and many crises of confidence in my first years running my own business, I found my true calling.

Over the past 16 years since launching my firm, I have had great years and good years, but no bad years. I've added fulfilling pieces to my work, ranging from teaching career-related workshops for graduate communications students at the University of Washington to podcasting and writing a book titled *Dare to be Deliberate*. Words I have always lived by, I suppose. When an opportunity would come my way, I would often ask, "Why not now?"

Turning someday into today

The freedom of being my own boss also allowed me to make another giant leap. Those years on the cruise ship include ports around the world. My first visit to Lisbon, Portugal left an impression. For two decades, I would quip to my friends, "Someday, when I move to Portugal . . ." I thought maybe if I really did it, it would be after I retired.

Then I was confronted with some health issues that pointed to the possibility that I may not be as mobile in my retirement years, and I knew I should consider making that move to Portugal while I still felt good enough to enjoy it. My new mantra was, "Why not now!"

Boxes were packed in my dining room in February of 2020. My plan was to go to Portugal, find an apartment, and return to complete my visa application. I would sell my house in Seattle, visit my family for a couple of months in Iowa, and be gone by the fall of 2020. Well, we all know what happened in 2020.

Delayed but not denied, I finally left Seattle at the end of 2020 and did return to Iowa. It had been nearly 40 years since I lived there. I made my extended family my "bubble people," a common term during COVID years for those few people with whom you spent in-person time. I got my visa and moved to Ericeira, Portugal in the fall of 2021.

I continue to recruit and do career coaching. Thanks to technology and a willingness to work across time zones, not much has changed when it comes to delivering great service to my clients. But I have noticed that I have changed. Instead of leaping at opportunities to do big things, I'm more prone to saying "why not" to the simpler things in life. Coffee with friends after a beach walk with the dogs or a drive to one of the many historic palaces to explore the gardens.

As I dared to be deliberate, I realized it was my mom who modeled and encouraged curiosity as one of the most important traits to be someone interesting and attract others who are as well.

That curiosity took me to more places than I could have dreamed. It allowed me to make bold choices in my career and my life. It provided me the capacity to be open to people, places, and experiences that have made my life rich. The answer is always "no" if you don't ask the question. So, go for it. Why not now?

Learn More: Angee is the author of *Dare to Be Deliberate: Level Up Your Communication Career*—available anywhere books are sold online.

CHAPTER 12

Compass Heading 5 — Be a Zelensky

In early 2020, I had a spirited conversation with my good friend and former client Marta Newhart about the consequential times we live in. In the years that followed, our discussion has inspired me to write and speak a lot about the need for what I call "consequential leadership."

History has presented us with many examples of consequential leaders. Abraham Lincoln, Angela Merkel, Earnest Shackleton, Eleanor Roosevelt, John Lewis, Nelson Mandela, Rosa Parks, and Ruth Bader Ginsburg are a few names that come to mind.

More recently, as I watched Russia's unprovoked invasion of Ukraine unfold night by night, attack by attack, and tweet by tweet, the gut-wrenching and heartbreaking scenes exposed an unimaginable magnitude of inhumanity. At the same time, I witnessed an unforeseen spirit of resilience, patriotism, and heroism emerge that reveals the best of humanity.

No one personifies consequential leadership more than Ukrainian President Volodymyr Zelensky. It has been said that a crisis doesn't build character. It reveals it. The heroic response to this crucible has demanded much of Zelensky and his people. But it has revealed even more about the character of this unfamiliar leader and country than any of us ever expected.

As we combat our own firestorms in life and business, there are six virtues of consequential leadership Zelensky and his brave comrades are illuminating for us that we can learn from:

Conviction: Whether you are facing a personal or business challenge, it is essential to summon the courage and confidence to navigate the storm. It will be scary, but we must be brave for ourselves and all those depending on us. Consequential leaders know and honor their purpose. They recognize their responsibility to use the talent, health, education, opportunities, and influence they are blessed with to solve big problems and do very hard things. In rare circumstances—like Zelensky's—we are called to do things no person should ever have to do. While most of us devote our lives to preparing to be the person we want to be, in moments of consequence, we must become the people and leaders the world needs us to be.

Courage: Consequential leaders have the resolve to live their purpose, even under life-threatening conditions. It's easy for us to talk about our convictions when times are good, from the comfort and safety of our homes and offices. But when the world turns on us, how many of us and our political leaders would—or could—summon the primal valor Zelensky models for us? The heroism demonstrated by Zelensky and countless others in Ukraine present an example of courage we can all strive for in moments of distress.

Collaboration: Good leaders believe we can fly faster alone. Consequential leaders know we can fly farther together. In these consequential times, our organizations are confronted with monumental challenges and opportunities. In most cases, they are too big for us to take on alone. They summon us to work across our teams and organizations. In many cases, we need to collaborate across businesses, industries, and institutions. Zelensky understands winning the consequential battle he is fighting won't be won alone: victory will require a united coalition of likeminded nations.

Compassion: Consequential leaders put serving others ahead of serving themselves. Zelensky and leaders like him put the public interest ahead of their self-interest. While most leaders measure their *success in the world*, consequential leaders measure their *significance on the world*. It is never too late for any of us to rethink how we gauge our individual impact. When it comes to addressing our own personal struggles, we don't have hundreds of customers to take care of, we have the most important customer of all to care for: ourselves.

Composure: In a moment of crisis, it is also imperative that we confront our struggle with poise, even-keeled temperament, and fortitude. Consequential leaders thrive under fire and in times of great uncertainty. There is no blueprint for moments of consequence like the one Zelensky is facing. There is no playbook for responding to the unprovoked invasion of your country by a neighboring world superpower. However, leaders of consequence like Zelensky don't panic. They stay calm, rational, and in control. They know that panic fuels fear and that composure catalyzes confidence. The equilibrium Zelensky and his country are demonstrating provide us with a battle-tested blueprint for unshakeable composure for the adversities in our own personal and professional lives.

Connection: Above all, consequential leaders don't just communicate, they leverage the power of storytelling and influence to authentically connect with their stakeholders. They speak to our minds, move our hearts, and have the intuition to know when and how to deliver the hard truth, as well as realistic hope. Consequential leaders like Zelensky are brutally blunt about the abundance of resources they are lacking, but they also remind us of the prosperity of blessings we have, things like family, friends, country, and faith. Good leaders communicate. Consequential leaders connect.

We bought a hotel—now what?

While few, if any, of us will ever have to muster these consequential leadership virtues in the way Zelensky has, there are examples all around us of ordinary people unleashing their "inner Zelensky" to achieve extraordinary milestones. My former Starbucks teammate and friend Kristen Deptula and her husband, Bryan, are an illustrious example. After residing in Florida for several years, they were ready to press control-alt-delete on their life in the Sunshine State and restart life with their young family in Delaware, where Bryan grew up.

Kristen shared with me, "Having grown up in Leavenworth, Washington—also known as 'The Village of Lights'—I could never get used to Florida's intense heat and humidity. Adding to that, despite living in a nice area, our home and neighborhood were repeatedly broken into. With the rising cost of living, hurricane threats, environmental concerns like rising seas, and increasing worries about human trafficking, it became impossible for me to imagine a long-term future there. These topics aren't just headlines, these are everyday events happening. So, after debating all these issues we were left with a tough decision and no other choice than to make the move north."

In 2019, they sold their Florida home and resettled on the Delaware coast. As an acclaimed author, leadership consultant, and business professor, it wouldn't have been hard for Bryan to find similar work in Delaware. However, their move north was about far more than a geographical "reset." It was a metamorphosis of sorts. They aspired to start a business and control their own entrepreneurial destiny.

So, the 40-something couple bought a rundown motel along Delaware's central coastline not far from President Biden's beach home. They spent several months renovating the property, transforming it into a welcoming and charming upscale destination property.

Their dream was taking flight. Then the global pandemic slammed into their plans head on. They were forced to close the Canalside Inn for several months during a statewide lockdown. They weren't sure they would make it.

However, Kristen and Bryan summoned their inner Zelensky to not only survive this consequential period in their lives and our world, but ultimately thrive.

They stuck to their conviction, never wavering from their purpose-inspired mission to build a better life for their family. They exhibited immense courage to never give up, even as the global pandemic paralyzed their business. They exhibited a graceful and unshakeable composure through it all. And they demonstrated a selfless compassion for their employees by keeping them employed throughout the lockdown despite a 100% vacancy at their property.

Today, the Canalside Inn and Deptula family are thriving.

"When we first moved to Delaware, we had no idea what the future held. We certainly didn't expect a pandemic, but we are proud of how we adapted. It took courage, flexibility, and resilience, and through it all, we taught our children how to tackle hard things. What could have been a setback became a journey of growth. I wouldn't trade the experience for anything," Kristen shared with me.

Are you a Zelensky?

It is unclear how the battle over Ukraine will play out, but it is unambiguously clear this moment will redefine leadership for generations. As in all moments of great consequence, history will judge Zelensky and Putin, as well as other world leaders, by how they acted and the consequences of their humanity and inhumanity.

As *New York Times* columnist David Brooks tweeted shortly after the start of the war: "Would you be Zelensky? Would I? What a high and heroic standard that guy has set for us in the years ahead."

Stormriders

Kristen and Bryan Deptula

How we pressed control-alt-delete to reboot our life.

In life, we often face choices, some easy, some challenging. We hope that taking a chance on the harder choice will bring greater rewards. My husband, Bryan Deptula, and I were living in South Florida when we began seriously debating a move out of state. Being closer to family, whether in Washington State or Delaware, became a priority.

Having grown up in Leavenworth, Washington—also known as 'The Village of Lights"—I could never get used to Florida's intense heat and humidity. Adding to that, despite living in a nice area, our home and neighborhood were repeatedly broken into. With the rising cost of living, hurricane threats, environmental concerns like rising seas, and increasing worries about human trafficking, it became impossible for me to imagine a long-term future there. These topics aren't just headlines, these are everyday events happening. So, after debating all these issues, we were left with a tough decision and no other choice than to make the move north.

The easier choice would have been for Bryan to continue his career as a professor at Nova Southeastern University while we both continued working on consulting projects through our company, BKD Leaders.

Conviction

Instead, we made a bold decision: we sold our house. The hardest part wasn't selling. It was abandoning everything we had worked for, the life we had built, and the comfort of familiarity, all for the welfare of our family and the pursuit of the entrepreneurial dream at the expense of a salary and Bryan's tenured position.

On February 27, 2019, we drove in the sweltering 99-degree heat toward our new, unfamiliar home in Rehoboth Beach, Delaware. We arrived on March 1st, my birthday. Though it was cold compared to Florida, the crisp ocean air felt invigorating. Even with uncertainties about how Bryan would manage his teaching and consulting from afar, we trusted it was the right move for our growing family.

As summer approached, Rehoboth Beach, "The Nation's Summer Capital," began to reveal its vibrant energy. A lifelong friend, who was also a real estate agent, helped us search for a home, knowing our furnished rental was only temporary. When we pulled into the parking lot of Canalside Inn, I laughed and said to Bryan, "I don't think I want to live in a hotel."

Bryan replied, "I've told Blair about our idea for a consulting and retreat center focused on leadership. This small inn has been on the market for a while and needs some work. Let's tour it and see if it could be a good fit for us."

We could live as entrepreneurs, free ourselves from corporate jobs, and raise our kids our way.

Courage

After careful consideration, we purchased the inn in September 2019 and began our journey into hospitality. Excited but busy, we juggled tasks like planning which rooms to paint, replacing carpets, and learning basics like marketing and social media. We even took on minor maintenance, watching YouTube tutorials to handle jobs like cleaning sink p-traps and changing A/C filters.

Winter is a slow tourism season at the beach, with fewer guests and less revenue. By March 2020, our reservation numbers looked promising, and we geared up for the busy season, starting with the St. Patrick's Day grand opening at The Starboard in Dewey Beach. Then everything changed.

COVID-19 began spreading quickly along the East Coast. While I knew of its impact in Seattle, I hadn't anticipated how soon it would affect us. The Starboard opened early that morning, but by nightfall, Delaware's Governor Carney had issued a stay-at-home order, in place until June 15th. We had a full set of spring reservations, all of which had to be canceled or credited. Financially, it was the worst-case scenario: no rooms sold and no future revenue. This was scary, but Bryan and I leaned in and faced it together.

Composure

Our family relocated to the basement of the inn on March 31st after our landlord decided not to renew our lease. We still hadn't settled on a new home, and with pandemic uncertainty, moving into the inn seemed like the best choice. With bookings canceled and revenue plummeting, the future seemed bleak.

On our first night, we felt utterly defeated. There were moments of "what-ifs." Here we were, with a 13-room inn, two toddlers (and Sky the Husky), and a daunting future ahead. To lift our spirits, I decided we should sleep upstairs in rooms 3 and 4. I took my children's hands and said, "Now that we're here, let's explore."

We opened the adjoining rooms, and I jumped onto the bed, bouncing from one to the next. We made it a point to sleep in every room, testing the beds and making the best of our new situation. We really did play hard and learned a bunch about our inn.

Living in the inn revealed the small details we needed to address: which beds to replace, which rooms needed new pillows, and what other renovations were essential. I spent months tearing out carpets previously soiled by pets, something I wouldn't have noticed had we not lived in the inn.

Our dire circumstances and the worst choice we faced turned into a series of amazing choices that reshaped our business. From deciding whether to stay a "bed and breakfast" to becoming a vacationer's paradise and corporate retreat center, we made countless decisions every day. Each choice, big and small, helped us transform the way we ran our business and our lives.

Compassion

As small business owners, the financial strain of the pandemic was terrifying. With no guests and a barrage of refund requests, we had to make tough choices. We opted not to refund money but offered guests a one-year credit instead. Thankfully, most agreed. We also launched a virtual T-shirt shop to support the business, sending shirts to guests who bought gift cards.

Once Governor Carney allowed travel on June 15, 2020, our booking calendar exploded. We were almost fully booked from mid-June through October. People needed to escape, and Rehoboth Beach, with its open air and beach, became a refuge.

We adapted our business to meet travelers' needs. We already had keyless entry, but we upgraded to a system that synced with our reservations for easier turnovers. We also invested in texting software to send check-in info, eliminating in-person interactions for health and safety reasons.

During these difficult months, every decision felt like a gamble. We often had to choose between paying ourselves or our employees, holding onto cash reserves or paying bills. We always prioritized paying our team. This uncertainty led to creativity; we launched an internship program, bringing in students from across the country and even one from Chile. Our first intern, Marissa, eventually became a full-time employee.

We learned to innovate, turning to interns to handle social media, email campaigns, and even write standard operating procedures. These initiatives helped us survive the pandemic.

By August 2022, we moved out of the inn. With our children now in school, we were burnt out. The virtual model had helped us reduce overhead, but it also meant guests could reach us 24/7, which was exhausting. However, we quickly found ways to automate responses to common questions.

Meanwhile, Bryan's consulting business, BKD Leaders, began to pick up again. As companies returned to work, many sought leadership advice. Juggling two businesses, we found a way to manage remote employees across different time zones.

Connection

Although the virtual model has worked well, our time at the inn remains special. We built friendships with our guests, celebrated their milestones, and shared in their special moments. Canalside Inn will always have a special place in our hearts. Our children lived in an inn during a pandemic while doing Zoom kindergarten, and we managed to overcome all the obstacles thanks to returning guests and support from our community.

When we first moved to Delaware, we had no idea what the future held. We certainly didn't expect a pandemic, but we are proud of how we adapted. It took courage, flexibility, and resilience, and through it all, we taught our children how to tackle hard things. What could have been a setback became a journey of growth. I wouldn't trade the experience for anything.

Learn More: Bryan Deptula's latest book *Leaders Are Born To Be Made* is available anywhere books are sold online. Also, discover more about the Canalside Inn at TheCanalsideInn.com.

CHAPTER 13

Compass Heading 6 – Do Hard Things

"Men wanted for hazardous journey. Small wages, bitter cold, long months of complete darkness, constant danger, safe return doubtful. Honor and recognition in case of success."

Legend has it this is the copy from the advertisement placed by Irish explorer Captain Ernest Shackleton to recruit a crew for his 1914 trans-Antarctic expedition. The ad is believed to have attracted more than 5,000 applicants for the two-year journey. Regardless of the authenticity of the ad, it lived up to its promise: Captain Shackleton's arctic journey turned out to be one of the greatest survival stories of modern times.

Following a failed 1907 attempt to reach the South Pole, the 40-year-old arctic adventurer endeavored to be the first person to cross Antarctica, the coldest and windiest place on earth. Shackleton's proposal would be one of the most ambitious expeditions at that time.

However, the dreams for fame and fortune of the 28 men aboard the Endurance quickly turned into an unimaginable nightmare after the ship was trapped and ultimately crushed in the jaws of drifting ice north of Antarctica. The crew was stranded for a year, enduring sub-zero temperatures, gale-force winds, dwindling food supplies, and little hope of rescue. Yet, they persevered with courage, resilience, and grit monumentalized as one of history's grimmest tests of human survival.

With the odds stacked against them and no path to safety, Captain Shackleton and his crew found themselves marooned for more than a year in one of the most unforgiving places on Earth. In the wake of their eventual rescue, Captain Shackleton's quest for survival stands as a testament to endurance pushed to its limits and an extraordinary level of resilience and heroism.

Captain Shackleton's story is one of many remarkable examples of humanity summoning the courage, grit, and perseverance to "Do Hard Things."

Why the Moon?

On a sweltering hot day in early September of 1962, U.S. President John F. Kennedy gave a historic and inspiring speech at Rice University to bolster support for his vision to land a man on the Moon and return him safely by 1970. Much like the recruitment ad Shackleton may or may not have penned, President Kennedy inspired support for his moonshot mission by evoking the courageous, pioneering, and frontier-discovering virtues of America's destiny-choosing identity.

In the 20-minute speech, President Kennedy emboldens us to "Do Hard Things:"

"But why, some say, the Moon? Why choose this as our goal? And they may well ask, why climb the highest mountain? Why, 35 years ago, fly across the Atlantic? Why does Rice play Texas? We choose to go to the Moon. We choose to go to the Moon in this decade and do the other things, not because they are easy, but because they are hard; because that goal will serve to organize and measure the best of our energies and skills, because that challenge is one that we are willing to accept, one we are unwilling to postpone, and one we intend to win, and the others, too."

Keep going!

I was reminded of President Kennedy's speech in early 2019 when I met Fred Swaniker. Fred is the Founder of the African Leadership University (ALU). I reached out to Swaniker on LinkedIn, congratulating him on ALU's *Fast Company* recognition as one of the world's 50 most innovative organizations and offering to serve as a PR sounding board. Several weeks went by with no response.

Then, one day in April, Fred replied. We spoke on the phone a few days later, at which time he invited me to meet him in New York City and accompany him for a couple days to meet with potential ALU supporters. He was also in New York to attend a ceremony where he would be honored as one of *TIME*'s 100 Most Influential Leaders. At the ceremony, Fred was invited to make a toast. Surrounded by other honorees, including Michelle Obama, Taylor Swift, Glenn Close, Nancy Pelosi, Tiger Woods, and Mark Zuckerberg, Fred evoked Kennedy's calling to "Do Hard Things" in his inspiring remarks:

> *"For all of us who are privileged enough to be healthy, to be alive, to have education and influence, our role is not to do small things and to solve small problems. The only way we can justify our privilege is to solve big problems and 'Do Hard Things.' In my case, I've chosen to do a very hard thing. To develop three million leaders for Africa who will bring leadership capacity to 40% of the world's population by the end of this century. That's a very hard, impossible thing. All of you have chosen to do very hard things to be on this list. But of all the hard things we have to do, the most difficult thing is to keep going. When everyone else is telling you it's not going to work and no one believes in you, keep faith and keep the passion to keep going."*

The next morning, as we sat in the hotel lobby, Fred invited me to join his mission. "I've really enjoyed spending the past couple days with you. I've realized I need a Chief Communications Officer. What do you think about moving to Africa?"

Without much hesitation, I responded, "I would love to fly back with you tonight, but I should probably check with my wife and daughter first."

I returned home to Chicago that evening and after two weeks of persuading my wife Stephanie and 14-year-old daughter Kaitlyn, we put our North Shore home on the market and prepared for our move to the remote Indian Ocean island nation of Mauritius.

Not surprisingly, on my first visit to ALU's campus, I was greeted by a big red sign painted on the wall that read: "Do Hard Things." These words are also emblazoned on Fred's other three campuses in South Africa, Kenya, and Rwanda. It is a reminder to the students of the responsibility they will carry as Africa's future leaders and as the privileged 8% of Sub-Saharan Africans who will hold a university degree.

I was destined to be part of this university. My life has been defined by doing hard things.

Sometimes we choose the hard things to conquer in our lives. Sometimes the hard things choose us. Throughout my life, I've chosen the road less traveled and the fatigue, bruises, and sacrifice that accompany making the choice to "Do Hard Things."

My passion for doing hard things started when I was eight and living with my family in Cartagena, Colombia. A 20-foot coconut tree stood at the entrance to the red-tile driveway of our home. For the two years we lived in the Caribbean coastal city, I was obsessed with climbing that tree. Every weekend, I would attempt to scale the narrow, bending trunk. With each passing week, I would hug the tree with my skinny legs and arms, pulling myself slightly higher with each attempt.

Early on, I was discouraged as bystanders laughed at my futile attempts to scale that tree, but I kept at it. A couple weeks before we moved back to the U.S., I clambered my way to the top, snatched a fuzzy brown coconut, and slid back down to cheering family members and onlookers.

It's about the climb—not the summit

I didn't choose to climb that tree because I had to. I took this self-imposed challenge not because it was easy, but because it was hard. Like riding the Cartagena buses alone, this was another early lesson in determination I gained from our time in Colombia. These childhood adventures gifted me with the pride and confidence that accompany doing hard things.

Twenty years later, that same "Do Hard Things" calling that summoned me to climb that 20-foot coconut tree called on me to climb Africa's tallest mountain, the nearly 20,000-foot glacier-capped Mount Kilimanjaro. Like that breezy Cartagena tree, I chose to climb Africa's equator-straddling peak because it was there and it was hard. In September of 1999, at the age of 30, I made it to the top of Kili as the sun awakened the expansive Serengeti below.

There are many other choices I've made to "Do Hard Things" over the course of my life which I discuss throughout this book: pursuing an Executive MBA at the University of Southern California while simultaneously leading global communications for a fast-moving tech startup; co-founding a strategic communications consultancy at the age of 28 with Nissan as a flagship client; accepting the role as VP of Corporate Communications at US Airways during one of the most turbulent periods in the airline industry with no prior airline experience; selling our beloved Chicago home and moving my family to Africa; and joining a startup airline as Head of Communications at the peak of the global pandemic.

I've also been confronted by an abundance of hard things that have chosen me. I was laid off from a senior executive position following a leadership shuffle; my family lost the majority of our household belongings from hurricane flooding of our storage unit during our move to Houston not covered by insurance; the unexpected passing of my father; a Stage 4 metastatic melanoma cancer diagnosis in my lung and brain; the loss of vision in both eyes following abrupt optic nerve damage; and caring for Stephanie during her 90-day recovery after she broke both shoulders and her wrist in an accident and supporting her through her own recent Stage 4 cancer diagnosis.

Challenge-ready resolve

Speaking of doing hard things, there are few people in this world I know with a stronger challenge-ready resolve than my longtime friend Paul Fejtek.

All of us have obstacles to overcome in life; some are just bigger and sometimes more obvious than others. Paul was presented with a difficult challenge on the day he entered the world. During birth, the nerves connecting his right arm to his spine were torn, resulting in partial paralysis of the arm.

Growing up with this challenge, Paul was forced to find solutions to simple tasks that other kids find easy, like tying shoes, buttoning a shirt, or participating in sports. Overcoming challenges with a solution-focused mindset became Paul's lifelong personal resolve.

Paul figured out a way to do these things and overcome more daunting personal trials like climbing to the top of Mt. Everest and all Seven Summits, the highest mountains on each of the world's seven continents. Despite the limited functionality of his right arm, Paul even managed to complete the Ironman Triathlon World Championship in Hawaii.

Paul shared with me that the satisfaction we receive from accomplishing things we once doubted we were capable of doing holds an incredible power. It gives us the confidence to keep striving for more and expel our perceived limitations.

"It seems strange to say this, but I feel fortunate I was given a big life challenge at birth. I'm accustomed to dealing with obstacles and adversity, and these are precisely the things that shape us into who we eventually become as individuals. Sometimes the big setbacks don't surface until later in life, but when they do occur, it helps to have some experience to draw upon from successfully dealing with our prior hardships. There is always a lesson that can be learned from any difficult situation and an opportunity for growth. After the initial shock of the bad situation, I try to take some comfort in knowing there is a purpose for this in my life and a silver lining to be discovered."

Paul has transformed his adversity into a purpose-fulfilling resolve to support others with similar physical challenges to his through adaptive sports. After volunteering at a triathlon organized by the Challenged Athletes Foundation (CAF), Paul discovered the rewards of helping kids and adults with missing limbs and much greater disabilities than his to participate more fully in life through sports.

Over the years, Paul and his wife, Denise, have organized dozens of fundraising events, as well as group charity climbs to places like

Mt. Kilimanjaro and Mt. Everest Base Camp, all in support of CAF. Since the organization's inception in 1994, CAF has raised nearly $200 million for prosthetic limbs and specialized sports equipment to help those in need to get off the sidelines and back into the game of life.

Paul embraced a "Do Hard Things" mindset and turned the monumental challenge confronting him since birth into his legacy-defining destiny.

Whether we choose the hard thing, or it chooses us, the path forward is the same. As Captain Shackleton, Fred, Paul, and Stephanie remind us—the most important thing is to keep moving forward, surround ourselves with other Stormriders, and, most importantly, never lose hope.

It is this persevering mindset that inspired me to memorialize "Do Hard Things" with a tattoo of the three words on my right shoulder. Every day, as I'm drying off from my morning shower, these three powerful words remind me, on my good days and the bad ones, to keep going!

Stormrider

Paul Fejtek

How I turned a paralyzing birth injury into a "Do Hard Things" resolve to climb life's tallest mountains.

All of us have obstacles to overcome in life; some are just bigger and, sometimes, more obvious than others. I was presented with a difficult challenge on the day I entered the world.

During birth, the nerves connecting my right arm to my spine were torn, resulting in partial paralysis of the arm. Known as an *obstetric brachial plexus injury*, or OBPI, this preventable injury occurs at an alarmingly frequent rate, with a higher incidence than muscular dystrophy, Down syndrome, and spina bifida. Growing up with this challenge, I was forced to find solutions to simple tasks that other kids find easy, like tying shoes, buttoning a shirt, or participating in sports.

Next-level craziness

Overcoming challenges quickly became a way of life, a solution-focused mindset based on personal resolve. I figured out a way to do these things and overcome more daunting personal trials like climbing to the top of Mt. Everest and the Seven Summits, the highest mountains on each of the world's seven continents. Despite the limited functionality of my right arm, I even managed to complete the Ironman Triathlon World Championship in Hawaii, which begins with a 2.4-mile ocean swim. I'm more proud of that portion of the race than the following 112-mile bike ride and 24.2-mile marathon segments required to reach the finish line. Successfully completing the Hawaii Ironman, along with reaching the summit of Everest, earned me a spot in a rare and obscure club termed the "Peak to Heat Double," which only four known individuals at the time had ever accomplished.

Along with my wife Denise Fejtek, who also completed both feats, we represented half of the people in the world who possessed this next-level craziness. I couldn't have done this without her. As with any ambitious goals we may pursue, or large obstacles in life presented to us by choice, or not, the strong support of others is essential.

For me, that early support in life and foundational development came from my mother—Stela Fejtek. Throughout my childhood, she constantly supported and encouraged me with positive reinforcement, which I found to be very empowering. Growing up, my mom enrolled me in everything she could that would help strengthen my right arm: drum lessons, swim team, judo practice—she even taught me how to waterski. As she subjected me to one physical activity after another that required dexterity, coordination, and strength from my arm that I didn't possess, I would often think to myself, *Didn't anyone tell this lady that my arm doesn't work like all of the other kids?*

Transforming doubt into determination

What I didn't know or appreciate at the time was that she was creating a new mentality for me through these small victories. The satisfaction we receive from accomplishing things we once doubted we were capable of doing holds an incredible power. It gives us the confidence to keep trying for more and expanding our perceived limitations. Into adulthood, I was lucky enough to make a habit of this pattern of achieving small but progressively larger goals in all areas of my life, both personal and professional.

Before standing on the summit of Mt. Everest, the highest point on Earth, Denise and I spent eight years climbing the Seven Summits and reaching progressively higher and higher peaks. Before that, we hiked the 14,500-foot Mt. Whitney, the highest point in the contiguous United States, which, at the time, was a big goal after climbing many peaks of much lower elevations.

It seems strange to say this, but I feel fortunate I was given a big life challenge at birth. I'm accustomed to dealing with obstacles and adversity, and these are precisely the things that shape us into who we eventually become as individuals. Sometimes the big setbacks don't surface until later in life, but when they do occur, it helps to have some experience to draw upon from successfully dealing with our prior hardships. There is always a lesson that can be learned from any difficult situation and an opportunity for growth. After the initial shock of the bad situation, I try to take some comfort in knowing there is a purpose for this in my life and a silver lining to be discovered.

My life has been shaped and designed for the better because of my various trials, both the chosen and unchosen ones. I feel fortunate to have achieved great success following a career path in investment banking and mergers and acquisitions, which rewards those with creative problem-solving skills and the disciplined resolve to continually overcome challenging obstacles to close a deal.

Life is a team sport

Another area of my life positively molded by my birth injury has been my involvement in adaptive sports. After volunteering at a triathlon organized by the Challenged Athletes Foundation (CAF), I discovered the rewards of helping kids and adults with missing limbs and much greater disabilities than mine to participate more fully in life through sports.

Over the years, Denise and I have put together dozens of fundraising events, as well as group charity climbs to places like Mt. Kilimanjaro in Africa and Mt. Everest Base Camp, all in support of CAF. Since its inception in 1994, the San Diego-based organization has raised nearly $200 million to provide grants for prosthetic limbs and specialized sports equipment to help those in need get off the sidelines and back into the game of life.

Today, we are both on the board of trustees (where I serve as president) for a much smaller nonprofit, Ogden Valley Adaptive Sports, in Northern Utah, furthering a similar mission to remove barriers for those with disabilities through life-changing outdoor sports and recreation opportunities.

Learn More: Paul's book *Steps to the Summit* is available where books are sold online. You can discover more about Ogden Valley Adaptive Sports at OgdenValleyAdaptive.org and the Challenged Athletes Foundation at ChallengedAthletes.org.

CHAPTER 14

Compass Heading 7 – Discover Your Next Mountain

Twenty seven years ago, I set out to scale Africa's tallest peak: Mount Kilimanjaro. The equator-straddling dormant volcano stretches nearly four miles into the sky. I succeeded in summiting the cloud-piercing mountain, but I descended with so much more than a photo atop this glacier-crowned pinnacle on the Kenya-Tanzania border.

In 2019, I returned to Kenya for the first time in nearly two decades. As my flight began its descent into Nairobi, Kenya's bustling capital, I could see "Kili" poking through the clouds in the distance. As I reflected on my five-day trek two decades earlier, I started to think about all the parallels between mountaineering and my professional ascent.

Whether you are at the trailhead of your career or preparing to summit, there are three parallels worth considering.

Moving forward does not require moving up

In our high-performance culture, we are led to believe that achieving professional nirvana requires a continuous upwardly mobile career progression. In-house recruiters question resumes with lateral career changes and headhunters dismiss candidates with anything but a drumbeat of back-to-back promotions or title-elevating leaps.

However, as the most accomplished mountaineers in the world will advise, the only way you will make it to the top of the highest peaks is by descending several times to properly acclimate. In fact, failing to backtrack will often lead to altitude sickness and, in many cases, death. Career climbing requires the same patience and acclimation; climbing the corporate ladder too fast without the necessary descents to base camp along the way is a recipe for professional, and often personal, tragedy.

Let's look at the purpose-embracing transformation of Jillian Hastings. While I was leading communications at United Airlines, Jillian was a rising star at our Chicago PR Agency, Edelman. She was whip-smart, always a step ahead, and brought a smiling, positive attitude to everything she touched and everyone she met. Of the more than a dozen Edelman account team members, she is one of the few that made a significant impression on me. I was certain this 20-something account supervisor was destined for a senior leadership post at the agency or elsewhere.

Jillian shared with me that a couple years after I left United, she experienced a severe anxiety attack on the heels of a heartbreaking relationship split and intensifying pressure at work. With the support of her Edelman leaders, she took an eight-week medical leave of absence to tackle the anxiety. It was during this period she got the medical treatment she needed, worked out, and simply took time to invest in her general wellbeing.

It was during this "in-between space" when Jillian realized something was off and it wasn't anything a doctor or personal trainer could fix. Jillian contemplated her purpose. She shared with me that her therapist asked her, "What do you really care about? What would you do if money didn't matter?"

Jillian replied, "Camp."

Like many Jewish American children, Jillian attended a Jewish summer camp as a child from ages nine or ten to 17 and continued to be a counselor and unit head throughout college. It's a traditional summer camp, where campers eat s'mores, swim, rock climb, do arts and crafts, sing silly songs, and make lifelong friendships.

"It was my happy place," she told me.

Shortly after returning to Edelman, Jillian cold-called the Director of her childhood camp and asked if they needed any PR help. They offered her a job. She resigned from Edelman, took a steep pay cut, and left Chicago for rural Indiana. Today, as the Associate Camp Director, she is traveling the world, training a new generation of camp leaders and combatting antisemitism.

Jillian rediscovered her purpose and, in doing so, traded her fast-track corporate career for a soul-fulfilling role that reconnected her with an organization she loves, in a role she is great at doing, and advances a mission that is making the world a better place.

When I asked Jillian about the biggest lesson she took away from this journey, she told me, "I've learned it's never too early or too late to make a change that betters you and your life. You can do what you're excellent at and find a job you are passionate about that is fulfilling. Making both a career and lifestyle change has made me into a better version of myself. I am happier than ever and continue to learn and be challenged in my role."

The air is thin at the top

In August 1999, when I reached Uhuru Peak, the highest point on Kilimanjaro's glacier-coated rim, our guide warned us that we would only stay on the summit for a few minutes. At 19,308 feet above sea level, it was cold, windy, and the air was razor thin. The sunrise views of the vast African savanna below were breathtaking. So was the altitude. After taking a few pictures, signing the summit registry book, and taking a moment to absorb the milestone, we turned around and started our descent. An accomplishment that I had trained for and anticipated for six months was over in a flash.

The air is equally thin at the top of the corporate ladder. With average CEO and C-suite tenures getting shorter and shorter, the same cold, windy, and breath-stealing conditions can be found on the top floors and in the corner offices of most corporations.

In 2016, I joined United Airlines as Chief Communications Officer during one of the most turbulent and transformative periods in the airline's 90-year history. Attaining the CCO role at a major global airline had been a career-long dream. It was the pinnacle of my public relations career, and I enjoyed every breathtaking moment and experience that accompanied this role. But just like the top of "Kili," the air was thin at the top and, following a corporate restructuring, my two-year tenure at the world's largest airline was over in a flash.

There's always another mountain

When I talk to others who have climbed the world's tallest mountains, they all share a similar sentiment: "There's always another mountain." Even those who have conquered Everest will tell you their mountain-climbing odysseys do not end there. Indeed, there are lower altitude yet far more challenging summits to slay.

The same can be said for career climbing. Even for those of us who have attained some of the highest posts in our profession, there is always another mountain. It may not be as lofty or prominent as our prior summit, but it may be far more rewarding in so many other ways.

Take Mount Kenya, for example. The central Kenyan majestic peak has always lived in the shadow of the taller, more famous Kilimanjaro. Yet, those who have climbed both mountains will tell you that Mount Kenya has a far more enjoyable and rewarding vista. In other words, the best experiences aren't always the biggest or most coveted ones.

Knowing that there is always another mountain should also give mountain- and career-climbers alike the courage to turn around in the face of threatening conditions.

Consider the story of a former colleague who shared my passion for mountain climbing. He set out to scale South America's tallest peak, Aconcagua. As he approached the top of the 23,000-foot summit, his group stumbled across the snow-covered body of another trekker. The guide advised the group they should turn around; he warned that proceeding could result in loss of limb from frostbite or even death. Upon his safe return home, he told me, "There is always another mountain, but you only have one life."

After summiting at United, I explored the world in search of my next mountain. This search led me to roles as an Executive In Residence at African Leadership University on the remote Indian Ocean Island of Mauritius, a PR Professor at Syracuse University, and Head of Communications at a startup airline. Like Mount Kenya, these roles are not one of the Seven Summits of the corporate PR world, but the opportunity to help empower a new generation of African leaders, educate a new wave of PR professionals, and launch America's first new airline in 15 years are far bigger in many ways.

To say that I have taken a quantum leap forward since leaving United would be an understatement, and I did it without moving up. If the air is starting to thin in your world, it's probably a sign to descend to basecamp to acclimate or, better yet, discover another mountain to climb with a brighter vista or more challenging terrain.

Country music stars Bailey Zimmerman and Luke Combs reminded me of this in their recently released hit single "Backup Plan." Falling down doesn't change who you were born to be.

What is your next mountain?

Stormrider

Jillian Hastings

*How I turned my high-flying career into
my purpose-fulfilling happy place.*

When I decided to study PR and advertising, a professor took us on tours of top-tier agencies throughout Chicago. At the time, many of them were scattered throughout the skyscrapers that make up the Chicago skyline. In the end, we probably toured five or six firms, and they were impressive places. There were beautiful meeting spots, jaw-dropping views of the lake, meditation and game rooms—things that seem important when you're 19. But one agency stood out, and I can remember saying to myself, *This is where I want to be.*

That place was Edelman, a global PR/communications marketing firm. I was impressed with their clients, the work that was being produced, and the office that overlooked both Lake Michigan and Millenium Park.

Landing my dream job

After a series of internships, right-place-right-time introductions, and luck, I landed a job there at age 21. It was a dream come true and an incredible opportunity. I was young, green, and eager to learn. Edelman, and more specifically, my team, paid me to learn and become an *actual* PR professional. I had excellent mentors and managers who developed me into a confident Assistant Account Executive who rose to an Account Supervisor (there were a lot of titles for junior staff so there's room for growth). I worked with world-renowned clients on brand management and reputation, crisis management, content development, media relations, executive positioning, and much more. I traveled to new places, continued learning and growing, landed a seat with the C-suite during a major crisis, and more.

Of course, stress was also part of the experience. You don't get to work for this type of firm with these types of clients without understanding stress and the pressure for perfection. Luckily, I am a bit of an anxious perfectionist, so, most of the time, this worked in my favor. But there were hard moments.

About five years in, I experienced a rough patch in my personal life. I ended a relationship with a boyfriend I was living with, which was heartbreaking, even though it was my decision, and I was struggling with anxiety. The same anxiety that pushed me to strive for perfection was also wreaking havoc on me physically and emotionally. The timing, surprisingly, was great in that my parents had just gotten an apartment about a five-minute walk from the Aon Center, where Edelman was located at the time, and I moved in while I figured things out.

Rediscovering my purpose

Long story short, I ended up requesting medical leave from work. Edelman and my supervisor were beyond supportive. They helped me take the proper steps to secure my position, and I ended up taking about eight weeks off from work. During this time, I exercised, worked with medical professionals and therapists, and had endless support from family and friends. I returned to work, my team welcomed me back with open arms, and I picked up right where I left off. Great clients, great colleagues, and more incredible opportunities. But something was off.

During this "off" time, a therapist asked me what I really cared about. My answer was "camp." She asked what I would do if money wasn't a concern. My answer was, again, camp.

As many Jewish American children, I attended a Jewish summer camp as a child from ages nine or ten to 17 and continued to be a counselor and unit head throughout college. It's a traditional summer camp, where campers eat s'mores, swim, rock climb, do arts and crafts, sing silly songs, make lifelong friendships, and so on. It's long been my "happy place." This camp that I grew up going to is where I met some of my closest friends, and where, eventually, I met my now-husband and got married in 2022. There was always a joke with my parents that "you can't work at camp forever," so I never really considered it as a potential career path. However, this therapist asked me, "why not?"

I cold-called the Director, asking if the camp needed help with communications or marketing. It turned out they did. Fast forward a few months and there was a job posting for a new Assistant Director role at the Goldman Union Camp Institute (GUCI), with a focus on marketing and communication. When I received an offer following the interview process, I told the Director that "I wanted in."

Answering my calling

It was very emotional leaving Edelman. This was a place that took a chance on me, trained me, and provided countless opportunities for growth. I was sad to leave, and a little nervous. I had more than one friend question if I was in the right headspace to make this change. One even suggested that this was the end of my career. How could I take a salary cut this big? These thoughts, of course, weighed on me. I was giving up a career I saw a path to success in, all in a city I loved. And for what? To move to Indiana to work on a very small team.

What about future growth? There's only so far you can move up in a small camp.

But this change gave me so much energy and excitement. I knew I was doing the right thing. So, I took a gamble and won. My parents (thank goodness for them and their support, I don't know where I would be without them) helped me move from Chicago to Carmel, a suburb in Indianapolis.

I am entering my eighth year working for camp and now serving as the Associate Director. As I mentioned, I ended up meeting my now-husband through work and am the best version of myself I have ever known. I am still an anxious perfectionist, and our Director will laugh at my sometimes-too-corporate emails. (What can I say? I was trained well.) I am so proud of the work I have done with camp and the amazing, though different, opportunities it has provided.

My old professional wardrobe is mostly obsolete, as athleisure is the name of the game in the camping world. I still get to travel to new places, learn new skills, and expand upon my initial skillset. And I still get to work with amazing colleagues and clients.

Trading my dream job for my dream life

While I was advancing quickly at Edelman, I also believe I am excelling in this role. This year, I am part of two spectacular professional development programs, one on combatting antisemitism (which, given the world we are living in now, is more important than ever) and one for rising Jewish summer camp leaders hoping to grow in their career path. Through these programs, I will be traveling everywhere from LA to Boston, New York, Poland, Hungary, and Israel. I am also humbled to share that I have been recognized as one of the 2024 Jewish Federation of Greater Indianapolis' "36 under 36."

Making both a career and lifestyle change has made me into a better version of myself. I am happier than ever and continue to learn and be challenged in my role. I work each day to help camp get better and provide life-changing experiences for the next generation of staff and campers. This change helped me realize that you can do what you're excellent at and find a job you are passionate about and that is fulfilling.

I find it fascinating to talk to people who consider making a major career change 20 years into their career. It's a scary thing to do. I also talk to my peers who are looking for a change five or ten years into their career. That is also scary. Though I have learned it is never too early *or* too late to make a change that betters you and your life.

Just last year I had a friend I've known (from camp) since I was 12. He texted me, "I'm quitting my corporate job to take a leadership position at a Jewish summer camp!"

Sound familiar?

Learn More: You can discover more about Jillian and the Goldman Union Camp Institute at Guci.org.

HAPTER 15

Compass Heading 8 — Turn Your Resolution into Resolve

2022 was an exciting year at Avelo, the startup airline where I led brand and communications. As we soared into our second year of service, we quadrupled the number of people we carried, flew our first million customers, added 15 new destinations, and tripled the number of flights we operated. I buckled in for nearly 100 flights that year as I crisscrossed the country almost every week, announcing new routes, inaugurating flights, and memorializing monumental milestones.

That October, as I was suiting up for a high-profile press event that necessitated wearing a tie (which we loathe at Avelo), I was unable to secure the top button of my shirt or comfortably button my suit jacket. When I returned home, I tried on several other shirts and jackets.

Houston, we have a problem, I thought to myself as I stood in my suburban H-Town closet.

I loaded my car with a third of my wardrobe and headed to a local tailor. A week later, everything fit like a glove as I continued hopscotching across the country cutting ribbons and christening new destinations. Mission accomplished, I declared to myself.

Fast forward to December. While celebrating the holidays with my family in San Diego, I had the revelation that my wardrobe rehab was simply masking the symptoms of a much bigger issue: the extensive travel, eating out, and irregular exercise had caught up with me. I stared reality in the eyes and made a New Year's resolution to devote the month of January to ditching alcohol, carbs, and high-sugar temptations.

I wasn't on a "30-day plan." There were no pills or health shake regimens. I didn't have a weight loss sherpa coaching me. Frankly, I had no idea what I was doing. What I do know is I could feel and see the pounds flying off. Family and colleagues were noticing a thinner face and a leaner core. I didn't just look better. I felt better.

Dry January turned into damp February, and I relaxed some of the draconian dietary restraints I had imposed on myself.

As the pace of travel ramped back up, I harnessed an intentionality and discipline that kept my personal wellness movement alive. I was eating better and took my workout routine on the road. Best of all, I lost my desire for many of the indulgences I had frequented in the past: my daily Starbucks mocha, bagels and cream cheese, and overstuffed burritos (although, I couldn't shake my craving for a basket of warm chips and handcrafted guac).

The shallow, short-term destination of my New Year's resolution transformed into a life-changing resolve.

What started as a physical quick fix morphed into an enduring wellness mindset. Over the course of the first 90 days of 2023, I lost 30 pounds, shed two to three inches in waist size, and reclaimed the fierce and fast "battle-ready" physique that I had abandoned.

While I am immensely proud of the weight I lost, it's what I gained along the way that energized me the most. Little did I know, the health-restoring quest I embarked on in early 2023 was preparing me physically and mentally for the battle of my life. My Oncologist told me from the start that one of the reasons he had great confidence I would win my cancer battle and be as responsive as I have been to the treatments I've undertaken is because of the strong state of fitness I was in at the start of my fight.

Here are my five big takeaways from my 2023 wellness turnaround that I hope will help you prepare for the big fights in your life, or simply enjoy a happier and healthier life:

1. Take the hill.

Once I made the decision to change, I fully committed. Like an army battalion that commits to seizing the foothills occupied by an entrenched enemy, I resolved to achieve my wellness ambitions. There was no hesitation or contemplation. No second thoughts. Any doubts were replaced by determination. I was all in! As John Wayne proclaimed, "Courage is being scared to death, but saddling up anyway."

2. Embrace the suck.

When my family relocated to Africa in 2019 and my teenage daughter was experiencing anxiety about the move, my friend and mentor Mark Stouse encouraged her to "embrace the suck." He explained to Kaitlyn that her fears would turn into barrier-slaying courage and life-defining stories. Avoiding so many of the culinary pleasures I've enjoyed for years was not easy. One week into this journey, my body revolted with a withdrawal that grounded me for a weekend with energy-zapping nausea and headaches. Resisting dining out, a daily glass (or two) of wine, and my morning Starbucks mocha was tougher than I ever imagined. Quitting is easy. "Do Hard Things!"

3. The bigger our challenge, the greater our destiny.

The change we endure is a compelling measure of the potential we are capable of. Was this the most daunting challenge I've faced in my life? No. But it certainly tested my discipline and commitment in new and different ways I never expected. I am seizing each day with greater physical and mental fitness, vibrancy and fortitude, with the certainty that my destiny is that much greater now.

4. Seek out other change seekers.

Nothing will diminish our resolve more than *complacency enablers*. They are the doubters, discouragers, and distractors who prefer the path of least resistance to the road less traveled. We know who these people are; they surround us every day. Instead, I sought the *change seekers* in my life: the family members, friends, and colleagues who pressed me to honor my commitment and lean into the crucible of change I was confronting. You are the people you hang with. Choose wisely the people who will push you to be the dream maker you want to be and the difference maker the world needs you to be.

5. Accept being perfectly imperfect.

So many people I know who start a "New Year's diet" are chasing a specific weight target, waist size, or physical improvement. The reality is we never will achieve perfection. We are in an eternal state of imperfection. Perfection is a mirage; the true measure of our progress is the magnitude of our improvement. We keep getting better. We keep improving. We keep grinding and moving forward. We are all beautiful disasters on a never-ending quest for excellence.

Few people in this world have an ironclad resolve as unbending as Jason Teitler. We worked together at a global PR firm in the '90s. We became friends after Jason was dispatched from New York to LA to assist me on a client project. Jason's career flourished in the years and decades that followed, culminating as the sports and entertainment global specialty leader at Burson, one of the world's most prestigious PR agencies. Jason was flying high, serving as a communications counselor for some of the sports world's biggest names.

Unbending determination

On June 15, 2017, Jason's world changed forever. On this postcard-perfect Southern California Thursday afternoon, Jason was in LA on a business trip. After picking up his son at the University of California Los Angeles (UCLA), the two were on their way to Venice Beach for a meeting when a full-size pickup plowed into their Hyundai rental car while they were stopped on a freeway exit ramp. Their small sedan was crushed beyond recognition by the substantially larger truck.

The first thing he remembers about the accident is waking up in the ER at UCLA Medical Center.

"The truck plowed into us from behind, hitting the driver's side with dramatic force. Glass broke, metal twisted, and flesh was torn," Jason recalls hospital staff telling him after regaining consciousness.

His son, who was on summer break from college at the time, received many stitches on his ear and was quickly discharged from the hospital. Unfortunately, Jason's situation was far more serious. After having glass removed from his head and several stitches later, he was released from the hospital. However, he was back in the ER 24 hours later after experiencing severe pain in one of his legs.

Doctors ultimately determined a blood clot had formed in his leg and subsequently traveled to his lung, threatening Jason's life. The blood clot coincided with a partially collapsed lung, making it very difficult for Jason to breathe, thanks to a pulmonary embolism. He spent the next several days in the hospital's intensive care unit, where he was attended to by doctors and nurses around the clock.

Jason recalled, "I surprised myself, and perhaps others, by embracing an optimistic spirit and resolve. I contributed to the hospital-administered healing by adding my determination to the mix. This came in the form of pushing beyond the recommended walking and breathing exercises to strengthen my breathing. I reminded myself that the impact of the crash could have easily stopped my life and my son's too short."

After returning home to New Jersey, another blood clot threatened Jason's life. Doctors successfully treated this latest setback, and my friend was back on the road to recovery. Following several more weeks of rest and rehabilitation, Jason was ready to return to work.

He had a renewed appreciation for life and desired to use the combination of his expertise in communications and passion for sports as a force for good in the world. He found his way to the Special Olympics movement, where he led the life-changing organization's global communications and brand function across nearly 200 countries and territories. For the next several years, Jason helped people with intellectual disabilities across the world live healthier, more productive, and more rewarding lives. Today, Jason continues to help organizations grow with purpose as a senior communications consultant, supporting agency clients and clients directly as they navigate formidable opportunities and challenges.

Jason turned his resilience to survive into a resolve to help others thrive.

As you saddle up to take the next hill in your journey, I hope these lessons will inspire you to turn your next elusive New Year's resolution into a life-changing, and potentially life-saving, resolve.

Stormrider

Jason Teitler

*How I turned a life-threatening car accident into
a life-catalyzing resolve.*

It was supposed to be a simple and quick trip to Los Angeles for a business meeting and to spend some time with my son, who was attending the University of California Los Angeles (UCLA) as an undergrad; however, it was neither simple nor quick. Little did I know, what I expected to be an ordinary visit to the West Coast was about to become one of the most unexpected and extraordinary experiences of my life.

It was June 15, 2017. Another postcard-perfect Southern California Thursday afternoon. I landed at LAX, fetched my rental car, and picked up my son in Westwood. We headed to Venice Beach, where my son was joining me for a business meeting and the hope of a summer internship with the firm hosting us.

We never made it.

Colliding with destiny

The last thing I remember is our car was stopped at an exit ramp on I-10, also known as the Santa Monica Freeway. I was later told a full-size pickup plowed into our much smaller sedan from behind at a high rate of speed. The truck virtually climbed over us, hitting the driver's side with dramatic force. Glass broke, metal twisted, and flesh was torn.

My son woke from the collision first. A bystander offered his phone to him after asking if he was alright. Blood dripping from my son's ear was all that was needed to confirm that he was anything but alright. After unsuccessfully trying to wake me, he called my wife on the borrowed phone and received advice to instruct EMS workers to take me to UCLA Medical Center.

As I awoke in the ER, I still was not certain what had happened. A coworker and good friend of mine from my agency's LA office was by my side. This was a good thing, given it was quite unsettling to wake in a busy ER without understanding what had taken place. I quickly asked about my wife and son. I was told my wife was on her way out from New Jersey. Hospital staff also shared with me that, after a checkup and several stitches on his ear, my son was in decent shape and had been discharged.

On the other hand, my situation was far less optimistic. A major gash on the back of my head required the removal of several pieces of glass. Even after being stitched up, bits of glass remained in my head.

My incredible wife made it to Los Angeles in record time and was by my side through the entire ordeal in the hospital. Eventually, I was discharged from the ER and on my way to my wife's cousin's house to spend a few days before taking a flight back to New Jersey to recover. Given the impact the accident took on my body, my doctors directed me to avoid flying for several days.

My wife's family was quite hospitable and understanding, given what we had all been through. Their home was close to the hospital I had just left, which was very lucky, considering the second shoe that was about to drop. Less than 24 hours later, my body sounded an urgent alarm in the form of a staggering amount of pain in one of my legs. The pain grew agonizingly worse as the hours passed. The pain became unbearable, and we rushed back to the hospital.

After several tests and scans, it was confirmed a blood clot traveled from my leg to my lung. The clot's journey was causing severe pain and threatening my life. A life-threatening pulmonary embolism and a partially collapsed lung were hindering my breathing. The doctors were concerned this could be the first of many clots. I was immediately put on blood thinners, pain medication, and connected to a variety of contraptions in the ICU.

For the next few days, I resided in a quasi-bubble in the ICU, with nurses attending to me around the clock and doctors visiting at all hours. The staff at the UCLA Medical Center were incredible, with many of them gracefully enduring my sarcasm, horrible jokes, and relentless questioning as I tried to understand what was transpiring and the short- and long-term future of my health. I was also grateful to have business colleagues visit me to check on my spirits and wish me well.

My life-saving prescription—optimism

I surprised myself, and perhaps others, by embracing an optimistic spirit and resolve. I contributed to the hospital-administered healing by adding my determination to the mix. This came in the form of pushing beyond the recommended walking and breathing exercises to strengthen my breathing. I reminded myself that the impact of the crash could have easily stopped my life and my son's too short.

Despite the fortitude and a healing lung, complications challenged the vigor of my recovery, extending my hospital stay. With the help of my wife, son, and friends on the West Coast, I pushed through the setback of my healing lung needing to be drained regularly courtesy of a chest tube inserted into my lung through my neck. Given my improvement and a little luck, I was able to move past this new issue and relocate from the hospital to an affiliated recovery center in Westwood.

With my extended stay came an even greater desire to improve, return to New Jersey, and begin the extended healing process. I pushed myself even harder, reluctantly listening to my wife's warnings that

I was pushing myself too hard. Each day, we walked to the center of Westwood to get a coffee, enjoy lunch, and visit the shops as an excuse to escape the copious amounts of horrible television reruns and decades-old movies that were available on local stations.

When it was time to go home, that was an adventure in itself. I made it safe and sound back to Old Bridge, New Jersey. I was greeted by friends, neighbors, and family. There was a steady stream of visitors to my home, and my local Pulmonologist was patient with me, explaining every little detail, being available when my optimism waned and anxious inquiries required a quick response to not rock my positive outlook. Of course, my wife continued to be my bedrock.

I walked extensively each day, using the treadmill when the weather was less than ideal to keep the improvement at an optimum level. All seemed to be lined up for a full recovery.

At least, until one evening, when a nagging pain in my legs became unbearable. While I initially attributed it to excessive walking, I didn't want to risk anything, and my wife drove me to the local hospital. After several tests, many of which I've become quite familiar with, we learned that another large clot had formed and was now threatening my other lung. I was admitted and was instantly administered blood thinners.

I was told this clot was so large, it could have been catastrophic if I hadn't gone to the hospital.

The recovery was strenuous, at times, painful, and, above all, critical. I had the full support of friends and family near and far, and incredible doctors who were patient and generous with their time and explanation of what I was experiencing. I pushed myself every day to get back to normalcy, which I am proud to share that I reached.

With the exception of a daily dose of blood thinners, keeping up with my cardio workout schedule, making special preparations when I travel, avoiding sitting for long stretches of time, and being mindful of my surroundings, I'm able to work and play as I did in the past, knowing full well my lung capacity will never be 100%.

While I am enjoying and cherishing the pastimes that I enjoyed prior to the accident, such as scuba diving, I am conscious of what could have been. I could have lost way more than I did: my limbs, my life, my son. I'll never let down on the commitment I made to myself—to live!

Turn pain into purpose

As I returned to work, I desired to use the combination of my expertise in communications and passion for sports as a force for good in the world. I found my way to the Special Olympics movement, where I led the life-changing organization's global communications and brand function, supporting colleagues across nearly 200 countries and territories. For the next several years, I helped people with intellectual disabilities across the world live healthier, more productive, and more rewarding lives. Along the way, I helped change public policy and bolster the allocation of resources that advanced the Special Olympics' mission.

Today, I continue to help organizations grow with purpose as a senior communications consultant, supporting agency clients and clients directly as they navigate formidable opportunities and challenges.

There were many scary moments and some discouraging setbacks along the way, but I never lost my resolve to live. I learned there are many things we don't have control over in our lives, but our unbending determination to live is one thing we always have control over.

Learn More: You can discover more about Jason on his LinkedIn profile page.

CHAPTER 16

Compass Heading 9 — Hopelessness is Finite. Hope is Infinite.

Few comeback stories are as miraculous as that of Daniel Jacobs. In 2011, Daniel was considered one of the world's most promising young professional boxers. The Brooklyn-born 26-year-old had the world middleweight championship belt in his sights.

That was, until he was unexpectedly diagnosed with a rare form of paralyzing bone cancer. Following a six-hour surgery and ten weeks of cancer treatment in a New York hospital, Daniel's team of doctors told him he would never fight again. They warned him to stay away from the ring or risk a life of paralysis.

His dream of being the middleweight champion of the world was shattered.

However, Daniel never lost hope. Despite his doctors' guidance, he returned to the gym. Day by day, punch by punch, and round by round, over the course of 18 months he grinded his way back to peak fighting condition.

Daniel shared with me, "Without hope, I would not have gotten through this. Hope is what inspired me and made me feel like I could have another shot at victory—and more importantly, a second shot at life."

Nicknamed the "Miracle Man," Daniel returned to the ring in 2013, knocking out his first professional opponent in the first round. In 2014, Daniel achieved his lifelong dream, claiming the world middleweight championship belt, a title he held for the next three years.

Daniel's story is an inspiring reminder no matter how hopeless our circumstances may seem, never lose hope.

Hope is not a strategy—hope is everything

"Faith is taking the first step, even when you don't see the whole staircase," encouraged Dr. Martin Luther King, Jr. Even in confronting the vicious adversity in pursuit of equality and social justice, Dr. King never lost faith:

"We must accept finite disappointment but never lose infinite hope."

Sadly, however, too many business and political leaders today insist that "hope is not a strategy." They contend that there is no place in business or public policy for something as aspirational, elusive, intangible, uncontrollable or, dare I suggest, human as "hope." Yet, this is precisely why hope should be the light guiding us.

Success fades—faith sustains

In 2019, I attended the 10th annual gathering of the African Leadership Network (ALN) in Accra, Ghana, what many describe as "the Davos of Africa." Each year, ALN convenes 300 leaders, political dignitaries, philanthropists, entertainers, and other luminaries from around the world who share a dream of transforming Africa through the development of a new era of young leaders. Former United Nations Secretary General Ban Ki-moon, Mastercard Foundation President Reeta Roy, Former PepsiCo President Zein Abdalla, Alibaba Founder Jack Ma, Conservation International CEO Dr. M. Sanjayan, and Toronto Raptors President Masai Ujiri are just some of the global changemakers that were drawn to ALN.

For me, one participant stood out more than the others: Zimbabwean billionaire entrepreneur and philanthropist Strive Masiyiwa. By way of background, Strive is the Founder and Executive Chairman of Econet, Africa's largest telecommunications, media, and technology company, as well as one of the continent's most admired corporate leaders. He also serves on the boards of Unilever, The Bill and Melinda Gates Foundation, The Rockefeller Foundation, and The Conrad Hilton Foundation. During a fireside-style discussion with Strive, he was asked to share his "keys to success." While I was expecting to hear the usual "secrets"—imagination, resilience, courage and so on—the soft-spoken business titan shared these simple but profound words:

"Success is about faith. It creates opportunities. Some call that luck, but that's what I expect from faith."

Strive is right. Faith is the oxygen that breathes life into our biggest dreams and most audacious moonshots.

Speaking of dreaming, we need not look any farther than one of the business world's biggest dreamers, Walt Disney. Indeed, it was Walt who declared "if you can dream it, you can do it." A few years ago, we visited The Walt Disney Family Museum tucked away in San Francisco's Golden Gate National Park. As we toured the exhibits, which were chronologically arranged to map Walt's life, I was moved by the role hope and faith played in making his dreams a reality at virtually every turn in his illustrious journey.

Leap-of-faith mindset

There is no better example of Walt's "leap-of-faith mindset" than the creation of *Snow White and the Seven Dwarfs*—perhaps one of his greatest achievements. The creation of the world's first animated feature-length film was an extremely complex and expensive endeavor. The two-hour film required the illustrating, photographing, and synchronizing of 250,000 frames. At the time (1934), no one thought such a production was feasible, except Walt.

"We decided there was only one way we could successfully do *Snow White*, and that was to go for broke. Shoot the works," wrote Walt. "I had to sit alone with Joe Rosenberg (Executive Vice President at Bank of America) and try to sell him a quarter of a million dollars worth of faith. After the lights came on, he walked out of the projection room, remarked that it was a nice day, and yawned. . . then he turned to me and said 'Walt, that picture will make a potful of money.' To this day, he's my favorite banker."

In the end, it was faith that made possible the impossible—and provided the essential hope Disney's investors and employees needed to transform his vision into reality.

Follow your heart

Disney is far from alone. Apple is another example of a company powered by the unflinching hope and faith of its founder. Steve Jobs was fired from the company he co-created shortly after the debut of the world-changing Mac. After leaving Apple, he started two more companies (NeXT and Pixar) and was ultimately rehired by Apple to lead the greatest corporate renaissance of our time.

"Sometimes life is going to hit you in the head with a brick," Steve warned. "Don't lose faith."

We all get thrown off our horse at some point in life—even Steve Jobs. Learn from the experience, dust yourself off, and jump back in the saddle. He acknowledged that getting fired from Apple was the best thing that ever happened to him.

"You have to trust that the dots will somehow connect in your future . . . because believing that the dots will connect down the road will give you the confidence to follow your heart even when it leads you off the well-worn path."

Steve lost everything. But he never lost hope.

Selling the moon

Of course, this discussion would not be complete without reminding ourselves of the rocket fuel that hope and faith provided President John F. Kennedy's vision to go to the Moon.

In his now famous speech delivered under a sweltering sun at Rice University on September 12, 1962, President Kennedy pulled back the curtain on his moonshot. He secured the nation's buy-in to his dream, not by articulating every meticulous detail of the mission, but, like Disney, by selling America $150 billion worth of faith in a space program, rocket, and technology that had yet to be invented.

"We have given this program a high national priority, even though I realize that this is in some measure an act of faith and vision—for we do not now know what benefits await us," President Kennedy avowed.

JFK's same moonshot mindset can be found at the African Leadership Group, where I served as an Executive In Residence and Chief Communications Officer. Our dream, to transform Africa by empowering 3 million young leaders by 2035, sounds like an impossible mission to most people. But for those who work for, study at, and invest in this innovative ecosystem of high school, university, and lifelong-learning institutions across the continent, we share the same unshakeable faith that put *Snow White* on the big screen, put two men on the moon, and put computers on our wrists.

Embracing hope is paramount to unleashing the highest levels of our potential. It will propel us to our destiny through whatever barriers stand in our way. After all, nothing great in our world has ever been achieved without hope and faith. Aiming for anything short of our purpose-fulfilling destiny is a shallow aspiration.

No matter how elusive our dreams may be, or how terminal our circumstances may seem, we can never lose hope.

Daniel Jacobs returned to the boxing ring to achieve his dream of a world championship title after recovering from a crippling cancer diagnosis. He never lost hope. Walt Disney pitched a banker a $250,000 dream that would change the world. He never lost hope. JFK sold America a vision to put a man on the Moon. He never lost hope. Steve Jobs was fired from the company he created and returned several years later to build one of the most valuable and world-changing companies in the world. He never lost hope. And MLK urged America to dream of a free and equitable country. He never lost hope.

The setbacks that blindside us can leave us feeling hopeless. Yet, hope is perhaps the one thing we need more than anything as we ride the respective storms in our lives towards the purpose-fueling potential we are destined to achieve.

In a letter to a friend, blind and deaf author Helen Keller wrote, "Hope sees the invisible, feels the intangible, and achieves the impossible."

Stormrider

Daniel Jacobs

How I knocked out cancer and became the middleweight boxing champion of the world.

I grew up in a tough neighborhood in Brooklyn, surrounded by a lot of gang activity and drug use. I knew there was something very wrong with all of this. I also appreciated so many good things about Brooklyn: the family reunions, community gatherings, and the many music and sports legends my neighborhood gave birth to.

I knew Brooklyn wouldn't be my be-all and end-all. I wanted more. I wanted to explore and travel the world. As a child, I was always trying to find my niche. I was never good at the sports other kids were playing, like football, basketball, or baseball, but I wanted to be great at something. I just didn't know what that would be.

A defining moment in my life occurred when I was 14. The neighborhood bully turned his attention to me. I stood up to him and we ended up in the principal's office—and left with a stern warning. I learned this other kid was working out at the local boxing gym. I decided I would give it a shot myself and take care of this bully the proper way. So, I went to the gym, met with the coach, and learned the basics of boxing. A few days later, I had the chance to box the other kid, and let's just say he didn't do so well. I surprised him and, more importantly, I surprised myself. I discovered my calling. Being in the ring just felt natural.

Living my dream

That bully never bothered me again and boxing became my mission. I stuck with it, and I was able to travel to places across the U.S. and, eventually, around the world. In many ways, that bully was the best thing that ever happened to me. Our confrontation became the affirmation of my destiny, and a life of discovery, joy, and glory I never imagined.

I remember graduating from high school feeling like the LeBron James of boxing. All the promoters and the boxing world were excited about me going pro. It went from me just boxing to be cool or get some form of revenge to fulfilling my dreams and becoming a world champion.

I had nine or ten consecutive first-round knockouts as a young pro, and I quickly emerged as the next sensation everyone was talking about. I recall gazing at the ocean from the balcony of my Long Island condo, thinking, *This is it—I made it, I have everything I ever wanted.* I was grateful. I was living my dream.

Not long after that, I began experiencing a pain in my back. This continued for several months. I complained to my trainer about it, but he was one of these "old school guys" who was all about dedication and pushing through the pain. The pain continued to intensify and, during an exhibition trip to Iraq to teach our troops how to box, I got very sick. I was having a hard time eating and walking.

The fight of my life was the fight for my life

A few days after returning to the U.S., I fell while getting out of bed. I was paralyzed from my waist down. My godmother took me to a Neurologist, who diagnosed me with bone cancer spreading from a tennis-ball-sized tumor growing in my lower spine. They immediately sent me to the ER at New York Presbyterian Hospital. In the days and weeks that followed, I underwent six hours of surgery where portions of my spine were replaced with titanium rods, endured dozens of hours of chemotherapy to kill the cancer, and logged countless sessions of rehabilitative physical therapy to relearn how to walk.

I was admitted to the hospital thinking my career was at stake. My life was at stake. There were moments where I would cry in my hospital bed and dark thoughts haunted me. It was a very rough time. However, I confronted my treatment journey as though I was training for the fight of my life. In this case, it was the fight *for* my life. I had a new opponent: it was me vs. me. Cancer became the biggest and toughest opponent I would ever face. I knew I would emerge victorious with my hand raised in the air.

Ten weeks later, I was discharged from the hospital. However, prior to leaving, I met with my doctors, who warned me, "Boxing is out of the equation. You are going to have to find something else to do with your life. If you get hit the wrong way, you could be paralyzed for the rest of your life."

I felt like my back was against the wall.

The hero of my own movie

The doctors ordered me to "stay away from the gym." That was probably the first thing I did after I left the hospital. The idea of never being able to box again sparked something in me. Boxing was my life. It allowed me to see the world and provide for me and my family. Now I was worried whether I would step foot in the ring again, let alone achieve my dream of claiming the world title.

As I headed home from the hospital, I made the decision I wasn't going to be a victim—I was going to be the hero of my own movie. The whole journey was physically and mentally excruciating. I had to summon the strength from the depths of my body and soul to move forward. Step by step, punch by punch, and round by round, over the next 18 months, I grinded my way back to peak fighting condition.

Boxing gave me the mentality that no matter what you do, you have to work hard and have the proper dedication, and you have to make sacrifices. The only thing I wanted to do was train and push myself. I envisioned having my hand raised. My life turned into a movie to see how far I could go. I became my own inspiration. I wasn't worried about inspiring others—it was to motivate myself. Boxing gave me the mindset to dig deep. You never know what you are made of until you go through something like this. In many ways, it was the best thing that ever happened to me.

One of the best feelings I ever had occurred when I stepped foot back in the ring for the opening of the Barclays Center for my comeback fight. I remember being in the dressing room, recalling the moments of hopelessness I felt in the hospital. I felt a motivational spirit to be back doing what I loved doing. I always wanted to say I could come back for one more fight.

The "Miracle Man"

In 2013, I knocked out my first opponent in the first round. A year later, I became the middleweight champion of the world, a title I held for the next three years. After that, the boxing community nicknamed me the "Miracle Man."

I ran with it. I had a new identity. I had a new mindset. And I had a new understanding of what it took to put yourself in the right mental capacity to do anything. I became my own biggest fan. I became a sensation not because of my talent, but because of who I am and what I represent. I've always wanted to be somebody people identified with, like Muhammad Ali or Sugar Ray Leonard. That gave me hope, purpose, and drive. I knew my victorious fight against cancer and my return to the ring were an inspiration to millions of fellow cancer warriors around the world. I knew I was doing something righteous.

Starting the Getting in the Ring Foundation after hanging up my gloves was the ultimate victory for me. Helping kids with cancer, as well as supporting kids who are being bullied, has proven far more rewarding than any victory I achieved inside the ring. The Foundation allowed me to be that beautiful person I always wanted to be. Helping these kids is a full circle experience from the playground bullying I experienced as a kid to the cancer battle I waged as an adult.

You must understand how big of a role you play in dictating your own future and being the one who creates the life you want to live. You are never going to truly know what you are made of until you live through a really difficult experience. It made me the best version of myself, and I emerged the man I always wanted to be. You can go through anything in life if you have the right mindset of hope, a strong faith in God, and have love surrounding you.

I'm grateful for hope. Without hope, I would not have gotten through this. Hope is what inspired me and made me feel like I could have another shot at victory and, more importantly, a second shot at life. I've always had a great relationship with "The Most High" power. A few months before I was even diagnosed with cancer, I remember asking God to show me what being humble and graceful means. To show me how to be inspirational to others.

To now be the Miracle Man with a story to tell, I have a newfound responsibility. That responsibility was granted to me by God because I pleaded with him to allow me to be humble, grateful, and an inspiration to others. My cancer diagnosis was truly a blessing in disguise.

In boxing, they say, "the fight is never won inside the ring. It is won during training." Training is how you keep your mind sharp and how you prepare for getting through anything in life. If you are mentally and spiritually prepared, anything is possible.

Learn More: You can follow Daniel on Instagram at danieljacobsTKO.

CHAPTER 17

Compass Heading 10 – Share Your Blanket

On my 2019 orientation trip to the remote Indian Ocean island of Mauritius, I had the good fortune of meeting Susanna Dalais. She served on the board of African Leadership University, where I would soon be starting as an Executive In Residence. During our visit, she welcomed me to her home and the island. I departed our sunset conversation overlooking the Indian Ocean's turquoise waters inspired by the story she shared of her own journey to Mauritius, as well as by the life-improving impact she and her husband, Marc, have had on scores of people across the island.

Only later, once my family and I were planted on the island, would the full abundance of Susanna and Marc's grace, generosity, and humanity reveal itself to me.

Susanna's journey took her from the U.S. through 25 African countries to eventually put down roots in Mauritius, one of the continent's tiniest nations. She shared with me that the excuse for this pan-African odyssey was pursuing studies and a research fellowship in the strange confluence of economics and political change. It was a personal, professional, and academic quest that would expose Susanna to the various adventures in investment banking from Angola to Malawi.

"It was fun," she told me. "But perhaps, more importantly, a good preparation for the wild ride of running nonprofits on a remote African island awaiting me."

The birth of a child gave birth to a school

Like a lot of parents, the birth of Susanna's first child made her very philosophical and dreamy about what her daughter's education could look like. Friends were asking where they planned to send her to school. Government schools in Mauritius left much to be desired, so those who could afford it—only about 6% of families—opted for the small handful of private schools on the island that required tuition well beyond the means of most parents.

"Those schools were fine, safe choices. Yet our minds wrestled with two ideas. First, as people whose faith has deeply marked our own paths and calling, we wondered about a place of learning that could also be a place that helps young people explore the reality of a good God, to better inform and direct that learning. We also wondered how we could include kids across the socioeconomic spectrum of our country, not just those who could afford it. Only about one third of Mauritian children earn a secondary (high school) degree."

Susanna quit her lucrative investment banking career, and without any formal training in education or running a nonprofit, she launched The Lighthouse School. In the meantime, Marc was starting a new company and Susanna was raising their three children, including their newborn baby.

Like all great endeavors, they started small: with one grade, one student (their first daughter), one teacher, and one cook in a small, rented house. Sixteen years later, Lighthouse is a thriving K-12 school, educating 600 students on a charming 12-acre purpose-built campus. To this day, the school continues to honor its founding mission to provide full scholarships to 25% of those students and financial support to many beyond that.

Place shared-interest above self-interest

To help fund those scholarships, the Dalais' dreamed up a second complementary nonprofit: The Good Shop. Their idea was simple. They would open a retail store offering the public donated second-hand clothing, electronics, and other products for free or at a very low cost. The proceeds are used to provide employment opportunities, 30% of which are offered to individuals with disabilities, and to fund Lighthouse scholarships.

"My incredible American mother was a thrift shop maven, and I grew up on secondhand magic, but for Marc, as for any Mauritian, the idea of a whole store just selling secondhand items was a new concept."

Seven years later, there are four Good Shops across the island which, today, fund 20% of Lighthouse scholarships.

What began as a simple experiment in 2010 has flourished into a shining example of how our blessings can be transformed into meaningful gifts for those around us. Above all, Susanna reminds us, "Deciding to give up a salary can be daunting, but it has a different— and very often more gratifying—payoff."

I'm proud to say our daughter Kaitlyn attended Lighthouse during our year in Mauritius. The school played a pivotal role in a transforma-tive childhood experience she continues to reflect upon as a thriving college junior today. Lighthouse offered Kaitlyn far more than an edu-cation. It made her an enlightened citizen of the world and introduced her to classmates who have become lifelong friends, including the school's first student, Susanna and Marc's eldest daughter.

Susanna's story reminds me of another powerful story of placing shared-interest above self-interest.

The blanket story

This tale begins on a day in early 2015, one that started like so many others I experienced during my five-year tenure leading global corpo-rate communications at Starbucks Coffee Company. On this occasion, I was accompanying Starbucks Chairman and CEO Howard Schultz to a speaking engagement: Sheraton's global leadership conference, attended by 1,000 hotel general managers from around the world.

I met Howard in the lobby of the hotel chain's flagship Puget Sound property, the Sheraton Grand Seattle. We were greeted by a Sheraton executive who escorted us to the second-floor ballroom where the event was being held. As we waited backstage for Howard's turn at the dais, I reminded him of a few key points to highlight in his remarks.

"It is now my pleasure to introduce a leader who needs no introduction, Howard Schultz: the Chairman and Chief Executive Officer of Starbucks Coffee Company."

Dressed in a sleek black suit, crisp white shirt, and his signature navy blue tie, Howard stepped on stage, shook hands with Sheraton's CEO, gripped the podium, and smiled widely at the audience, who welcomed him with a standing ovation.

In the meantime, I discretely skirted my way from backstage to the back of the ballroom so I could have a wide-angle view of Howard and the audience's reaction. I had heard him deliver this inspiring leadership stump speech many times before. So, I used the time to tackle a few of the emails crossing my screen that morning.

Twenty minutes into his remarks, Howard began telling a story that was unfamiliar to my ears. I put my phone down and pulled out the palm-sized reporter's notepad I had tucked away in my inside jacket pocket for moments like this. I started intensely scribbling notes.

He had veered off-road. Most corporate communications execs would panic at this point, but I was excited. I had a new story to work with. In my world, storytelling is not part of the game, storytelling *is* the game!

Howard proceeded to share what I now fondly refer to as "the blanket story."

It went something like this:

Howard set the stage by sharing how a few years earlier he traveled to Israel with a small cohort of fellow Jewish CEOs. While there, a prominent Rabbi took the leaders to Jerusalem's Old City, the Wailing Wall, and several other significant religious landmarks.

The true meaning of the Holocaust

On the final day of their visit, the Rabbi met with the American business titans to share some parting wisdom. The Rabbi asked, "Gentlemen, do you know the true meaning of the Holocaust?"

Howard told the hotel managers it was an unexpected and uncomfortably intimidating question that left the CEOs speechless. None, Howard recalled, had the courage to try and answer such a soul-stirring question posed by one of their faith's most influential leaders.

After a moment of pin-dropping silence, the Rabbi explained the Holocaust illuminated "the best of humanity." The CEOs, Howard recalled, were stunned by this proclamation. How could one of modern history's darkest periods of inhumanity be characterized as a model for humanity, especially by one of the Jewish faith's most distinguished leaders?

"Let me tell you a story," the Rabbi continued.

We are all haunted by the chilling images of Jewish families being rounded up and herded into cattle cars destined for Nazi extermination camps. It was not unusual for a single poorly ventilated railcar to be packed with 150 people. The journey would often take eight or more days, without food or water. This led to numerous deaths along the way from illness, suffocation, and exposure to frigid conditions.

The Rabbi went on to explain that one blanket was typically dispersed to one out of every six prisoners for the long and horrifying journey.

"This meant that each prisoner who was handed a blanket had a choice," he told the CEOs. "They could keep the blanket for themselves. Or they could share it with someone else on the train."

The Rabbi explained that it is well-documented in virtually every case, the treasured blankets were shared.

"Gentlemen, in the face of imminent torture and death, humanity prevailed. The human gift of caring and sharing was never more evident." In these brief moments of kindness, great humanity eclipsed grave inhumanity.

The Rabbi concluded his story by leaving the CEOs with a profound question. "As you fly home, I want you to think about the blankets each of you have been blessed with. Who will you share yours with?"

Howard concluded his speech by imploring the hotel managers to contemplate the Rabbi's challenge. "As you return to your hotels and communities around the globe, I want each of you to think about the blankets you've been blessed with—and who will you share yours with?"

Everyone in the ballroom that day received a powerful lesson in servant leadership—including me.

Good stories change us—great stories change the world

Six months later, I found myself on the opposite side of the country staying at the New York City Times Square Sheraton. A couple days into my visit, I bumped into the hotel's General Manager on an elevator ride down to the lobby. After I mentioned I worked for Starbucks, he started telling me about a conference he attended that included a speech by our CEO.

"He shared this remarkable story that has stuck with me and that I have told many times over to my hotel staff."

I quietly replied, "The blanket story?"

He smiled, nodded his head affirmatively. We shook hands and went our separate ways.

Good stories have the potential of changing us. Great stories have the power to change the world. As we reflect on our own purpose-fulfilling journeys, we should all consider the blankets we have been blessed with. Howard, Susanna, and Marc are sharing their blankets. Who will we share ours with?

Stormrider

Susanna Dalais

How I discovered the more we give, the more we can give.

My journey has taken me from the U.S. through 25 African countries to eventually put down roots in one of the continent's tiniest nations, Mauritius. My excuse for embarking on this quest was pursuing studies and a research fellowship in the strange confluence of economics and political change. This was followed by various adventures in investment banking from Angola to Malawi.

It was fun. And perhaps good preparation for the wild ride of running nonprofits on the remote African island awaiting me.

I'm not a trained educator, but, like a lot of parents, the birth of my first child made me get very philosophical and dreamy about what her education could look like. Given that a child's primary and secondary education potentially represent some 14 years or so of their life and take up about 20%–40% of their waking hours, school seems to have a high-stakes influence on what kind of person we might become (at least, from the perspective of a naive first-time parent). That's why I guess people were asking us where we planned to send her to school from the time she was still in the womb. In our context, government schools left much to be desired, and people who could afford it, some 6% of the population at the time, opted for private schools that charged tuition beyond the means of most families.

Those schools were fine, safe choices. Yet our minds wrestled with two ideas. As people whose faith has deeply marked our own paths and calling, we wondered about a place of learning that could also help young people explore the reality of a good God to better inform and direct that learning.

We also wondered how we could include kids across the socioeconomic spectrum of our country, not just those who could afford it. It was bugging us that in the public system, after running a gauntlet of summative exams, only about a third of students ended up with their secondary (high) school diploma. Why should the futures of young people with no income be constrained by the income levels, and possibly life choices, of the adults who are raising them? This question kept us up at night. In fact, that niggling issue of the reality of a good God challenged us to think from this lens.

This went completely against my own market-driven supply-and-demand-curve education and thinking.

Trading my career for my calling

To up the ante, as a couple, we decided that I would not return to a lucrative career in the private sector. Rather, I would devote my time and unqualified experience to help this financially and personally risky endeavor fly. At the same time, Marc was navigating a major career transition and decided to launch his own company while I was carting around a newborn—our third child, by that date.

Very improbably, we launched what we thought would only be a primary (elementary) school. Well, to be more precise, we started one single grade in a small, rented house with one student (our kid), one teacher, and one person to prepare lunch. We had shopped the idea around to lots of people who gave us their enthusiastic feedback and assurance that it was just what their children needed, but, as it turns out, many of those people really meant "we'll wait and see." For various reasons, I believe one of these was an uneasiness with the idea of mixing up poor kids and those with means. There was a presumption that this would compromise educational quality. One parent told me that, while it was a nice idea, why not have a "good" private school that can then give some profits towards a separate nice little charity school? But this struck at the heart of the idea.

From the beginning, our conviction was that a significant portion of children in the school would receive financial need-based scholarships. The fourth child in the school was on scholarship, and every fourth one from there. We ended that first charmed year with 12 students.

If we build it, they will come

It was an experiment. We workshopped phonics flashcards in tin-roofed homes, helping parents with low educational levels support their children in going higher. Our kids had play dates. In year three, the school had to move to a bigger building: a former swimsuit factory that Marc discovered after inexplicably taking a wrong turn on his way home one day.

All along the way, children and exceptional educators kept coming. About 75%–80% of the operational budget of any school goes to paying its main resource: people. While we have remained guided by the conviction that people should earn solid salaries, no less than market-based, we have also noticed that they also rely on mission and organizational culture for strength.

Those mission-minded educators have been joined by other mission-minded people who give generously of themselves, many of humble resources. Our non-remunerated board. The octogenarian who literally reenacted the Biblical story of the widow's mite by giving us a non-interest-bearing loan with her savings. Many of our staff might be more comfortable in their home countries. The building contractor parent who offered contractor financing on very generous terms to get our next phase of classrooms done. It was weird for me, a former financier, to be on the other side of the table, explaining to our bankers why the school was a solid financing candidate on the basis of a history of generosity and our future faith in miraculous provision. Contrary to their stereotype, sometimes even commercial bankers can get dreamy.

Our own buildings were necessitated by families refusing to leave when their kids finished Lighthouse Primary School, and us realizing that the bemoaned teenage years are really a clincher. We scoped out land that could belong permanently to the school (within a charitable trust). We signed a purchase agreement without having the wherewithal to pay it, but we were able to raise the money in the eleventh hour. Some $2.8 million dollars of land and building investments later, the trust now holds a 12-acre school campus and school farm operating with some 600 K-12 students, and it still maintains the scholarship program according to its founding principles 16 years ago.

Goodness breeds goodness

Along the way, that scholarship program helped birth another idea. To provide for it in the long term, what if another nonprofit social enterprise could be started that could provide a needed, good service or product, one that would be financially sustainable and from which any surplus could help fund scholarships? The Good Shop was born.

My incredible American mother was a thrift shop maven, and I had grown up on secondhand magic, but for Marc, as for any Mauritian, the idea of a whole store just selling secondhand items was a new concept. We identified a particular juncture of history in the country, however: the growth of a consumerist society (much to my chagrin) and thus, more stuff; rising awareness of environmental degradation and waste management as a vulnerable island country; and, as ever, impoverishment. Though I had been involved with needy communities, I never felt comfortable with just bequeathing them odd bags of stuff that were not what they needed or wanted.

With the help of another gifted person with an entrepreneurial spirit who knew a bit more about retail than we did, together, we threw some resources behind starting a secondhand shop. The idea was to actually employ people to be a more efficient mechanism of getting people things they actually need, and want, at very low prices, or even free; The Good Shop works with dozens of NGOs to get them pre-sorted items that they really need and allows identified beneficiaries "free shopping."

Once again, the mission steamrolled, and as of 2025, we are celebrating seven years and four shops across the island. Once again, there are some counterintuitive hurdles we set for ourselves to make the whole thing better. My niece, who has Down syndrome, inspired us to see the value of dignified work for people with barriers to employment. The Good Shop sets a minimum bar of 30% of its employees falling in this category, who also have access to their own performance bonuses. This amazing workforce and the very low prices offered have now started to make significant donations from their surplus, about 20% of the school's whole scholarship fund in the last year.

What the Lighthouse School taught me

What observations do I have for others who might feel a tug to do something counterintuitive, for the good of others?

1. **It's all grace.** I can't help but share that our experience has convinced us even more that there is a sovereign God who loves people and wants their best, and that all the money and talent in the world belongs to Him. Crazily enough, He channels those resources to people to be part of His redemptive work. I am not sure why and how He entrusts us faulty, block-headed, fearful people, but He does.
2. **The more we give, the more we can give**. There have been many board meetings where I stare at spreadsheets and still wonder how this happens. Recently, The Good Shop spent half a day hosting women from a shelter for victims of domestic violence, enabling them to pick all the clothing items they wanted for free, and on that same day, that particular shop posted record sales. It's a mini-example of our "normal" and helped us to be bolder in generosity.
3. **Charity is not always deciding what to do with the extra**. Solutions that really uplift others in a sustainable, long-term way

might take a lot of time and usually up-front trust, as well as giving early and consistently, when the individual or organization thinks they can't afford it. Good intentions of first building up heaps of profits, making distributions, and then slicing off a percentage to "give away" can be misguided. Rather, consider making the "positive externalities," in the words of my old economics studies, *internalities*—part of the business model that incidentally makes the organization or product better. The school's students turn out better through the diversity of their student body; it's not just something we do to be nice or appear charitable.

4. **If it weren't hard or sacrificial, someone else would already be doing it.** My account may sound shiny and harmonious, but it almost goes without saying, like Jim's story, there are plenty of heartbreaks and roadblocks on the way. But also like his story, deep joy through the tough stuff is possible. Identify what helps you persevere and prioritize both its practice and the people committed to your accountability and encouragement.

5. **Teamwork.** No one person can ever take credit for a worthwhile endeavor. We all depend on each other. While I now see that I was permitted opportunities to acquire some unique skills and natural proclivities, I also see that, often, what I'm led to do or contribute is actually in areas where I'm weakest or least qualified, and I see that in others, too. Humility and honing our ability to discern and value the ways other people can jump in helps keep things going way beyond the limitations of self, and it frees other people to try things beyond what they think they can do. I continue to be surprised at how, if I keep moving toward something, just the right people come along the path, but it also kind of makes me expect the surprises.

Learn More: You can discover more about Lighthouse at Lighthouse.edu.mu and The Good Shop at TheGoodShop.mu.

Stage 3

Communicate

CHAPTER 18

Be a Gold Medal Storyteller

It has been said that we forget what people say, we remember what they show us, but the stories people share live in our hearts and minds forever.

Think about it. Most of us can't remember who won last year's World Series, which film claimed the Oscar, or the name of the seatmate we met on our flight back from New York ten minutes after they introduced themselves. Yet, we can retell the campfire stories, fishing tales, and family legends our grandpa passed down to us as kids with the same exacting detail as if they were shared with us yesterday.

That's because stories have been with us since the dawn of humanity. They have the power to unite us or divide us. Engage us or enrage us. Heal us or hurt us. And propel us from ordinary to extraordinary. Stories have the capacity to give our setbacks and comebacks a voice that not only stir our hearts, souls, and minds, as all great stories should, but also provoke conversation, inspire commitment, and invite action. Indeed, storytelling is the vessel that brings context, simplicity, relevance, and humanity to our greatest ideas, experiences, plans, and ambitions.

Stories make us laugh, they make us cry and, above all, they make us think. They prompt us to think about where we've been, where we are, and where we are going.

I wrote this book to share my story and those of the other Stormriders I've introduced along the way to help you author your own comeback plot.

Storytelling has been a cornerstone of my life since my earliest days. Growing up, my parents would set up their slide projector after Sunday evening dinner. They would click through slides from their time living in India and other adventures prior to my sister and I coming into the world. As our family moved from state to state, storytelling became my currency for connecting and relating to new classmates, teammates, and friends.

So, it shouldn't be surprising that I aspired to become a journalist at an early age. I was editor of my high school newspaper. I loved discovering and sharing the experiences of my classmates. When I got to college, I majored in journalism my freshman year before switching to public relations as a sophomore. My PR education at Syracuse University set the stage for a communications career that has presented me with the chance to help shape and tell some of the world's most consequential business, technology, and social impact stories of our time.

As a professional communicator, corporate executive, public speaker, professor, columnist, and recently minted book author, stories are the lens through which I thrive at all these roles. I've relished the opportunity to use these storytelling platforms to chronicle how ordinary people have transformed into extraordinary heroes.

We see our challenges in their struggles

As I joined the world to watch the 2024 Paris Summer Olympic Games, I found myself more interested in the athletes' personal stories than the medals they won. I suspect I was not the only viewer more intrigued by the struggles these Olympians confronted than the races they were running. That's probably because we see ourselves in the challenges these competitors have had to overcome in their quest for gold.

More than anything, their narratives are the stuff dreams are made of. Because they move us, change us, and inspire us. They console us, make us laugh, and make us cry. They help us understand each other and ourselves, discover distant lands, explore different cultures, and contemplate the consequential issues of our time.

Their stories turn routine journeys into epic adventures. They transform ordinary people into eternal legends. And they convert everyday experiences into breathtaking moments.

That's because their stories motivate us to do hard things, challenge us to solve big problems, and show us that we don't have to be influential to have influence. Most of all, they unite us, provoke us, and give us hope. And every now and then, they remind us to believe the impossible is possible.

As alluring as the Olympics are to watch, they are an illustrative template of the stories of courage, hope, transformation, and impact we can share about our world, our communities, and, most importantly, ourselves.

Gold medal heart

Let's look at one of the most memorable comeback stories in modern Olympic history. Orphaned as a young boy in the Hill Country of eastern Kenya, Kip Keino was raised by his aunt and later became a police officer. Kip took up running in his early 20s and quickly emerged on the international track and field stage as one of the world's elite distance runners.

In the 1968 Mexico City Summer Olympics, Kip qualified for three events over the course of four days: the 10,000 meter, 5,000 meter and 1,500 meter races. During the 10,000-meter finals, he collapsed from severe stomach pain with two laps left in the race. As medics tended to him, Kip got back up and finished the race. A couple days later, still suffering severe stomach pain, Kip finished second in the 5,000 meters.

However, it was Kip's 1,500-meter victory that is regarded as one of the most triumphant comebacks in Olympic history. After his silver medal 5,000-meter finish, his abdominal issues worsened. Doctors ultimately diagnosed his condition as a serious issue with his gallbladder. The physicians ordered him to withdraw from his final race, warning Kip that continuing to run would not only aggravate his condition but potentially kill him.

An hour before the race, despite his doctors' orders, Kip decided to run. He suited up, hopped on a bus, and headed to the stadium. Along the way, the bus got stuck in horrible traffic. Time was running out, so Kip jumped off the bus and ran the final mile to the stadium, arriving at the starting line just as they were announcing the field of runners.

Despite being the underdog in this race against American distance running legend Jim Ryan, Kip surged from the back of the pack with just two laps left to win the gold by 20 meters—the largest margin of victory ever achieved in the 1,500 meters to this day.

Thirty-two years after his legendary comeback, I took three flights spanning 10,000 miles from LA to Kenya to meet Kip. I was halfway through my Executive MBA program at the University of Southern California (USC), where we were required to complete an entrepreneurship capstone assignment. Unlike the rest of my startup-focused classmates, I chose to focus my project on social entrepreneurship.

Kip was an ideal case study in social impact leadership. After retiring from running, Kip and his wife built an orphanage and secondary school in Eldoret, Kenya (near where he grew up). At the time, public education was only available through 8th grade. High school was a luxury reserved for those with the financial means to pay for the tuition.

Kip invited me to stay with him and his wife at the orphanage where they reside. I lived there for a week while I visited the school and the adjacent farm that fed the students and children at the orphanage. For me, this trip was an ideal convergence of my passion for running and social impact.

One evening, I asked Kip why he started the orphanage and school, while the other elite runners returning to Kenya with lucrative sponsorship deals were building mansions and buying exotic cars.

"We are helping kids with no future. If we don't help them, nobody will be there for them. There are a lot of people who think these kids will have no future—we can help them learn to think and learn to lead. Knowledge is the key; anyone with knowledge will have the key to help their country and the world."

Twenty five years after my trip to Eldoret, the Kip Keino School and orphanage continue to thrive. Kip's life is far more than an epic Olympic comeback story. He has transformed his success story on the track into a life-changing legacy of significance off the track.

10 gold medal plots

As we assess how to tell our own gold medal stories, consider these ten setback-to-comeback illuminating plots:

- **Stories of Origin:** Honoring our past is one of the best ways of revealing who we are today. It is an opportunity to recognize our heritage, give tribute to our values, and celebrate the people and moments that have shaped our current existence.
- **Stories of Possibility:** Paint a vivid description of where we are going. Ignite excitement and spark intrigue about what's next in our journey, the barriers we will break, the places we'll go, and the heights we'll soar to.
- **Stories of Purpose:** Showcase our commitment to a cause greater than ourselves. When we align our work with a higher calling, we don't just find meaning, we ignite it. Purpose-driven action inspires not only personal fulfillment, but a ripple effect that empowers others to help shape a better world.
- **Stories of Resilience:** Resilience goes beyond mere endurance—it is the unwavering commitment to keep showing up again and again. It is the determination to endure the unendurable and to continue believing in what's possible even when it seems impossible.
- **Stories of Hope:** Ignite our conviction that nothing is beyond our reach. Share how we achieved what once seemed impossible, persevered through what appeared unbearable, and overcame challenges that felt insurmountable.
- **Stories of Grace:** Shine a light on moments when our empathy has guided us, allowing us to hold space for others' struggles, listen without judgment, and respond with gentle authenticity. We illuminate how we've helped others navigate difficult decisions and painful struggles with open hearts, compassion, and understanding.
- **Stories of Collaboration:** Life is a team sport. Most of the biggest challenges in our personal and professional lives are too big for us to take on by ourselves. No one is as smart or as effective as all of us.
- **Stories of Impact:** Highlight the positive difference we have made in the world through our transformation. Retell the change we underwent to change the world.
- **Stories of Gratitude:** Celebrate the kindness, wisdom, and opportunities gifted to us over the years by friends, colleagues,

mentors, and loved ones. Often, the narratives of those who have walked beside us are even more powerful than our own. More than anything, these stories remind us we are not alone on our journeys.

- **Stories of Courage:** Spotlight the heroic actions we've taken and brave decisions we've made. These courageous quests have often summoned us to overcome an unconquerable challenge or defeat an invincible villain.

The hero's journey

Speaking of courage, the hero's journey is a story arc popularized by Joseph Campbell, a comparative religion professor, in the first half of the 20th century. In *The Hero with a Thousand Faces*, Professor Campbell suggests every plot to a great story begins with a character residing in a state of normalcy which is interrupted by an unexpected challenge. The character must make a choice which yields an outcome, and the outcome teaches a moral. Our heroes are often guided by real-life or spiritual sherpas who help them defeat the villain or navigate the storm confronting them.

Whether it's an Oscar-winning film, an Olympian's odyssey from personal tragedy to gold medal triumph, or our own transformation from victim to victory, the hero's journey offers a roadmap for spawning an inviting, intriguing, and inspiring story.

So profound is Professor Campbell's influence on the craft of storytelling, director George Lucas admits, "If it hadn't been for Campbell, it's possible I would still be trying to write *Star Wars.*"

The hero's journey can be boiled down to narratives that convey our journey from challenge to conquest and the emotional peaks and valleys we trekked to get there. I am certain you will be energized to start putting pen to paper and chronicling the lessons and inspiration from your quest for the world to benefit from.

As we contemplate sharing our own journeys, Kip Keino and his fellow Olympians remind us that everyone's story, no matter how big or small, is worthy of being told.

As Professor Campbell bequeaths in his 1988 PBS interview with Bill Moyers, "We have only to follow the thread of the hero path. And, where we had thought to find an abomination, we shall find a God. And where we had thought to slay another, we shall slay ourselves. And where we had thought to travel outward, we shall come to the center of our own existence. And where we had thought to be alone, we will be with all the world."

CHAPTER 19

Find the Story in Your Storm

Every great story is defined by a great storm.

Our favorite movies and novels are memorialized by the epic cyclones that turn our everyday characters into eternal heroes. *The Karate Kid, The Wizard of Oz, The Lion King, The Fugitive,* and *Rocky* are just some of the blockbusters that illuminate the transformative power of the storms that confront all of us.

In *The Wizard of Oz,* Dorothy and Toto are swept away by a F5 Kansas tornado. In *The Fugitive,* Dr. Richard Kimble evades the FBI to clear his name after being convicted of murdering his wife and being sentenced to death. Rocky Balboa slugged his way to the world heavyweight championship title.

However, we don't have to look to the big screen, our bookshelf, or Broadway to discover the seismic change that the personal tempests we face have the capacity to unleash. Their stories are all around us. They are being authored every day by our family, friends, colleagues, and neighbors. And we don't have to search any further than our favorite barista, teacher, bartender, or barber to find the real-life storm-riding plots in front of us.

Beyond my story, this book is brimming with the storm-riding stories of my own friends and colleagues, as well as the hurricane-taming tales of others I've discovered along the way. In each case, I've been moved by the strength, resilience, and hope each of these ordinary people have summoned from their respective struggles.

- Cheryl Laws, who I introduced you to in Chapter 7, rewrote her dark story of self-destructive struggle with alcohol and drug addiction into a redemptive story of healing to serve as a bright beacon of hope for other women confronting addiction.
- Caroline Bowen, the 50-year-old Georgia pharmaceutical sales exec we met in Chapter 9, found her story in a near life-ending heart attack that turned her passion for cooking into a thriving and purpose-fulfilling apple pie business.
- Pat Lore, the award-winning TV news journalist we met in Chapter 10, turned her story of shame into a life of significance by launching a thriving video storytelling business after freezing during a high-profile live broadcast.

Ride your storm—from shame to significance

What do each of these and most other great comeback stories have in common? Let's take a moment to look at these five "shame-to-significance" mileposts and how we can apply them to our own stories.

Shame

Most—but certainly not all—personal adversities kick off with some sense of shame. I use the term "shame" broadly. I recognize there is a clinical diagnosis. However, for the purpose of this discussion, let's consider "shame" to be the feelings of distress and humiliation resulting from situations we've intentionally or accidentally caused, as well as those distressing situations that have resulted from no action of our own, yet they are still our fault in our mind.

During this initial period of shame, it is not unusual for feelings of guilt, anger, betrayal, remorse, and denial, among others, to race through our veins like a heat of Indy race cars. As you frame your comeback story, it is essential to start your story with the emotions that rock you at the onset of your setback.

When I received my cancer diagnosis, I wanted to blame somebody or something for thrusting this deadly disease upon me. With no one to blame, I wanted to indict myself. But I couldn't even convict myself of this assault on my life.

As you contemplate your comeback story, start sketching out your plot from the stormfront. It is typically the leading edge of the storm that is the most cataclysmic. Everyone has faced a destructive storm in their life; expressing the shame or related emotions that swarmed you at the onset of your storm will entice your audience to connect with your experience.

Shared emotions are the key to creating a shared experience.

Surrender

As we advance deeper into the storm, a moment arrives where we consciously or unconsciously "let go" and let the jetstream carry us through the headwinds, tailwinds, crosswinds, downdrafts, and updrafts. Like the shared sense of shame so many of us experience at the forefront of our journeys, surrendering to the storm is another equally powerful moment others will relate to.

Think about the morning charity: water Founder Scott Harrison described in Chapter 7, waking up and realizing he had hit rock bottom after years of Manhattan all-nighters. At that moment, he surrendered—he let go—of his soul-draining past and let a purpose-fulfilling tailwind carry him to Africa as a volunteer on a hospital ship and return the founder of a life-saving global charity.

Surrendering demands vulnerability. I'll dive into this a lot more in the next chapter, but for now, I want you to dig deep and excavate the moment you surrendered to your storm. It may not be obvious at first, but we've all "let go" at some point.

This inflection point is critical to share with others; it will convey the courage and vulnerability that will carry your story forward. Too often, we think of surrendering as a sign of weakness. To the contrary—surrendering is very often the ultimate example of strength, courage, and fortitude. Put another way, walking away from a fight is very often braver than punching back.

Surrender. Let go. Move on. And move forward.

Struggle

The struggles that accompany our adversities are often the hardest part of riding our storms. Our struggles are also often the most interesting and inspiring part of our journeys. In the last chapter, I discussed how most of us tune into the Olympics for the stories, not the races, matches, and vaults (although, the Olympics do present some pretty breathtaking moments).

No one knows more about illuminating stories of struggle than *NBC Sports* executive Dick Ebersol, the legendary producer who pioneered modern sports coverage. In a 2024 *Inc* magazine interview, Ebersol said, "The Olympics is the crucible of storytelling. That's because most viewers don't tune in to get scores—they watch to get stories that touch their heart."

The biggest comeback story of the 2024 Summer Games was, of course, Simone Biles. The GOAT (Greatest Athlete of All Time), as she is known, pulled out of the 2020 Tokyo Games after suffering an anxiety attack known as "The Twisties" that prevented her from competing. For the next four years, Biles embraced her struggle, clawing her way back to the Olympics to peak performance and readiness for the 2024 Paris Games, claiming three gold medals and a silver.

"It was important to me because nobody forced me to be out there on that stage," Biles told *CNN* following her 2024 Summer Games performance. "I solely did it for myself and I'm in a really good spot mentally and physically. So doing this for just me meant the world."

Biles' high-profile struggle exemplifies Ebersol's belief that the harder the road an athlete travels, the greater their glory. Biles' setback-to-comeback strife is what he contends makes stories of struggle and hardship irresistible. And it is our own tragedy-to-triumph odysseys that will make our own stories captivating and inspiring to so many others.

Strength

As difficult and destructive as our respective storms are, it is indeed our biggest struggles that debut our greatest strengths. It is during these unimagined trials of life that we discover superpowers within us that we never knew existed.

Rocky grinded out predawn runs and knuckle-bleeding workouts at his gritty boxing gym to knock out his opponent and claim the world heavyweight championship title belt.

Similarly, remember Daniel Jacobs? He is the real-world boxer I introduced you to in Chapter 16 who knocked out a paralyzing cancer diagnosis to claim the middleweight world boxing championship title. Even after multiple surgeries, chemotherapy, and years of rehabilitation, giving up was never an option for Daniel. Instead, he mustered the mental and physical strength to get up every morning. Step by step and punch by punch, he returned to professional boxing, something his doctors told him was not possible.

Daniel found the primal strength in his struggle to win the fight of his life. The strength he has heroically exhibited serves as an example for all of us as we search for the toughness, tenacity, and durability to share in our stories. So, dig in and dig deep to find the strength in your struggle. The courage, grit, and vigor that has fueled your storm-riding comeback odyssey may very well be the inspiration your neighbor, teacher, or bartender needs to hear about to overcome their own life-derailing adversities.

Significance

Of all the lessons I've drawn from my comeback journey, as well as the others I've included in this book, it is the gift of significance that emerges from our struggles. This is the final stage of plotting our story that reveals itself as we exit the darkness of our respective storms.

Few embody a story of significance more than my former colleague, Lucy Helm. Lucy is a retired Starbucks executive who suffered a life-threatening brain aneurysm that left her nearly blind in one eye. She translated her storm into an even more significant leadership role at the global coffee giant upon her return.

Lucy shared with me, "From the minute I received my surprise diagnosis, I felt nothing but grateful: that it was caught, when the odds of that are astronomical; that even though it would require risky and complex brain surgery and a long convalescence, I would likely recover without significant complications or ongoing issues; that I lived in a city with fantastic medical care; that I was surrounded by loving people in my life who supported me through each day; that my employer was unbelievably supportive and made sure I knew that no matter how long my recovery took, I would return to my same position and not lose a step in my career journey."

Shortly after Lucy's return, she was promoted to General Counsel, the company's top lawyer, and a few years later was elevated to Chief People Officer, overseeing the HR employee experience for Starbucks' 300,000 employees around the world. While at Starbucks, she created the nation's first pro bono legal services program, which became a model for other companies.

For 12 years, Lucy was the Global Chair of the board of Mercy Corps, a global relief and development organization. Today, she serves on the Board of Trustees of the Seattle Foundation and is a Board Member of the Campaign for the Fair Sentencing of Youth. Lucy also serves on the Advisory Boards of the Endowment for Equal Justice and Disability Rights Advocates. Additionally, she is the Co-Director of Camp Parkview, a residential camp for adults with developmental disabilities, where she has volunteered for nearly 25 years.

Lucy told me that, through this life-altering experience, she became braver. When confronted with her own mortality, Lucy was not afraid to die. She had no regrets. She had no need to say or write "last words" to family or friends, to fix or make things right. Lucy shared with me she felt at peace spiritually and emotionally, knowing that she had an amazing, meaningful life.

"My life's work has always been about 'doing good,' whatever that means in any given situation. To give more than I take, to be kind always, and to be of service. Facing my own mortality has meant living each day knowing that my life is finite, and that what I do with each minute is important. And I wake up every single day so grateful for each minute."

Every story has a moral and yours is no exception. Sharing the significance of your storm-riding journey is the culmination of your story, and the magic others you share your story with deserve, want, and need to hear. Summoning the courage to share how your journey reframed your story will flip someone else's script. So, if sharing your story scares you, it's precisely the story the world needs to hear.

Who is your Obi-Wan Kenobi?

As we learned in the last chapter, every great hero is guided through their storm by a wise mentor, spiritual guide, or supernatural sherpa. Indeed, it is these enlightened teachers who lead us to the gifts of significance awaiting us.

In *The Karate Kid*, Mr. Miyagi mentors Daniel in karate and life. The elder karate master equips his protégé with the discipline and wisdom that ultimately results in the defeat of his bullying rival. Then there is Rocky's trainer, Mickey—a retired professional boxer himself—who guides the young boxer to his world championship title. And, of course, who can forget the teachings of the omniscient Obi-Wan Kenobi, the Master Jedi who served as the supernatural guide to Luke Skywalker in *Star Wars*.

In the case of my friend Rachel Gerber Kule, her late father (Alan Gerber) has been the spiritual guide whispering in her ear as she coped with his unexpected passing and the medical hurdles complicating her dream of bringing a child into this world.

In 2019, moments after awakening from an IVF procedure, the 30-something founder of Pursuit PR received a call that her beloved father had died. She acknowledged the double punch to her gut "hit me like a Mack truck."

Approaching the first anniversary of her father's passing, Rachel took a long walk along the Jersey shore. "I pondered how I would move forward, bearing the unbearable pain of my dad's death and the uncertainty of ever bearing a child. In despair, I prayed to God for an antidote to my pain."

As she walked along the beach, Rachel told me she cried out to her dad. "What do I do? I need your help!"

A few moments later, she glanced up and saw the sun dancing across the crashing waves "just as Dad liked it." At that moment, her dad whispered in her ear, "Rachel, make it a great day."

She recalled the texts he would send her family each day, signing off with those five simple yet motivating words. "He wasn't saying have a great day—he was reminding me that no matter how tall the mountain was confronting me on any given morning, I have the power to make it a great day."

Rachel's dad has been an ever-present voice whispering in his daughter's ear each morning to never give up, to make it a great day. That's become her mantra for life, opening up new possibilities to embrace each day.

On July 11, 2025, Rachel had a really great day. After seven years packed with medications, procedures, and cumulative grief, Alanna Dane Kule was born (named after her father Alan).

Today, Rachel honors her dad's legacy with her self-empowered and grateful outlook on life. To share coping strategies with others, she highlights other inspiring storm riders and healers on her podcast appropriately titled *Make It A Great Day*. Her book about applying her dad's lessons and learning to embrace her own intuition to navigate grief, including fertility, is coming soon.

Who is your Alan Gerber? Who is your Mr. Miyagi? Who is your Mickey? Who is your Obi-Wan Kenobi? Our stories would not be possible without them. Telling your comeback story is your chance to acknowledge this consequential partner in your journey. It's also your chance—and dare I say obligation—to share their significance-enlightening wisdom and inspiration with those captivated by your story.

In doing so, you and your story become the sage for your audience.

As I was distilling my concluding thoughts for this chapter, I ached like so many others hearing the news of Robert Redford's passing. In a 2017 *Esquire* interview, this master storyteller spoke about the pleasure found in the struggle, in the process and the work, rather than the final destination:

"To climb up the mountain *is the fun*, not standing at the top. There's nowhere to go. But climbing up, that struggle, that to me is where the fun is. That to me is the thrill."

Every unforgettable story is shaped by a defining storm. What storm shaped you?

CHAPTER 20

Tear Off Your Mask

There has been a lot of hype over the past couple years about AI—artificial intelligence. Let there be no mistake, AI will continue to change our lives and world in unimaginably positive and, at the same time, terrifying ways. The medical, educational, security, and business breakthroughs AI is enabling through its lightspeed calculations and information aggregation are indisputable. In fact, it will very likely be AI-powered medical breakthroughs that extend my life and restore my vision.

However, the most notable and noble benefit of AI in my view is the democratization of information, knowledge, and education. As a former university Professor, I believe there are unequivocal benefits to in-person instruction, collaboration, discussion, and debate. Nevertheless, billions of people now have free and ubiquitous access to the same books, articles, case studies, models, theories, and other knowledge that many pay upwards of $100,000 per year for at elite universities.

Amidst the transformative and world-changing benefits of AI lurks the mirage of AI-powered authoring and content-generating tools, such as ChatGPT. Yes, these are powerful aggregators of massive sums of world-spanning content that are proving immensely helpful in accelerating problem solving and time-consuming research. And, yes, generative AI creative and authoring tools make it cheaper, easier, and faster than ever to produce reports, articles, photos, videos, and—for the scores of unimaginative hopeless romantics out there—seductive texts and love letters.

The messy cutting room floor

Unfortunately, the undeniable efficiency we gain from tools like ChatGPT is accompanied by the irreversible depletion of humanity's critical thinking, ideation, and imagination. As a writer, I've relished the messiness of shaping and expressing my ideas. I love rolling around in the muddy swamps of words. It is here where I refine, iterate, and polish my sentences, narratives, and plots.

AI may generate the perfectly manicured message—the Tesla Model S of copy—but the best writing is often rough around the edges and bears a few scars or blemishes. This is what gives great writing character, much like my late father's Alfa Romeo roadster. The clutch would often get stuck, and it wasn't the smoothest ride on the road. But I would take my dad's gritty Alfa, with all its imperfections, over the sterile perfection of a Tesla any day.

Taking our audience (whether one person or a thousand) on a stroll through the messy "cutting room floor" of our lives are the best stories. After all, it is there where we discover the truth and inspiration quietly pulsing beneath the polished narrative we all feel pressured to tell.

That's a long-winded way of saying AI offers us a lot, but when it comes to writing, AI-generated content cannot evoke the authenticity, vulnerability, and soul that is essential to great storytelling. That's because being authentic demands that we dig deep into our story and ourselves to excavate the uniquely human emotions our journey has unleashed. Only we know what those feelings are, and for our story to be enticing and believable, it must first and foremost be real.

AI by its very name and nature is the opposite of real—*it's artificial*.

So, what does this mean for us as we endeavor to tell our comeback stories?

Stop chasing approval—start being authentic

For many of us, we've spent our life projecting a desired image. For some, that might be an identity of power and influence. For others, it may be an image of beauty and sophistication. And for some, it may be an appearance of wealth and popularity.

In the age of social media, keeping up with the Jones' is elevated to new heights. In our image-driven, follower-collecting, and "likes-obsessed" world, too many of us race through life worried about what our neighbors, work colleagues, and friends think about us. Are we driving the biggest truck, carrying the "in" purse, wearing the right shoes, or looking fit enough? Whether we are walking our dog, at the gym, out to dinner, or at work, we are worried about what everyone else thinks about us.

Of course, there is nothing wrong with having a successful career, living in a nice neighborhood, driving a nice car, staying fit, or wearing a new pair of boots. But for too many of us, our identity-obsessed lives mask our authentic selves. We put on our masks and pretend everything is great, that we are happy and living our best life. But sadly, in many cases, we're not.

In February 2024, a large plastic mask was customized for my head the day before my radiation treatment to eliminate my brain tumor. Before the procedure began, the mask was placed over my head and bolted down to prevent it from moving during the high-precision laser strike on my brain.

After the 15-minute laser show concluded, they unscrewed the mask. A few seconds later, I reached up and removed the face covering. As I drove home that afternoon, I realized that when I took off that mask, I removed far more than that snug-fitting piece of plastic from my face. I set aside the insecurities, fears, shame, doubt, regrets, and denial I was hiding from the world—and myself. At that moment, I tore off my purpose-concealing mask and took on my legacy-revealing calling.

Hiding in plain sight

Speaking of masks, no one cast aside their mask of shame to embrace their true self more courageously than my friend Phil Nardone, the Founder and CEO of the global PR firm PAN. For most of his life, Phil played the part he thought he was supposed to play. He had a successful career, a loving wife, and two incredible sons. From the outside, everything looked right. But inside, Phil was hiding a truth he had been carrying since he was a kid.

"I was gay, and no one knew," Phil recently revealed to me. "I grew up in a traditional Catholic Italian family where 'gay' wasn't something people talked about. Instead, it was joked about or dismissed."

That environment made Phil push his identity deep underground. He wasn't angry at his family. He loved them and told me he always will. But their language made it hard to imagine living as his full self.

"I spent decades living a divided life. At home, I was a husband and father. At work, I was a leader. But in both places, I was never fully myself. I had trained myself to be compartmentalized, always guarded, always performing."

Coming out didn't happen early or easily. Phil was in his 40s. His wife had just left him. That loss was devastating for him. But it also cracked something open. "I went from hiding in plain sight to standing fully in who I am."

No one helped Phil muster the courage to come out more than his now-husband Scott. "He didn't just love me; he helped me find myself. Scott introduced me to the parts of life I had missed. He brought me into the LGBTQ+ community, helped me understand its history, its joy, and its struggles."

With Scott, Phil felt a version of life that felt real, and he realized how much he had been holding back. Through the help of Scott, family and friends, therapists, and others who have taken this path before Phil, he was able to unlearn years of hiding.

"I learned that it's okay to celebrate who I am and not just survive with it."

Coming out didn't just change Phil's personal life; it reshaped how he leads. "The mask I had worn for decades fell away, and a new kind of clarity came with it. I realized that the most effective leaders don't separate who they are from how they lead; they integrate. My journey of hiding has become a part of my leadership style: less armor, more authenticity."

That shift allowed Phil to connect more deeply with his team, champion inclusivity, and create a space for others to bring their whole selves to work. He now sees leadership as something deeply personal. He strives to be the kind of leader who listens, who sees people for who they are, and who helps them grow not just as professionals, but as people.

"Today, I am a proud, confident gay man. I cry more easily. I lead with more empathy. I no longer feel like I'm living in pieces. I'm able to live my life fully, and I'm proud that every individual I encounter, especially my sons, get to see me living my truth."

Now, Phil mentors other men who come out later in life, many of them fathers, most of them executives. "I tell them it's okay to be fearful and grieve what you've lost. But I also tell them, your story is yours to write."

Like Phil, telling our authentic story starts with the vulnerability, humility, and courage to be real. This brutal self-awareness demands that we be honest and transparent about the peaks and troughs of our journey, and all the emotional volatility saddling up with us. This doesn't mean we have to reveal every dark secret or medical record since fifth grade. However, being authentic does command us to ditch our perfection-projecting masks and, in doing so, show the world who we really are behind the veneer of our titles, cars, clothes, and addresses.

Embrace a real AI—your Authentic Identity

As bestselling *New York Times* author and master storyteller Bob Goff implores, "If you take away what you are known for, whatever is left is who you are. Let's be the kind of people who are interested in who someone is, instead of what they do."

When you toss your mask, you will stop worrying about the approval of other people and refocus on the only validation that really matters—your own. Before you can stir up the courage to share your rawest emotions with the outside world, you need to muster the courage to reveal these emotions to yourself.

You can be sure that when you trash your mask, those "dream slayers" I've mentioned previously in this book will be waiting to condemn your flaws, broadcast your mistakes, and reinforce your self-doubt. However, I assure you, your story is far stronger than these detractors. So, jettison your mask, lean on the dream-enablers around you, and charge forward.

The courage to ditch our mask is only outweighed by our bravery to be vulnerable. We are all works in progress. It is ultimately our willingness to be vulnerable that is the genesis of the authenticity of our story.

Remember, if telling your story doesn't scare you, you're not revealing enough. You're not being real enough.

And don't count on AI to help. We need not look any further than HAL 9000, the fictional AI antagonist in the epic 1968 sci-fi blockbuster *2001: A Space Odyssey*. During a critical scene, in a soft and calm voice, HAL rejects astronaut David Bowman's request to open the spacecraft's door:

"Dave, I'm afraid I cannot do that."

I'm certain I would have received a similarly dispassionate rebuff from one of HAL's modern-day AI offspring had I sought help crafting my own authentic story for this book:

"Jim, I'm afraid I cannot do that."

In this new era of artificial intelligence, it's crucial we lean into an even deeper, more potent form of AI—our *Authentic Identity*.

CHAPTER 21

Don't Let Your Story Go to Waste

"You never want a serious crisis to go to waste. And what I mean by that is an opportunity to do things that you think you could not do before."

This is the advice from President Barack Obama's former Chief of Staff Rahm Emanuel.

By now, you have hopefully formulated your storm-riding comeback story. As Rahm implores, we cannot let the crises in our lives go to waste. And you certainly can't let the story—and the lessons and inspiration that accompany it—land on the cutting-room floor.

I devoted the last three chapters to describing the time-honored and wilderness-tested ingredients for crafting your own authentic and compelling comeback story. Now it is time for me to share some of my pro tips for sharing your story with the world.

I've boiled these story-sharing strategies down to five best practices.

1. **Write a Book**

   A number of surveys have reported that upwards of 80% of Americans want to write a book. However, the actual number of people who do it is south of 1%. I was one of those 80% of people for many years. It's not easy to write 300 pages that will be of interest to strangers across the globe.

   Yet, authoring a book is very likely the best and most comprehensive way to document and share your storm-riding journey. Everyone who has written a book has their secrets for getting it done. Here are mine:

- **Declare a Master Narrative:** Start your writing journey by writing a one-sentence mission statement for your book. Not two sentences or a paragraph, but one tight sentence that encompasses who you want to read your book and how it will help them. This is not the title of your book, but the elevator pitch you will tell people who ask what your book is about. For example, the master narrative for this book is:

  Tailwind is a compass for helping people, leaders, and organizations turn their setback story into their comeback legacy.

- **Download Everything:** Carve out blocks of time over the course of a month and write down on sticky notes, in a notebook, on your iPad, or whatever your journaling medium of choice may be all the potential topics, ideas, stories, emotions, lessons, characters, and settings you will potentially include in your story. This is intentionally a messy first stage in writing your book. Don't worry about organizing your ideas in chronological order or bucketing them in particular categories at this point. The important thing is just capturing all your thoughts.

- **Create a Story Map:** Now comes the organizing. Take your massive database of memories and ideas and start searching for similar themes, topics, and experiences. Create headings for these "shared themes" and then log your memories and experiences under each of those. You'll start to see some patterns emerge. This will be your "Story Map"—the cornerstone of your book-writing journey.

- **Develop Your Book Outline:** Next, take your story map and start distilling the outline for your book. You can refer to the first three chapters of this section to help you chart your story's plot, characters, and moral. Start at a very high level. Your first outline will be similar to an architect's artistic rendering of the home he is designing. After that, start adding bullets or subsections to your outline. If your outlining journey is anything like mine, you will reorganize over and over again. In fact, I went through 50 iterations of my outline before I put pen to paper on the first chapter of my book.

- **Build Your Table of Contents:** Once you are comfortable with and energized about your outline, it's time to translate and consolidate it into your book's table of contents. This is a much more important stage than most people imagine. It's important to develop a compelling title for each chapter that serves as the tentpole for holding your chapter together. More importantly, your table of contents becomes the roadmap for the authoring journey you are about to embark on. As the saying goes, every great journey begins with a single step. In book writing, every great book begins with a first chapter. For me, each chapter in the table of contents for this book became a daily goal to slay.

- **Start Writing:** The hardest part of writing a book is writing the book. Nothing will be more daunting than staring at that blank screen as you contemplate those first words. I've been there. I know the feeling. The best advice I can give anyone at this stage is to just start writing. You will rewrite most of your early drafts anyway, so give yourself a deadline for your first chapter—one week or even a weekend is very realistic. Word by word, sentence by sentence, and chapter by chapter I got my book done and so will you.

- **Find a Writing Muse:** One of the best tips I can offer once you have started writing is to find a trusted friend, colleague, or family member to help you focus and refine your writing. This person (or small group of writing mentors) doesn't have to be a writing professional. But they do need to be willing to be unapologetically honest. As you share your chapters with them, you need to deputize them to give you brutally truthful feedback on your work. Then you need to demand of yourself the humility to consider and accept their advice. It's very easy for us to get emotionally attached to our writing; after all, we've spent weeks and months on our book. But it's critical that we be objective about what will be inviting, interesting, inspiring, and, most of all, irresistible to your readers.

Writing a book is hard. And certainly, no harder than the set-back to comeback journey you have endured. It will be hard. But it will be worth it. If I could write the first draft of my book in 90 days—blind—you can write yours!

2. **Write an Article**

Great batting practice for authoring your book is writing an article (or two) about your storm-riding journey. There is a limitless number of online and print venues you can pursue for your article. Start with organizations you are familiar with and that are familiar with you: your college alumni magazine, your temple or church, your employer's intranet, professional associations you are a member of, or your community's weekly newspaper.

From there, you can work your way up to niche magazines and websites related to the topic you are writing about or your city's daily newspaper or website.

These channels are hungry for content. More specifically, they have a ferocious appetite for great stories like yours! You will likely face some rejection along the way. There is no guarantee that an organization or news outlet will post or publish your submission. But as hockey legend Wayne Gretzky said, "You miss every shot you never take."

3. **Pitch Your Story**

In addition to submitting articles you've authored about your story, you can "pitch" all the same channels I mentioned above to assign your story to one of their own writers or reporters. The editors and producers at these outlets will have the same interest in your story.

The best way to frame your pitch is simply to write a brief email proposing your interest in having them cover your story. Kick off your email demonstrating your understanding of the outlet's focus and audience. Then dive into your story and why you believe it will be appealing to their audience.

And don't forget podcasts. Like the conventional and online media outlets above, podcasts come in every color and flavor. There is literally a podcast on every topic and in every community. This means there is a podcast interview out there waiting for your story—the host just needs to know you are out there.

4. **Give a Speech:** I know this may be intimidating. Most people fear public speaking more than death. But it's one of the best ways to get your story out there.

   Similar to writing an article or pitching your story to news outlets, start small. Your presentation doesn't have to be a TED Talk. Kick your speaking career off somewhere familiar—your office, church or temple, the local nonprofit you volunteer at, or the high school or college you graduated from. From there, you can work your way up to professional organization conferences and other larger audience venues. Before you know it, you'll be delivering that TED Talk.

   If public speaking is new to you, there are numerous resources out there to help prepare you for delivering your story fearlessly and confidently and, in doing so, leave your audience informed, intrigued, and inspired. Consider checking out your local chapters of The National Speakers Association and Toast Masters International.

5. **Go Social**

   I saved this tip for last. It is very likely the easiest of all my suggestions because you are likely already doing it. As you build out your story, share it in "small bites" on your social media channels of choice.

   For instance, pick a photo from your phone that captures a compelling moment in your comeback journey and then wrap that image in a couple paragraphs of copy that illuminate your experience. Or tell part of your story through a short video. This doesn't have to be a Hollywood production; it can be as simple as a self-recorded vertical reel using your phone that you post on Instagram.

Once you start writing articles, giving speeches, and appearing in the news, your social channels and those of your friends and family are a powerful way to amplify this content.

It begs the question, is a story without an audience a story?

How much or how little you choose to share your story is up to you. But like a tree falling in a forest, did the tree make a noise if no one heard it fall? Your story is worthy of sharing. Don't let your Redwood-sized comeback story fall with no one to hear it.

As American poet Maya Angelou warns us, "There is nothing more agonizing than an untold story."

CHAPTER 22

Five Reasons Not to Tell Your Story

Last January many of my family, friends, and colleagues were jump-starting their New Year's resolutions. For some, it was enrolling in an unlimited Orange Theory membership to shed a few pounds. For others, it was diving into their first book of the year. And others still had already booked their flights to those elusive international bucket list destinations they had been dreaming of for years.

This year, I also observed an uptick in people resolving to be better storytellers. For some of them, it's to help grow their business. For others, it's a personal ambition. And for yet another group, it's both. Whatever their motivation, more people than ever are talking about storytelling.

In this section of my book, I have impressed upon you the importance of sharing your story. However, let me caution you with five reasons not to tell the story you think you want to tell:

1. **You want to tell a success story.** Instead, consider telling your setback story. Pulling back the curtain on a recent struggle in your life or that your organization faced will be far more interesting to your audience. As master storyteller Pat Lore (who I introduced you to in Chapter 10) opined recently, "The perspective you gain on the climb up the mountain is far more valuable than the view from the top." Indeed, it is the strength we summon in our struggles that makes for a far more rewarding—and dare I suggest seductive—experience for our audience.

2. **You want to tell a hero story.** Instead, share the stories of the unsung heroes around you. For example, when I was leading communications at US Airways at the time of the "Miracle on the Hudson," everyone wanted to hear Sully's story. This is understandable, and it rightfully deserved attention. However, as proud as I am of the positive coverage our team drove in the wake of that accident, which in large part can be attributed to Sully's courageous airmanship, some of the stories and interviews I'm proudest of were the profiles that illuminated the three unsung heroes on January 15, 2009. The three US Airways flight attendants who safely evacuated all 150 passengers aboard the Airbus A320 jetliner as it sank in the icy Hudson River—Donna Dent, Doreen Welsh, and Sheila Dail. Their composure, professionalism, and heroism played as much a part of this hero story as Sully's.

   Think about it. Some of our favorite books and movies are not about celebrities, presidents, or Hall of Fame athletes, they are about the underdogs. For example, the unknown story of Oakland A's baseball coach Billy Bean featured in *Moneyball*, or the backstory of NFL offensive tackle Michael Oher chronicled in *The Blindside*. Michael Lewis, the bestselling author of these books (and many others), explains in his storytelling *MasterClass* that the secret to storytelling is always looking where others aren't—you want to surprise the reader with an unexpected hero.

3. **You want to tell a story of strength.** Rather, consider revealing a story of vulnerability. Our willingness to reveal our denial, doubt, shame, and faith is far more admirable and instructive than hiding these sensibilities behind a veneer of confidence, bravado, and happiness. Being vulnerable is very likely one of the strongest things we can do. Others may respect your strength and authority, but they will connect with your vulnerability and authenticity. And, at the end of the day, connection and authenticity are the currency of storytelling.

   In Chapter 16, I shared with you the story of retired World Middleweight Boxing Champion Daniel Jacobs. Daniel's meteoric rise as one of professional boxing's most promising fighters is an admirable story. However, Daniel's bout with paralyzing spinal cancer and the fight of his life—or should I say fight for his life—outside the ring is a far more powerful story. Indeed, the emotional and spiritual vulnerability Daniel reveals when sharing his cancer-conquering journey, from diagnosis to world champion, is far more inspiring than the many knockout stories he is known for inside the ring.

Daniel shared with me, "You are never going to truly know what you are made of until you live through a really difficult experience. It made me the best version of myself, and I emerged the man I always wanted to be. You can go through anything in life if you have the right mindset of hope, a strong faith in God, and have love surrounding you."

4. **You want to tell a story that improves your image.** A more compelling story is one that reveals your glowing heart or gracious spirit. This is precisely the reason *Beauty and the Beast* is the enduring blockbuster story that it is. The unexpected tenderness and inner beauty the beast reveals are far more enchanting than the vacant soul and barren morality of the handsome prince.

Consider the remarkable personal turnaround journey of Scott Harrison (who I spotlighted in Chapter 7), the founder of charity: water—a nonprofit on a mission to bring clean water to everyone on the planet. However, for Scott, fulfilling his destiny to start charity: water was a precarious odyssey. His 20s were spent perfecting his image and that of others as a New York nightclub promoter.

"I was spiritually bankrupt, emotionally bankrupt, and I was certainly morally bankrupt. I wanted things to be different," Scott describes in his autobiographical video. He decided to leave night life. Scott sold almost everything he owned and took one year off to volunteer on a hospital boat circumnavigating Africa. "It was time to start serving others instead of myself."

Scott flipped the script on his story from one preoccupied with improving his image to one devoted to improving the lives of others.

5. **You want to tell a conquest story.** Instead, share a time you surrendered. Walking away from a fight is far more powerful and brave than punching back. Consider the humbling story of imprisoned South African President Nelson Mandela. For three decades, President Mandela surrendered his freedom and authority. He lost the battle. But he won the war. President Mandela's forfeiture of his individual liberty was ultimately the fortitude South Africa needed to surrender apartheid.

In Bono's 2022 biography *Surrender: 40 Songs, One Story*, he cautions us that winning isn't always worth the fight, and that the deeper victory comes from releasing the arguments you no longer need to have—especially the ones you've been carrying inside your own life.

Regardless of the story you aspire to tell, think carefully about your intentions. On a recent business trip to Connecticut, I had the privilege of meeting Moira Squier, a lead storyteller and narrative developer for a major Hollywood studio's gaming division. I asked her what she believes is the secret to great storytelling. Moira's answer was elegantly simple, "I always start the story development journey with a single question: How do I want my audience to feel at the end of the story? Sad? Happy? Inspired?"

As writer Maya Angelou reminds us, "I've learned that people will forget what you said, people will forget what you did, but people will never forget how you made them feel."

So, if you aspire to tell your story, ask yourself these three questions:

1. **Am I telling the story I want to tell—*or the story the world needs to hear?***
2. **Am I obsessing over how good my story will make me feel—*or how I want my story to make others feel?***
3. **When is the right time to tell my story: today, next month, or possibly never?**

As a greeting card I recently stumbled across beamed, "Your story is the hug the world is waiting for."

You are the pen to your story. Make it count.

Stage 4

Appreciate

CHAPTER 23

Ubuntu

I was recently on a walk catching up with an old friend—Doug Camp— who was also blinded a few years ago from an issue with his retinas. We covered a lot of ground that morning, but nothing stuck with me more than our discussion about the critical role that our support networks have played in helping us navigate our respective storms.

Doug reminded me of a heartening scene from *The West Wing*, one of my all-time favorite TV series. In this episode, the President's Deputy Chief of Staff, Josh Lyman, is discussing a personal trauma with his boss Leo McGarry, the President's Chief of Staff. After listening to Josh explain the anxiety and isolation he was experiencing, Leo shared what *West Wing* fans affectionately call "the man in a hole" story. It goes something like this:

This guy's walking down a street when he falls in a hole. The walls are so steep, he can't get out. A doctor passes by, and the guy shouts up, "Hey you, can you help me out?" The doctor writes a prescription, throws it down in the hole, and moves on. Then a priest comes along, and the guy shouts up "Father, I'm down in this hole, can you help me out?" The priest writes out a prayer, throws it down in the hole, and moves on. Then a friend walks by. "Hey Joe, it's me, can you help me out?" And the friend jumps in the hole. Our guy says, "Are you stupid? Now we're both down here." The friend says, "Yeah, but I've been down here before, and I know the way out."

We all have friends who have leaped in the hole with us "who know the way out." Without these storm-riding copilots, our comebacks would not have been possible.

Several years ago, during a visit to the Bill and Melinda Gates Foundation's Seattle headquarters, I saw a sign on a hallway wall quoting an African proverb that read, "If you want to go fast—go alone. If you want to go far—go together." Life is a team sport and never is that more true than when we are confronting the adversities in our lives.

The crew of dream-enablers that envelops us on our journeys help us in many ways. They help us live our daily lives by bridging the gaps with our physical needs. For those of us with visual challenges, they help us drive and read. The wingmen and wingwomen in our lives also provide critical emotional support. They lift us up when we are down and push us forward when we backslide. And in many cases, our storm-riding companions have fallen into a similar hole before us and know the way out.

I am because of you

When I traveled to Africa for the first time 25 years ago, I was introduced to another inspiring proverb from this beautiful continent: *Ubuntu.* This simple but heart-filling six-letter term means "I am because of you."

Embracing an Ubuntu mindset starts with an attitude of humanity and gratitude. This outlook begins with a duty to care—caring for those who have cared for us. This covenant reveals itself in many ways. However, it's not the scale of our words or actions that ultimately demonstrate the magnitude of our gratitude. As 19th century American author Edward Everett Hale reminds us:

> *"I am only one, but still, I am one. I cannot do everything, but still I can do something, and because I cannot do everything, I will not refuse to do the something that I can do."*

Or consider the words of 14th century Dominican theologian, philosopher, and mystic Meister Eckhart. He was best known for his preaching, in which he provided theological and practical wisdom for living a life grounded in contemplation and witnessed through action.

"One must not always think so much about what one should do, but rather what one should be. Our works do not enable us—we must enable our work."

I was first exposed to Eckhart's contemplation teachings in 2023 as a freshly minted Trustee at Albertus Magnus College in New Haven, Connecticut. Albertus is a 100-year-old Roman Catholic university founded by the Dominican Sisters of Peace. Through the vision and leadership of Albertus President Dr. Marc Camille, and in collaboration with the Board of Trustees and the Dominican Sisters of Peace, the university established the first of its kind Eckhart Center, which engages the school and neighboring community in dialogue by integrating the Dominican values of contemplation and action with the calling to promote a more just and peaceful world.

I've been contemplating "contemplation" a lot since joining the Albertus board. My enlightenment was further illuminated during the opening blessing at a recent quarterly board dinner delivered by the university's VP of Academic Affairs, Dr. Rosa Rivera-Hainaj. She reminded us that the fastest path to finding a peaceful heart is sharing our heart with other people. She concluded the blessing by appealing to each of us to contemplate, "Who will you share your heart with?"

We all want to be heard. We want to be seen. Recognizing others is the essence of caring, whether it's at home, at work, or with our friends.

Leading with an attitude of gratitude

Over the years, I've received dozens of letters and emails carrying genuine expressions of appreciation. The care and kindness these notes conveyed did not go unnoticed. To this day, I keep a shoebox in my home office preserving many of these gestures of gratitude from over the years.

One of the most treasured messages came in the form of a handwritten card from my boss at US Airways, where I led corporate communications at the time. What made this note so special was that the card was not addressed to me. Following three months of being held captive at work preparing for a potential merger with another air-line, US Airways' EVP of HR and Public Affairs Elise Eberwein sent my wife and daughter a thoughtful and thankful note expressing her deep gratitude for the sacrifice our family was making for the airline. Elise chose the right words, but more importantly, evoked the right feelings.

In many cases, however, the most enduring expressions of grati-tude don't come in the form of an email or Hallmark card—they are simply spoken.

One of the most memorable expressions of gratitude I've been the recipient of came when I was a 24-year-old junior associate on the Nissan account at the PR agency I worked for at the start of my career. One of my primary responsibilities was creating and advancing the slides for the automaker's top U.S. executives at company press events. This included Nissan North America's CEO, Bob Thomas.

At the time, I wasn't certain Bob knew who I was, let alone knew my name. That was, until the day after his Chicago Auto Show press conference. We were waiting in the lobby of our hotel for our respec-tive rides to the airport. Bob turned to me and said, "Jim, are you heading to the airport?"

I replied with a quick "Yes!" I thought to myself, *Bob Thomas knows my name.*

He quipped, "Well, let's go, then!"

Moments later, I found myself sitting in the backseat of a black Suburban next to my client's top executive and one of the auto indus-try's most influential leaders at the time.

"Jim, that was a great event yesterday. I really appreciate everything you and your team do for Nissan," he shared as our plush SUV blazed toward ORD.

At that moment, I felt seen. I felt appreciated. Bob recognized me and what I had done in two simple sentences. That's gratitude. That's authentic leadership.

Then there was the time I was sitting in the corner office of Nissan North America's Chief Communications Officer, Don Spetner, a few months before graduating college. I had completed an internship at the automaker's LA headquarters the previous summer and was meeting with Don to discuss potential entry-level job opportunities.

Sitting behind his oversized desk, Don explained his team didn't have any immediate entry-level openings. However, he told me how much he appreciated my contributions as an intern and wanted to help jumpstart my job search. At that moment, his assistant summoned him to an unexpected meeting. Don slid his towering carousel of business cards across the desk and said, "Look through this—pick three people you want to meet."

Don's Rolodex was a treasure chest of PR and political elites. I didn't recognize the names, but they had big titles. After Don returned, I nudged the three cards I had selected across his desk.

He said, "Great choices; I'll send out letters of introduction in the next few days."

Two decades later, I had the occasion to ask Don why he did that.

"Jim, when I was your age, I had a boss at the NY agency I was interning at who did the same thing for me. I was simply paying forward the gratitude I received from my first boss. I knew you would do the same thing down the road."

Elise Eberwein, Bob Thomas, and Don Spetner demonstrated an Ubuntu mindset. These three giants of leadership set the bar for me early in my career for what caring and gratitude looks like in the corporate world.

These stories of gratitude should serve as motivation for the appreciation we can and must show those who have made our personal comebacks possible. Indeed, we are well on our way to fulfilling our destiny because of them. Embrace your Ubuntu mindset today. We don't have to wait until the next holiday, birthday, or anniversary. We can convey our gratitude with a quick handwritten note, a spontaneous call, or even through a long and silent hug.

The emotional, physical, and social benefits of gratitude—for both the giver and receiver—are becoming increasingly clear thanks to recent research on the topic.

The science of gratitude

One of the more prominent studies on gratitude was conducted in 2016 by Dr. Glenn Fox, a researcher at the Brain and Creativity Institute at the University of Southern California (USC). Dr. Fox led a study that explored what happens in the brain when people experience gratitude. They used the unexpected testimonials of gratitude Holocaust survivors have shared as a cornerstone of their methodology.

The USC brain researchers recruited 23 study participants, most of them in their 20s, who had no personal connections to the Holocaust. After showing these participants documentaries about the Holocaust, researchers shared 50 stories from the survivors' gratitude-expressing testimonies with them. The participants were asked to imagine themselves in similar situations then rate the depth of their gratitude in each one.

Using an MRI scanner, the researchers mapped circuitry in the brain that were activated when the participants felt grateful. Activated areas of the brain included those responsible for feelings of reward and fairness. The study suggests the participants who experienced gratitude benefited from better psychological and physical health, improved sleep, greater empathy and friendships, and more.

"With the Holocaust, we only typically associate the awful things," Dr. Fox acknowledged in a press release announcing the study. "But when you listen to the survivors, you also hear stories of incredible virtue and gratitude for the help they received."

In 2023, I visited the National Holocaust Museum in Washington, D.C. Towards the end of the exhibit, there is a video gallery of survivor testimonials. I watched several of them, but one stuck with me more than the others:

> *"One morning, as I prayed and gave thanks to God for the great life he blessed me with, a fellow prisoner seated next to me asked how I could be so grateful to God for the life of hell we are living. I told him, I'm grateful I was not born as one of our guards."*

An attitude of gratitude does not get more powerful than that.

Who are the fellow Stormriders who jumped in the hole with you during your comeback journey? Who are the fellow hope-spreading illuminators who are already familiar with the hole you are in and know the way out?

Who are you grateful for?

Many say life is about the journey, not where it leads us. Personally, my greatest joy and fondest memories are tied to those who have accompanied me along the way: my friends, family, and colleagues who have walked beside me to the highest peaks, through the darkest valleys, and everywhere in-between.

Ubuntu!

CHAPTER 24

A Magnitude of Gratitude

Like 80% of people, I had a dream of writing a book for many years. I drafted and redrafted dozens of iterations and titles in my head. However, I was never able to land the right narrative on the stripes. My storylines and outlines were always a few degrees off course.

In August of 2024, eight months after my cancer diagnosis and a month after losing my sight, the storyline for this book came into focus. I was ready to write. And 90 days later, my initial manuscript was done.

There are far too many people who have helped me get where I am today to recognize here. Your absence from this tribute is not an absence from my heart.

As I mentioned at the start of this book, my setback-to-comeback journey has been fueled by a trifecta of world-class medical professionals and breakthroughs; an unrelenting positive attitude fueled by my own resilience, as well as the love, care, and prayers of hundreds of family members, friends, colleagues, and strangers; and an unbending faith in God.

Let me begin by thanking God for the gift of a remarkable life brimming with adventure, friendship, joy, love, and good health for most of my years. I wouldn't trade my life—and all the twists and turns that have accompanied it—for anyone else's. God has led me through some rough storms over the years, and I'm certain the storm I'm currently navigating will be no exception. There is simply no mountain too tall for me to climb with God as my guide. No matter how dark my days get, there is always a flame burning in the distance—God's inextinguishable torch of hope illuminating my path forward.

Let's turn to my family now. The magnitude of gratitude and love I have for my wife Stephanie, our daughter Kaitlyn, my late father George, my mom Barbara, and my sister Krista is immeasurable. As an expression of my gratitude, I've written you the following letters (which I suspect capture only 1% of the love and appreciation I have for you). We Swedes, as you know, are not great at wearing our emotions on our sleeves.

Dear Stephanie,

A tentpole of this book and my life has been embracing a "Do Hard Things" mindset. If there is anyone in my life deserving of "Do Hard Things" recognition, it's you.

You have been at my side in sickness and in health. In good times and bad, for 30 years, you traveled the world with me. Along the way, we have lived in seven cities spanning six states and the African nation of Mauritius, and we've visited more than a dozen countries spanning six continents.

But it has been my "on-the-move" career that has demanded more sacrifice from you than I know you were expecting at the start of our marriage, and that few others would have endured. Along the way, you have surrendered friendships, communities, and homes that I know you loved. But you did the "hard thing" and always joined me as I departed on the next leg of my professional journey, always with a smile and enthusiastically standing ready to orchestrate the move.

Simply put, your curious and adventurous spirit are unmatched, which I will forever adore and admire about you.

Your "Do Hard Things" love for me and our family came into vividly clear focus in 2024 as unimagined health crises confronted both of us. It was a dual-engine failure neither of us could have ever imagined would blindside our relatively smooth ascent in life (sans a few of the expected turbulences accompanying most three-decade marriages).

My Stage 4 cancer diagnosis and blindness, compounded by your catastrophic stairway fall (which resulted in the dislocation and shattering of both your shoulders and wrist), was a medical nightmare no one should have to endure. Yet, you summoned the grace, grit, and resilience to courageously recover from your own medical trauma that initially included two weeks in the hospital, including a week in the ICU, a six-hour surgery on both shoulders and your wrist, and the horrific relocating of your shoulders in the trauma center upon your arrival at the hospital.

Despite all this, you continued to focus on others more than yourself: helping me navigate the final leg of my cancer battle (which included several radiation treatments and brain surgery), being present during your mom's final hospice journey, and, most importantly, ensuring Kaitlyn's wellbeing at college for her sophomore year six hours from home. All while continuing your day job as the Director of Marketing and Communications at The Woodlands Christian Academy.

That's called "Doing Hard Things!" Not for your benefit, but for the benefit of others. Because that's how you roll. You transformed your pain into a passion for helping and inspiring others.

Of course, our choices to ignore the easy routes have also come to life in some really fun ways.

For example, when we decided to buy a boat in 2000 while living in LA. The easy choice would have been to purchase a simple power boat that would have driven on the water like a car. But that's not how we operate. Even back then, we did the "hard thing," custom building a 34-foot sailboat, not having ever taken so much as a sailing class in our lives. But we did it. We took sailing classes together and when the boat arrived, we were ready to captain our new vessel together, taking long weekend voyages in the sun-kissed breezy Santa Monica Bay. Aside from a few missed dockings that blemished our shiny white hull, you were an exceptional Co-Captain.

"Doing Hard Things" is always more rewarding than the easy things. We found comfort and strength in each other by focusing on discomfort. We've grown far more from doing hard things than from the easy things in life.

I was reminded of this recently when my dear friend, mentor and fellow executive from United and Avelo Airlines, Michael Quiello, shared with me the toast he delivered at his son's wedding several years ago:

"Today is a wonderful day and when he was a boy, I would look out and wonder who was the young girl out there that would catch his eye. But remember this day for how happy you both are but know you'll have some very trying times, that's life. You will hear people say that a good marriage is 50/50. I'll also add that in a good marriage, you'll try to out-serve each other. But I will tell you that marriage is not always 50/50, sometimes it's 90/10, sometimes it's 10/90. And then there will be times that when you are walking down life's trail together that you'll turn around and see only one set of footprints. That's because one of you will literally be carrying the other."

Michael's sage advice to his son reminded me of what has made our marriage and our love for each other so resilient and renewable over the years.

Lastly, this letter would be incomplete if I didn't thank you for the time and love you've poured into this book. It is unmistakably stronger because I had you at my side through it all.

Neither of us knows what the universe will throw at us next. But I know one thing is as certain as the sun rising tomorrow. We will move forward together with the same gracious, compassionate, adventurous "Do Hard Things" ideals that I have admired, cherished, and loved about us since our earliest days together.

With deep love and gratitude to Mauritius and back,

Jimmy

P.S. When I wrote this tribute in June 2025, I never imagined two weeks later you would be diagnosed with Stage 4 appendix cancer—an adversity requiring immediate surgery, and eight months of intense chemo and immunotherapy. Yet, you faced this latest medical crucible with the same "Do Hard Things" spirit that enabled you to overcome the many other obstacles you have faced over the years. This resilience, coupled with your deep faith, equipped you with the sword to slay this rare cancer diagnosis in less than a year. Kaitlyn and I will continue to be at your side every step of the way, just as you have selflessly stood by us.

———

Dear Kaitlyn,

As you start your junior year of college, the door continues to open wider to an extraordinary new world, a place known as "The Real World." It is a beautiful disaster of a place. Yet, no one is more equipped to slay the challenges you will encounter and seize the opportunities ahead than you.

As you step into adulthood, I have five pieces of advice for you:

Embrace the suck: Life is going to throw some fastballs and curveballs at you along the way. Some may even strike you in the head and knock you to your knees in pain and tears. But no matter how hard, disappointing, or fatiguing things get, don't run from them—embrace them. Because it is these moments that will make you stronger, braver, and smarter. Become comfortable with being uncomfortable. Because your life will more likely be defined by how you handle periods of uncertainty and discomfort than periods of certainty and comfort. In short, the bigger the challenge, the greater your destiny.

Share your blanket: You are going to be gifted with many blessings throughout your life. While I have no doubt you will be the recipient of many treasures along the way that will give you great happiness, I am equally certain you will find even greater joy from the gifts you share with others. So, as you receive the abundant gifts of life, continuously ask yourself, who you will share these with?

Hopelessness is finite. Hope is infinite: You are the poster child of positivity. However, the world is filled with detractors that will try and pull you down and demoralize you. They will tell you hope is a mirage. Hope is not a mirage—hope is everything. The world is powered by dreams and dreamers. As Bruce Springsteen appeals to us, dream, baby, dream!

Switch off your GPS and turn on your curiosity: It is easy in today's world to have an algorithm or app chart your path for you. In most cases, it will plot the path of least resistance. As tempting and safe as that sounds, I encourage you to choose the path less traveled. It is on this journey you will meet the most interesting people, discover the most unexpected places, and experience the most memorable moments of your life. So, when you find yourself at a fork in the road, remember it's often the wrong turns that lead to the right places—and people—in life.

Avoid asking *What If* and declare *Why Not*: The biggest barrier to achieving your dreams and happiness is fear. And the vast majority of times, those fears will not come to fruition. A hesitant life is the enemy of a vibrant life. The world is filled with "what-if-ers," the friends, family members, classmates, and colleagues who discourage you from taking chances in life, from rolling the dice, from pursuing your dreams. Find the dream-chasers in your life and abandon the dream-killers. Remember, moderation is for monks—take big bites in life.

As you walk through this door, remember Ferris Bueller's advice:

"Life moves pretty fast. If you don't take time to look around once in a while, you could miss it."

Indeed, some of the most majestic views, epic experiences, and treasured people you will encounter may be above you, below you, or behind you.

Most importantly, know that your family is your rock. Like a sailboat at sea, you always have a safe harbor to return to when the storms of life capsize your boat. Or, if you simply need to regain your bearings or restock your galley.

Let me close with these words of wisdom from Mark Twain:

"Twenty years from now you will be more disappointed with the things you didn't do then by the things you did do. So, throw off the bowlines. Sail away from the safe harbor. Catch the trade winds in your sails. Explore. Dream. Discover."

I love you to Mauritius and back, Kaitlyn Rose Olson!

Dad

———

Dear Dad,

It's been almost two years since your passing and I want to honor you—the man who breathed life into me 56 years ago and who was there for me at every turn with the right words, advice, and encouragement to keep charging forward.

It has been said that we should live the life we want to be remembered for. Over the course of your 84 years, you lived a story worthy of telling.

There are far too many memories and lessons to share here. But, as I contemplate the impact you had on my life and so many others, there are five illuminations from our five decades together I will carry with me until my final days.

You were a pathfinder

Put another way, you were my compass—not a GPS. You never directed me to a specific destination or pushed me in a particular direction. Rather, you were my sherpa on the trails I chose to blaze, illuminating the way forward with your unequivocal wisdom, experience, judgment, and foresight.

In high school, when my passion for writing and storytelling came into focus, you bought me a double-floppy PC before virtually any of my classmates knew what a word processor was. This allowed me to master my obsession for more efficiently and imaginatively weaving narratives together than was possible on the typewriter I was using at the time. You would often stay up with me into the early hours of the morning, pressing me to purge unnecessary words and sentences while challenging me to find more illustrative and interesting ways to express my thoughts.

As I embarked on my professional journey, you were there again to help me draft my first CV and craft interview-enticing cover letters. And as I embarked on my search for a summer internship my sophomore year of college, you encouraged me to spend spring break canvasing LA to introduce myself, in-person, to the city's top 20 PR agencies.

Your guidance landed me seven interviews and five job offers before the start of summer.

Of course, how could I forget the lively business lunches and dinners you invited me to accompany you to during my 20s, exposing me to the nuances of holding engaging conversations with worldly business executives, and, perhaps more importantly, how to navigate the splashy dinner and cocktail menus at the swanky LA eateries we would frequent with your colleagues?

In short, you taught me the ropes of traversing the career I chose to pursue—not one you thrust upon me.

You were a character builder

You taught me the virtues of hard work, loyalty, integrity, and standing your ground. I remember you telling me about the time your most important client asked you to do something you felt was unethical. You shared with me the fear you felt standing up to this client and the risk it posed to the account and your job. In that moment, you revealed to me the strength that conviction, courage, and vulnerability harvest.

You also taught me the value of perseverance and, no matter how perilous things may seem, to never give up. You would implore: "Don't worry about it until you need to worry about it. You always have options until you don't have any options. So, focus on keeping your options open."

For example, when I turned 15 and failed the vision test for my driver's license, I was devastated. I couldn't contemplate a life not being able to drive. But you reassured me we would find a positive path forward. We worked with my eye doctor to find a contact lens prescription that met the state standard. I've been driving ever since until the onset of last year's blindness.

You were a storyteller

Many of my earliest memories of you, Dad, are the stories you told. Whether it was gathering around our family cabin's fireplace, where you would share fanciful tales of spearheading African lion hunts (even though you were not a hunter), or convening our family after Sunday dinners to watch projection slide shows chronicling your two years living in India or our early family travels across Central and South America, you were a masterful storyteller who kept family and friends on the edge of their seats.

At the same time, you had a voracious appetite for the enticing stories of others. You introduced me to alluring fictional tales like Bartle Bull's *The Café on the Nile* and *The White Rhino Hotel*. I'm certain you had a best-selling adventure novel in you beckoning to be told.

You were an adventure seeker

One of the greatest gifts you instilled in me is the courage to travel, meet other people, and understand and respect different and distant cultures. No one modeled the virtue of having, following, and filling an "explorer's heart" better than you. After all, you were only in your young 20s when you moved to India, shortly after finishing graduate school.

Or when you relocated our family to Colombia, renting us a house on the Caribbean adjacent to a steakhouse I'm certain was a front for Pablo Escobar's drug cartel. This, coupled with your piranha-spearing sojourn to the Amazon, explains why you didn't discourage my first-grade Saturday morning solo bus rides across Cartagena.

It was these and so many of your other brave diversions in life that inspired me to visit 60 countries across six continents over the years, including living on the remote African Indian Ocean island of Mauritius for a year.

You were a difference maker

More than anything, you dedicated your life to making the lives of others better. Whether it was your nonprofit urban planning work in India and Colombia, your public service work as an assistant state health director in New Mexico and West Virginia, or managing the health care plan for the United Mine Workers of America, you devoted your career to improving the lives of others.

Nowhere did you make a bigger difference than in caring for your own family. You worked exhaustively to ensure we always had comfortable homes to sleep in and delicious food on our plates. You and Mom made significant sacrifices so Krista and I could grow up in safe neighborhoods, go to good schools, pursue our personal passions, and have fun and fulfilling childhoods. You ensured we could attend the colleges of our choice and that there was always a welcoming home for us to return to during and after our university years.

There are not enough words to express the magnitude of gratitude and love I have for you.

Like the flight simulators pilots use, you served as a "life simulator" of sorts, preparing me for the headwinds, tailwinds, and crosswinds of life. Like the real-world flying experience that flight simulators replicate, you taught me how to pushback, taxi, and take off in life. You modeled for me how to climb, descend, throttle up, and decelerate. You demonstrated for me how to keep my eye on the horizon and land on the stripes. And you reassured me that when I experienced a hard landing, I would live to soar another day.

Similar to the high-fidelity simulators where pilots learn, you provided a safe environment where wrong turns and crashing weren't criticized or punished (at least most of the time), but rather were treated as important learning moments for the real world.

In our increasingly complex and uncertain lives, we need more "life simulators" like you, who gave me the courage to take life head on, seek fresh adventures at every turn, and navigate life's updrafts and downdrafts with confidence, composure, and contemplation.

Most importantly, you impressed upon me that at the end of our journeys, our success won't be measured in the miles we've flown or the treasures we've accumulated along the way, but rather in the richness of the connections we've made, the abundance of stories we've penned, and the positive impact on the world we leave in our wake.

I can only hope I've equipped Kaitlyn with the same wings of inspiration, courage, and judgement to fly high, fly far, and fly right, as you did for me.

Onward and upward, Dad!

Love,

Jimmy

———

Dear Mom,

Anyone who knows you will say one of your most endearing qualities is your memory. That's because there is simply no one on this planet who can recall the details of conversations and experiences dating back decades with your exacting accuracy.

This rare gift enables you to recall the names of my friends and their parents dating back to first grade better than I can. Not only do you recall their names, but you love replaying for me specific events from my life that you've observed that are foggy memories to me at best. In fact, there are a few experiences where I wish your memory wasn't so good.

To me, your greatest virtue is not your "elephant memory." Rather, it's your unmatched ability to listen. Your remarkable memory is only outshined by your incredible ability to listen. And it is your attentive listening that enables you to recall so much with such amazing detail.

No one appreciates your attentive listening more than I. Growing up, you were always there for me, often to simply listen to the traumas and triumphs of the day. You always made me feel seen, heard, and, above all, loved. You listened, took time to understand what I was dealing with, and then shared supportive words of advice or a reassuring hug.

The understanding and compassion you gained from listening to my challenges and contemplations also translated into your frequent advocacy for me with teachers, coaches, doctors, and many others. I was especially appreciative of the numerous times you were in my corner on the various family "decisions" that arose over the years.

Nothing warmed my heart—and stomach—more, however, than your treasured home-baked chocolate chip cookies and three-color "Red, White, & Blue" sugar cookies. To this day, they are my favorite cookies, because I know they are yours and baked with the same attention and love you filled our home with growing up and that you continue to envelop our family in.

That's a long-winded way of saying "Thank you!"

Thank you for bringing me into this world.
Thank you for helping explain the world to me.

Thank you for showing me the world.
Thank you for listening to me.
Thank you for understanding me.
Thank you for fighting for me.
Thank you for loving me.

I may not remember the twists and turns of my own life with the clarity that you do, but my memories of your love, courage, and cookies are unforgettable.

I love you!

Jimmy

P.S. A letter to you would be incomplete without a postscript honoring your postscripts. You are one of the last people on the planet who still enjoys sending handwritten letters and cards. You treat every message with the same attention as you do your cookies, baking love and thoughtfulness into every page of your often multi-page cursive-penned notes.

P.P.S. However, it is your concluding postscripts—which often top four or five in number, that distinguish your letter and cards. In fact, when you run out of space on a birthday or Halloween card, your post scriptums spill over onto multiple yellow sticky notes. These always bring a smile to our faces. So, keep 'em coming!

———

Dear Krista,

Growing up, I know I was not the big brother to you I should have been. I'm sorry.

I was jealous of how smart you were and how easy school came to you. But that's no excuse for falling short of being the protector and pathbreaker big brothers are supposed to be for their younger siblings—especially our sisters.

I am grateful that during our college years, while I was at Syracuse and you were attending Cornell, you would treat me to your school's world-famous cafeteria, which served as a training camp for aspiring chefs enrolled in the school's top-ranked hotel management program. During those years, you also realigned my misguided political views, which had drifted inexplicably and indefensibly to the right. While you have and will always lean farther to the left than me, I appreciate your persistent shaming to bend me back to the commonsense political ideology I had abandoned somewhere along the way.

Some of my most cherished memories were catching up over dinner or drinks on my frequent business trips to New York, where you live. And how could I forget 9/11, and the couch you loaned me in your apartment for several days after being stranded at JFK in the wake of the attacks.

Fast forward two decades and you were the only one of our family or friends who made the 10,000-mile two-day journey to visit us in Africa. This was an especially memorable time for our kids; Kaitlyn continues to talk about parasailing and tubing with Wade on the Indian Ocean.

Of course, your loving heart showed up in full force in the days and weeks following Stephanie's fall. Your frequent calls and texts, coupled with the steady flow of meals you arranged to help us over this hump, illuminate the caring soul that you are and how blessed I am to have you as my sister.
I'm a better person because of you. Thank you for pushing me to be a better husband. A better father. A better son. And a better brother. I know I can still do a lot better. I'll keep trying, and I know you will keep pushing me in the right direction—as you always have.

Love,

Jimmy

My Dream Team

Beyond my family, it is hard to know where to start in expressing my gratitude to so many who have accompanied me on this journey.

My miracle workers

I'll start with the immensely talented and caring team of medical professionals who saved my life and who continue to work diligently to save my sight.

First and foremost, I am grateful to Dr. Krishna Pachipala and Dr. Jason Berilgen for their attentive and meticulous orchestration of my highly complex cancer treatment. The highly personalized care you and your exceptional team at The Woodlands Cancer Institute provided me (and continue to provide to this day) is unrivaled. I owe you both my life. I would not be sitting here today writing this final chapter without you.

Then there is Dr. Sabih Effendi, my neurosurgeon who removed the final potentially cancerous brain artifacts, which were ultimately tested and confirmed to be nonmalignant radiation particles. You and your neurological surgical team at Memorial Hermann Medical Center turned one of the scariest moments of my life—brain surgery—into a virtually pain-free, rapid recovery experience.

Additionally, I'm thankful for everyone within the Memorial Hermann Medical System who has contributed to my care along the way, from the ER staff that initially alerted me to the super-sized spot on my lung to the nurses and doctors who cared for me day and night during multiple hospital visits over the past two years.

Finally, I would like to thank the pair of Ophthalmologists at Retina Consultants of Texas who have guided me through the vision loss that has accompanied my cancer battle. I am especially appreciative of Dr. Effie Rahman. You have been at my side since the onset of this collateral damage. Following weeks of testing and collaboration with Dr. Pachipala, you ultimately diagnosed the optic nerve damage and potential causes. You are one of the most compassionate doctors I've ever met. Confronted with the perilous irreversible blindness that I have, your prescription of understanding and empathy is very likely the best remedy any doctor could offer.

I'm also grateful to Dr. Stacy Smith, who complemented Dr. Rahman's care with her world-renowned expertise in neuro-ophthalmology. Your efforts have offered important confirmation of Dr. Rahman's optic nerve damage diagnosis and potential contributors.

While both doctors have been brutally honest about the absence of any near-term remedies for my condition, I know if there are any breakthroughs, these two vision specialists will be on the forefront of that knowledge.

My fellow cancer slayers

Beyond my "Medical Dream Team" are the remarkable individuals who have joined me in the foxhole of my cancer fight. This includes a mix of fellow cancer warriors and many other caring friends.

Three individuals who have played the biggest role in helping me navigate my cancer crisis are Lynann Bradbury, Steven Latham, and Dave Latham.

Lynann is a three-time badass cancer-slaying black belt. In late 2023, when the early indicators were pointing towards cancer, she was the first person I called. She has been with me every step of the way, virtually holding my hand and heart through the entire process. She was very often the first person I would call after radiation, immunotherapy, or surgery. She was there for me 24/7, promptly returning every call or text. Lynann, you are far more than a friend, mentor, and former colleague—you are an angel dispatched by God that gave my fight the wings it needed to soar through this storm.

In the early days of my cancer battle, I also found great resolve in the cancer-slaying story of Dave Latham. Dave is the brother of my longtime friend Steven Latham. Steven was one of the first people I called after my diagnosis and has been a beacon of encouragement ever since.

Dave's journey of determination, resilience, and renewal set a powerful example for me from the outset. While pursuing his high-flying career in movie production for some of Hollywood's top studios and logging hundreds of miles a week as an avid long-distance cyclist, Dave's world was upended in 2018 by a devastating diagnosis: Stage 4 esophageal adenocarcinoma that had spread to his brain, lungs, liver, and esophagus. The prognosis from his doctors was bleak, giving him just a 3% chance of survival and advising him to prepare for hospice care. But Dave refused to surrender. Eight years later, he stands in full remission, now dedicating his post-Hollywood life to supporting other cancer warriors, like me, through his work with the nonprofit Stand Up to Cancer.

Lynann and Dave, your courage and resilience are nothing short of heroic. You've transformed adversity into triumph, setting the benchmark for what it means to face hardship with unwavering strength. You are my cancer-slaying heroes. And Steven, your friendship is eternal.

My writer's room

I will now turn to the wingmen and wingwomen who have helped me pilot my writing odyssey and comeback journey.

Let me begin by thanking former United Airlines CEO and Chairman Oscar Munoz for his deeply personal and heartfelt foreword. I never imagined when we first met, during my interview to serve as your communications chief at United Airlines just two months after your life-threatening heart attack, that you would be penning the forward to a book chronicling my own medically induced comeback story. This may be a stage-setting foreword for those of you reading this book, but for me, this foreword is a life ring of inspiration and hope I will keep close by for the dark and challenging days ahead. A cornerstone of this book is the ideal that there is always blue sky on the other side of every storm. Oscar, you set the bar for servant leadership—your friendship, coupled with your own courageous turnaround story, are my blue sky. The depth of my gratitude to you runs deeper than you'll ever know.

This tribute would be incomplete without honoring the chorus of other esteemed friends and leaders who have championed my vision for this project: Starbucks Chairman Emeritus and Retired CEO Howard Schultz, Thrive Global and *Huffington Post* Founder Arianna Huffington, Retired US Airways Captain Chesley "Sully" Sullenberger, Levi Strauss President and CEO Michelle Gass, former Wella and Godiva Chocolatier CEO Annie Young-Scrivner, REI Chairman Chris Carr, Day 2 Media Founder and former *CNN* Anchor Poppy Harlow, African Leadership Group and Sand Technologies Founder Fred Swaniker, Burson CEO Corey duBrowa, Avelo Airlines Founder and CEO Andrew Levy, Southwest Airlines Retired Chief Administration and Communications Officer Linda Rutherford, and Amahoro Coalition Founder Isaac Kwaku Fokuo.

I am mindful of the time you have devoted to this endeavor, and I am truly grateful for your steadfast support and encouragement. The grace you bring into our world is matched only by the generosity of your spirit. I also appreciate that these contributions would not have been possible without the generous assistance of Alex Clemens, Brian DeSplinter, Jessica Dock, Amy Lindquist, Kelly McGinnis, Carie McGrane, Thandi Petersen, Vivek Varma, and Phil Zabriskie.

Of course, my gratitude to all of you who have contributed your own setback-to-comeback stories to this project is appreciated beyond words. The vulnerability and authenticity you impart will touch and change many lives. I ventured to write a book that anyone riding a storm in their own life would see themselves in one of you. Thanks to your stories, I succeed in offering my readers that mirror, instruction, and inspiration I set out to offer.

So, here's to my fellow "Do Hard Things" Stormriders and contributors: Caroline Bowen, Craig Caldwell, Doug Camp, Susanna and Marc Dalais, Kristen and Bryan Deptula, Elise Eberwein, Mawulom Essel-Koomson, Paul and Denise Fejtek, Dr. Rosa Rivera-Hainaj, Scott Harrison, Jillian Hastings, Lucy Helm, Tom Izzo, Daniel Jacobs, Kip Keino, Rachel Gerber Kule, Cheryl Laws, Angee Linsey, Pat Lore, Phil Nardone, Marta Newhart, Ken Ross, Don Spetner, Moira Squier, Mark Stouse, Jason Teitler, Russ Whitenack, and Christopher O.H. Williams.

Beyond my fellow "Do Hard Things" Stormriders, my determination to write and finish this book was fueled by the constellation of friends who saddled up with me for this ride. They generously invested their time as sounding boards and motivators to keep charging forward. Your collaboration made this a better book and, more importantly, an enjoyable and fulfilling process.

Throughout my journey, countless friends and colleagues stepped into my virtual "writer's room," offering encouragement and wisdom. Yet none challenged me to embrace my vulnerability and lean into telling my authentic story quite like master storyteller Pat Lore. Pat, you have been a steadfast thought partner at every turn of my authoring adventure, inspiring me to dig deeper and reveal truths that frightened me but needed to be told. I am especially thankful for the beautiful video you created documenting my comeback story—it is a testament to your talent and friendship (the video can be viewed at ComeBackCompass.com).

I would also like to thank my dear friends and former Avelo Airlines colleagues Vicky Stennes, Michael Quiello, Mary Coursey, Jim Lynde, Daniel Camejo, Giselle Cortes, and Lauren Rovella for their frequent and motivating calls and texts to keep charging forward. You pushed me to keep fighting, to keep writing and, above all, keep believing. There are no words big enough to express my gratitude for the care and love you have shown my family and me throughout this unimaginable and often lonely journey.

Additionally, I would like to thank *New York Times* bestselling author and storytelling sage Bob Goff for his wisdom and guidance in helping me shape my public speaking narrative. You rocketed my story from good to great, which has been rewarded with standing ovations. I'm also appreciative for the kind words of support you offered for this book and my story. I encourage you to check out Bob's website at BobGoff.com and explore how he can help you discover and share your story.

I'm also very grateful to Ryan Ross and Cody Vermillion with UNCMN Creative Works for the time and creativity they devoted to producing my alluring speaking "pitch video." You can view the video they created for me at ComebackCompass.com and discover more about their mission-inspired work at UNCMNCreative.com.

Last—but certainly not least—I would like to give a huge shout out to Everett O'Keefe and his team (including Zelda Fogle, Malia Sexton, and Elizabeth Arterberry) at Ignite Press for bringing my book to life. I would also like to give a very special shout out to Imran Khaliq for creating the perfect cover for this book—it's beautiful. Thank you for your guidance, creativity, and attention to detail to ensure this endeavor was a seamless supernova of editorial beauty beyond my wildest dreams. You can learn more about Everett's book publishing capabilities at IgnitePress.us.

My wing riders

Let me close by taking this moment to recognize the chorus of friends and colleagues who have joined me on my comeback journey. Each of you have contributed a unique note to the symphony of courage, ideation, and storytelling I embarked on. You ensured my recovery and authoring quest was not the solitary journey it could have been.

Thank you, from the deepest well of my heart: Albertus Magnus College (President Dr. Marc Camille, my fellow Board of Trustees, the Sisters of Dominican Peace, and the President's Cabinet), Greg Baden, Kim Berlin, Deborah and Meredith Beyer, Steve Blackwell, Brian Carty, Fred and Cheryl Cook, Dan Cravens, Tony D'Angelo, Rick Devine, Marianne Duong, Josh Earnest, Greg Elliott, Bill Flora, Dr. Rochelle Ford, Dr. Kelly Gaggin, Marthalee Galeota, Chris Graves, Mandeep Grewal, Jon Harris, Stefan Holt, Dana Hughes, Jim Hughes, Madison Jones, Keith and Kini Jorgensen, Jeremy Jorgensen, Katherine Juergens, Adam Kaplan, Sally Kassab, Tasleem Kassum, Craig Keller, Andrew King, Scott Kronick, Mary Landsfield, Beatriz Manchado, Mitch Messinger, Linda Mills, Jenn Moore, Julia Morgillo, Nicole Noll-Williams, Jessica Pantages, Neil Patel, Tony Plohoros, Jason Porath, Helen Ramirez, Dana Reinglass, Jaime Riley, Bill Roberts, Jorge Roberts, Courtney Rosenberg, Bill Rosenthal, Danny Rosin, Sharon Rozum and Special Olympics Connecticut, Dr. Maria Russell, Tom Schmedding, Maggie Schmerin, Naomi Seligman, Barby Siegel, Fran Shockley, Lindsay Smelser, Nerissa Sugars, Linda Thomas, Joe Thornton, Gerry and Gabrielle Tschopp, Scott Vazin, Barbara Webster, Heather Wilson, Trevor Yealy, Dana Zimmerman, and Matt Zimmerman.

You Are My Tailwind

This morning, as I retire the pen on this year-long authoring odyssey, it is impossible for me to quantify the gratitude I hold for all of you who have been at my side. My gratitude is only surpassed by your grace.

You breathed the strength into me to keep grinding, to keep fighting, and to keep flying high. You revealed to me that our darkest misfortunes are our brightest fortunes. You showed me who I am and why I'm here.

You are my tailwind. Because of you, I rose from every stumble with newfound resolve, fearless of the gathering storms. The path ahead, though uncertain, now feels like a gift, each step a testament to resilience, each breath a quiet promise to honor the courage you kindled within me.

Above all, it is in gratitude where we find the courage to face uncertainty and the hope to dream anew. Here's to the unwritten pages ahead and to the gratitude that will fill them.

So, wherever the road bends next for us, may we remember the simple, extraordinary power of thankfulness embodied in the familiar and gentle words of gratitude from "It's You I Like" regularly sung by Fred Rogers. Words so many of us treasure from our childhood days hanging out in Mr. Rogers' neighborhood.

Indeed, as the words painted on a wall in a shop I was recently browsing in San Diego radiated, "Stay close to people who feel like sunshine."

It's you I like - there will forever be a vacancy in my heart for all of you.

Disembarkation: Our Attitude Determines Our Altitude

A few years ago, as I was helping my daughter Kaitlyn with a high school English assignment, she described to me the time-honored performing arts ritual of turning on a small, single-bulb light to illuminate the stage at night while the theater is closed. Kaitlyn—an aspiring Broadway actress—told me it's called a "ghost light."

There are many superstitions expounding this custom—after all, the theater is home to many of history's most masterful storytellers. One of the most widely accepted myths is that every theater harbors a ghost, and the ghost light glows at night to provide these spirits with a place to perform.

Like so many other experiences, the COVID-19 pandemic forced most theaters to go dark in 2020, sidelining tens of thousands of thespians around the world. The closing of theaters also left scores of performing arts enthusiasts with nowhere to satisfy their voracious theatrical appetites. The ghost light served a more significant purpose than ever. From Broadway to the West End, ghost lights were left burning by stage managers around the world as a *torch of hope that the show must go on.*

If there is one thing the pandemic revealed, it is humanity's universal need for hope, and our distinctly human capacity to share it. Having a purpose, mission, calling, or whatever we prefer to call it is important. But *sharing it*—our hope for a better world and our selfless care for other people—is infinitely more rewarding.

This is precisely what inspired Swiss light artist Gerry Hofstetter to project a unifying message of hope onto the face of The Matterhorn during the pandemic. Every day, between March 24 and April 26, 2020, the world-renowned artist illuminated the 15,000-foot vista with a different inspiring symbol or phrase, including the words *Hope, Solidarity,* and *Together,* the images of a candle and red heart, and the flags of more than two dozen nations, including Iran, South Africa, Switzerland, Italy, India, China, and the United States.

"The light is a sign of hope that our six-person team is giving the world," Hofstetter told a Swiss news outlet.

However, there are few expressions of hope more enduring than Robert F. Kennedy's historic 1966 "Ripple of Hope" speech at South Africa's University of Cape Town during the height of apartheid:

> "Each time a man stands up for an ideal, or acts to improve the lot of others, or strikes out against injustice, he sends forth a tiny ripple of hope; and crossing each other from a million different centers of energy and daring, those ripples build a current which can sweep down the mightiest walls of oppression and resistance."

These words convey RFK's ideal that hope starts with a single brave act and becomes powerful when echoed by many—the aspiration that ordinary people can bend the arc of history.

20 beacons of hope

Throughout this book you've met many of the hope-spreading acolytes RFK exhorted us to be. They are our fellow Stormriders— each personifying a destiny-shaping comeback story worthy of sharing. The adversities they've conquered, the doubt and fear they've buried, and the courage they've mustered, kindle a beacon of hope for all of us. Their light slices through the darkness with the clean precision and brilliance of a master-crafted Japanese blade.

Captain "Sully" Sullenberger safely landed US Airways Flight 1549 on New York's Hudson River, *teaching us how to "Aviate, Navigate, and Communicate" when we are confronted with a major storm in life or at work.*

Susanna Dalais traded her lucrative investment banking career in the U.S. to start a nonprofit school and secondhand clothing boutique on a remote African island, *reminding us that the more we give—the more we can give.*

Jillian Hastings traded her career-climbing anxiety for the purpose-fulfilling life as the Camp Director she's dreamed of since childhood, *showing us we're never too old or too young to embrace our purpose and live our best life.*

Angee Linsey inspires us to *stop asking "What If?" and live a "Why Not Now!" life,* one brave dream-chasing adventure at a time.

Phil Nardone courageously cast aside his shame-concealing mask and embraced his true self as a proud gay man, *lighting the way for us to be our true selves.*

Howard Schultz built one of the world's most admired and valuable companies, proving that a business can thrive commercially while staying anchored in purpose. *He showed that profits and shared success not only coexist, but strengthen each other when people and values are placed at the center of the enterprise.*

Coach Russ Whitenack built one of America's most respected college track programs and sports camps. *His rallying cry—"What a Day"—still pushes us to find the grit to get up, suit up, and lace up each morning, no matter how stormy the day ahead may seem.*

Lucy Helm turned her life-threatening aneurism which left her nearly blind in one eye into a life devoted to helping others. The retired Starbucks executive *reveals how we can bring direction to the lost, comfort to the hurt, connection to the lonely, and hope to the hopeless.*

Daniel Jacobs claimed the world middleweight championship boxing title after knocking out a paralyzing bone cancer diagnosis. *He reminds us our fights are won long before we step into the ring—one punch, one pull-up, and one mile at a time.*

Ernest Shackleton led his stranded crew through 16 months of Antarctic isolation. Against impossible odds, he brought every man home alive—*teaching us that true leadership offers hope when circumstances offer none.*

Caroline Bowen bounced back from her flatlining heart attack to start a thriving home-baked pie business, *reminding us tomorrow is not promised.*

Bryan and Kristen Deptula swapped their comfortable Florida life for a family adventure as first-time Delaware boutique hotel owners. *They model how to apply the virtues of consequential leadership in our personal lives, exhibiting conviction, courage, compassion, collaboration, and connection at every turn in their entrepreneurial journey.*

President John F. Kennedy challenged his fellow Americans with a bold mission: to land a man on the moon and bring him safely home. In doing so, *he reminded us that we choose great endeavors not because they are easy—but precisely because they are hard.*

Rachel Gerber Kule chronicles how she confronted the deep sadness, betrayal, and doubt that accompanied the unexpected loss of her dad and her near decade-long quest to have a child. *She reminds us hopelessness is finite and hope is infinite when we choose to make every day a great day.*

Pat Lore transformed her high-flying broadcast journalism career into a vibrant video storytelling business. *She shows us how to flip the script on our story of shame into a life of significance, one curiosity-inspiring story at a time.*

Cheryl Laws reveals how she emerged from her substance-abusing addiction with a destiny-embracing conviction to help other women reclaim their lives, *promising us that no one is broken beyond repair.*

Scott Harrison turned his self-destructive nosedive into a life-saving global charity, *unveiling how our legacy-achieving strengths are often discovered during our destiny-obstructing struggles.*

Jason Teitler shares with us his resolve to turn a near-death car accident into a life-renewing job with the Special Olympics, *personifying for us how to turn tragedy into triumph.*

Fred Swaniker is on a mission to develop a new generation of 3 million entrepreneurial and ethical leaders across Africa. *He reassures* *us, if we don't discover our "Moment of Obligation," it will find us—we just need to keep our eyes open for it.*

Paul Fejtek embraced a "Do Hard Things" resolve in overcoming his arm-paralyzing birth injury, *demonstrating for us no mountain is too tall for us to summit when we embrace a "take the hill" attitude in life.*

What is your moonshot legacy?

Their stories, which illustrate small acts of kindness, are often the seeds that bloom the biggest stories of significance. As diverse as these individuals and their stories are, they share one lesson in common: they dreamed big. As former Liberia President Ellen Johnson Sirleaf declared:

"If your dreams don't scare you, they aren't big enough."

As the first female elected as a head of state in Africa and a Nobel Peace Prize honoree, she should know. This is the reason *New York Times* bestselling author and master storyteller Bob Goff recently shared with a small gathering of us at his San Diego campsite:

1. When we are deciding what we want to do with our lives, we need to ask *why we want to do those things?*
2. *As* we contemplate who we choose to spend time with, we need to ask ourselves *why are we hanging with those people?*
3. And, think carefully about our legacy—*what do we want to be known for?*—and then live a life and surround ourselves with people that bring that legacy to life.

In short, what do we want to be known for when our time is up? And are the people in our lives illuminating or distracting us from achieving our desired legacy?

How bright will your light shine?

In U2's "Song for Someone," Bono reminds us to guard the flame within us. In my case, I lost my sight, but I found my purpose. And it is my calling—which is helping you answer yours by writing this book—that is blazing my path forward through the fog that blinds me. Like the rotating white and green beacons atop airport control towers guiding aviators home in the darkness of night, our purpose is the lighthouse that leads us to our destiny's harbor.

So, the next time you see a light barreling towards you at the end of a dark tunnel—remember, *you are the light*.

As our journey together draws to a close, I hope you will carry with you the stories, lessons, and inspiration I've shared in this book. They equip us with the mountain-moving, legacy-discovering compass necessary for confronting our bitterness with boldness; our loneliness with connection; our emptiness with purpose; our brokenness with breakthroughs; our heartbreak with heart; and our hopelessness with hope.

A couple years ago, I attended the National Aviation Hall of Fame's annual enshrinement ceremony in Washington, D.C. It's an illustrious occasion, memorializing the aerospace world's most pioneering leaders and innovators. As part of the ceremony, the organization recognizes an extraordinary educator who is inspiring a new generation of aerospace leaders. During her acceptance remarks, the high school science teacher honoree shared the prized advice she implores to motivate her students:

"Your altitude in life is only limited by your attitude towards life."

How high will you fly? More importantly, how bright will your beacon of hope—your ghost light—radiate for others? Together, we can and will ensure the show will go on.

Thank you for the gift of your time and the privilege of sharing my story with you. Until we meet again at the next crossroads, I'll leave you with these words from 20th century Spanish poet Antonio Machado:

Traveler, your footprints are the only road,
nothing else.

Traveler, there is no road;
you make your own path as you walk.

As you walk, you make your own road,
and when you look back you see the path
you will never travel again.

Traveler, there is no road;
only a ship's wake on the sea.

Keep walking. Keep dreaming. Keep doing hard things. There is blue sky on the other side of every storm.

See you down the road!

Let's Keep in Touch

You can discover more about me, our community of "Do Hard Things" Stormriders, and how I can help you or your organization craft your own setback-to-comeback story at: ComebackCompass.com.

Will You Share the Inspiration?

Get this book for a friend, associate, or family member!

If you found this book valuable and know others who would find it useful (friends, family, colleagues, congregants, or students), consider buying them a copy as a gift. Special bulk discounts are available if you would like your whole team, organization or school to benefit from reading this book. Just contact Jim@ComebackCompass.com.

Would You Like Jim to Speak to Your Organization?

Book Jim Now!

If you would like Jim to join your organization's next gathering, you can learn more at www.ComebackCompass.com or by emailing him at Jim@ComebackCompass.com.

Credits

The author has made a good faith effort to acknowledge the creators and sources of content referenced in this book.

Foreword

Speech on assasination of Martin Luther King, Jr. — Senator Robert F. Kennedy (April 4, 1968)

Agamemnon — Aeschylus (458 BCE)

Hamlet — William Shakespeare (1601)

Divine Comedy — Dante Alighieri (1321)

Embarkation

"Nick Cave on singing with Johnny Cash and the joyful, uplifting vibe of his new album, 'Wild God'" — *The Late Show with Stephen Colbert* (August 13, 2024)

Chapter 1

"In a tough year: 25 companies that got it right" — *Businessweek* (February 18, 2009)

Chapter 3

"There are people who make things happen . . ." — Jim Lovell (from undated motivational speeches)

Chapter 4

"Welcome to the Jungle" — Guns N' Roses (1987)

"Thunder Road" — Bruce Springsteen (1975)

Second Battle at El Alamein Victory Speech — Winston Churchill (November 10, 1942)

Chapter 5

Citizenship in a Republic Speech — President Theodore Roosevelt (1910)

"Nose Dive" — Post Malone and Lainey Wilson (2024)

Chapter 6

The Prison Letters of Nelson Mandela — Nelson Mandela (2018)

Chapter 7

Scott Harrison Biographical Video — www.charitywater.org (undated)

Inside Bill's Brain — Netflix (2019)

"In Secret Hideaway, Bill Gates Ponders Microsoft's Future" by Robert Guth — *The Wall Street Journal* (March 28, 2005)

"How Much Information Project" — Roger Bohn and James Short, University of California San Diego (2010)

"Give Your Ideas Some Legs: The Positive Effect of Walking on Creative Thinking" — Marily Oppezzo and Daniel L. Schwartz, Stanford University (2014)

"History Teaches Us Three Essential Lessons for Our Current Crisis" — Eugene Kogan and Nancy Koehn, *Fast Company* (June 2, 2020)

Maxims and Arrows — Friedrich Nietzsche (1889)

Chapter 8

"Coldplay on their record-breaking world tour" — *CBS Sunday Morning* (September 29, 2024)

An Interrupted Life: The Diaries of Etty Hillesum (1943)

"From Teenage Headmaster To Building the Harvard of Africa" — Robert Howell and Phoebe Parke, *CNN* (September 1, 2016)

"Where History is Being Made" — David Brooks, *New York Times* (February 7, 2017)

"The World's 50 Most Innovative Companies" — *Fast Company (February 19, 2019)*

"The World's 100 Most Influential People" — *TIME* (April 24, 2019)

Chapter 9

Tom Izzo and Andrew Levy Leadership Interview — *Fly LAN First* (November, 2022)

Any Given Sunday – Warner Brothers (1999)

Tao Te Ching — Laozi (500 BCE)

Chapter 11

"Ina Garten: Recipe for success" — *CBS Sunday Morning* (September 29, 2024)

Chapter 12

David Brooks Tweet (February 26, 2022)

Chapter 13

We Choose to Go to the Moon Speech — President John F. Kennedy (September 12, 1962)

"2019 50 Most Innovative Companies" — *Fast Company* (February 19, 2019)

Chapter 14

"Backup Plan" — Bailey Zimmerman and Luke Combs (2025)

Chapter 16

Emancipation Proclamation Anniversary Speech — Dr. Martin Luther King Jr. (September 12, 1962)

Stanford University Commencement Address — Steve Jobs (2005)

Walt Disney Story — Disney Family Museum

We Choose to Go to the Moon Speech — President John F. Kennedy (September 12, 1962)

Helen Keller (1890)

Chapter 18

The Hero with a Thousand Faces — Joseph Campbell (1949)

"Joseph Campbell and The Power of Myth" — *Bill Moyers/PBS* (1988)

George Lucas Tribute to Joseph Campbell — 57th Academy Awards (1985)

Chapter 19

"How to Bring Olympics-Style Storytelling to Your Presentations, According to a Legendary NBC Sports Exec" — Carmine Gallo, *Inc.* (July 30, 2024)

"Simone Biles interview — Matias Grez and Coy Wire, *CNN* (August, 2024)

"The Natural" — Michael Hainey, *Esquire* (November, 2017)

Chapter 20

"When you take away what you are known for. . ." — Bob Goff, *Speakers Retreat* (2025)

2001: A Space Odyssey – Stanley Kubrick Productions (1968)

Chapter 21

"You never want a serious crisis to go to waste" — Rahm Emanuel, *WSJ CEO Council* (2008)

I Know Why The Caged Bird Sings — Maya Angelou (1969)

Chapter 22

Michael Lewis Interview — *MasterClass* (April, 2024)

Surrender: 40 Songs, One Story – Bono (2022)

Maya Angelou quote (undated)

Chapter 23

"The man in the hole story" — *The West Wing*, NBC Season 2 / Episode 10 (2000)

I Am Only One — Edward Everett Hale (1909)

"The Science of Gratitude Study" — Dr. Glenn Fox, University of Southern California (2015)

Enable Our Work — Meister Eckhart (1328)

Chapter 24

"It's You I Like" — Fred Rogers (1971)

"Stay close to people who feel like sunshine." — Wall Art, Life is Good store (La Jolla, CA)

Disembarkation

"Matterhorn Lights of Hope" — *SWI* (April, 2020)

Ripple of Hope Speech — Robert F. Kennedy, University of Cape Town (1966)

"Song for Someone" — U2 (2015)

"Traveler, your footprints" — Antonio Machado (1917)

About the Author

Jim Olson's calling is to help other people, leaders, and organizations answer theirs. He specializes in helping them turn their setback story into their comeback legacy.

Over the years, he's illuminated some of the most consequential business, innovation, and social impact stories of our time. Jim is the former Chief Communications Officer at United Airlines, VP of Global Corporate Communications and Public Affairs at Starbucks, and VP of Corporate Communications at US Airways (now American Airlines). He's also served as an Executive In Residence at African Leadership University, with campuses in Mauritius, Kenya, and Rwanda.

Along the way, Jim has been at the forefront of many of the world's highest-profile business crises—including plane crashes, terrorist attacks, cyber breaches, labor fights, and natural disasters. He led the crisis management response to the crash of US Airways Flight 1549 on New York's Hudson River and the terrorist suicide bombing of Starbucks' flagship store in Jakarta, Indonesia.

Jim is also a blind cancer-slaying warrior.

He has received numerous honors, including recognition as one of the World's 100 Most Influential Communicators, and was named one of Syracuse University's 50 most influential communications school graduates. Jim was also awarded a Certificate in Airline Disaster

Communications Management from the U.S. National Transportation Safety Board.

Jim is a coveted keynote speaker who has addressed some of the most admired organizations in the world. He was also a Public Relations Professor at Syracuse University and has guest lectured at Georgetown University, New York University, and University of Southern California.

Jim earned his MBA from the University of Southern California and Bachelor of Science in Public Relations from Syracuse University. A lifelong traveler, he has visited, lived, and worked in more than 60 countries across six continents.

Jim and his wife, Stephanie, live in Houston with their Bernese Mountain Dog, Carmy Bear. Their daughter Kaitlyn attends Abilene Christian University where she is a Musical Theatre major.

You can discover more about Jim at ComebackCompass.com.

www.ingramcontent.com/pod-product-compliance
Lightning Source LLC
Chambersburg PA
CBHW020723150726
48196CB00028B/807/J